Cause Analysis Manual

Incident Investigation Method & Techniques

Fred Forck CPT

Kristen Noakes-Fry ABCI, Editor

A Division of Rothstein Associates, Inc.

Brookfield, Connecticut USA
www.rothsteinpublishing.com

ISBN: 978-1-944480-09-7 (Perfect Bound)
ISBN: 978-1-944480-10-3 (ePub)
ISBN: 978-1-944480-11-0 (eBook - PDF)

ISBN: 978-1-944480-09-7 (Perfect Bound)
ISBN: 978-1-944480-10-3 (ePub)
ISBN: 978-1-944480-11-0 (eBook - PDF)
Library of Congress Control Number: 2016949785

A Division of Rothstein Associates, Inc.
Philip Jan Rothstein FBCI, Publisher
4 Arapaho Road
Brookfield, Connecticut 06804-3104 USA
203.740.7400 • 203.740.7401 fax
info@rothstein.com
www.rothsteinpublishing.com
www.rothstein.com

Keep informed of the latest crisis communication, crisis management, and business continuity news.
Sign up for Business Survival™ Weblog: Business Continuity for Key Decision-Makers from Rothstein Associates at www.rothstein.com

twitter.com/rothsteinpub
www.facebook.com/RothsteinPublishing
www.linkedin.com/company/rothsteinpublishing

Acknowledgments

As I bring *Cause Analysis Manual: Incident Investigation Method and Techniques* to publication, many people have supported my efforts and have earned my appreciation. To begin, I offer thanks to:

- My wife Deborah for her prayers throughout the years.
- My son Joshua for all his persistence and diligence in making my writing more understandable and jargon-free. Joshua was the major contributor to the editing and completion of this manual.
- My son Nathan for the excellent challenges to concepts I had believed for years.
- My daughter Kristin for being a living example of organization and drive.
- My son Joel for the steady, peaceful example of kindness he sets.
- My father for being a strong, principled, hard-working role model.
- My mother for her living example of love and devotion.
- My brothers and sisters for all their help and giving.
- My relatives, friends, and co-workers for all you have taught me through the years.

Special thanks to my cousin Bob Rackers for his encouragement during the writing of this manual.

Thanks to the following utilities and plants for sharing information at nuclear industry workshops and during benchmarking visits:

Callaway, Calvert Cliffs, Columbia, Comanche Peak, Commonwealth Edison, Constellation, Cooper, Detroit Edison, Diablo Canyon, Dominion, Duke, Entergy, First Energy Nuclear Operating Company (FENOC), Florida Power & Light, Ft. Calhoun, Georgia Power, Nuclear Management Company (NMC), Palo Verde, Progress Energy, San Onofre, South Texas, Southern Nuclear, Susquehanna, Tennessee Valley Authority (TVA), and Wolf Creek.

Thanks to the following individuals who had specific and influential impact on my career:

- Mark Reinhart for his mentoring in quality assurance concepts,
- Mark Paradies for my first useful course in root cause analysis,
- Heinz Bloch for his valuable course on equipment failure analysis,
- Tony Muschara for his work and instruction in human performance principles,
- Dr. Sidney Dekker for teaching me to focus on what happened vs. what did not happen,
- Mark Reidmeyer for his loyalty as a friend through hard times,
- Peg Lucky for her instruction in structured common cause analysis, and
- Ken Elsea for his example as an investigator who is kind, honest, and effective.

Thanks to the exceptional supervisors I have had through the years: Sister Josetta Eveler, CCVI, LTC Greg Smith, John Schnack, and Fred Lake.

Thanks to the St. Francis Xavier school nuns who taught me how to diagram a sentence and to the La Salette Seminary priests who taught me the writing principles of unity, coherence, and emphasis.

Thanks to my scripture teachers for laying the ideas of the Bible in my head line-by-line, precept-by-precept, as instructed in Isaiah 28:10.

Finally, thanks to the First Cause for every good thought I have ever received and every good behavior I have ever witnessed. Thanks for food, clothing, shelter, and health.

Preface

Cause Analysis Manual: Incident Investigation Method and Techniques provides a step by step process designed to help your business navigate through major incidents and minor inefficiencies. The manual is intended for individuals and organizations no longer willing to accept "simple" explanations for problems. As you use this book, you will receive precise instructions for:

- ▶ Pinpointing a problem (Step 1).
- ▶ Finding the factors that allowed the problem to exist in your organization (Steps 2-5).
- ▶ Developing action plans to fix and improve behaviors or processes (Step 6).
- ▶ Writing investigation reports for decision-makers (Step 7).

Purpose

Years of professional experience have shown me that significant business incidents have causes hidden within the organization and its programs. I recommend that, as an investigator, you use *Cause Analysis Manual's* techniques in combination with the systematic seven-step methodology outlined here. Used accordingly, you will be able to find underlying causes and develop corrective action plans that are effective in preventing similar business incidents in the future.

Once you have determined an incident's contributing factors, the manual focuses on achieving business Results (R) by assuring organizational Behaviors (B) are aligned. Changed, improved, business Performance (P) in the future is the overall goal of corrective action planning.

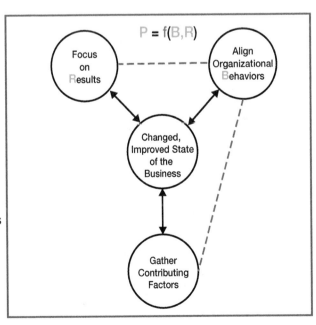

Personal Vision

This manual was built on the following personal convictions. I believe that:

1. Organizations reasonably plan for all job performers to succeed at their given tasks.
2. Businesses want to prevent problems and to learn all they can from significant incidents so lives, practices, and cultures can be improved.
3. Organizations routinely anticipate how a job performer might fail at a task and put plans in place to remove failure paths.
4. Despite these best efforts, organizations still experience significant incidents, near misses, or adverse trends.

My over-riding personal vision is "a world where people think Good* thoughts, work with Good* processes, and flourish on Good* teams."

Good (origin): Old English "god"

Basic Principles

I have worked to hold fast to the four principles of the International Society for Performance Improvement (ISPI) in writing this manual:

1. Focus on results and help clients focus on results.
2. Look at situations systemically, taking into consideration the larger context, including competing pressures, resource constraints, and anticipated changes.
3. Add value in how you do the work and through the work itself.
4. Use partnerships or collaborate with clients and other experts as needed.

How this Manual is Different

This manual is different than other cause analysis manuals on the market because:

▶ It's success-based cause analysis.

My colleagues and I focus on the planned success path — how the organization intended to get the desired result from people, processes, and programs.

▶ It focuses on structure and flexibility.

We are aware of and use structured models frequently. Because we have so many models in our mental toolkits, we are very flexible in finding beginning structures when we help people address issues.

▶ It celebrates the differences.

Many companies are looking at how they have different definitions or different processes and then dwell on why the other company's definition is wrong or why their process is flawed. We tend to see the differences as building blocks to grow better processes. We actually see the goodness and usefulness of what others do.

▶ It's a product of our own cooking.

Whether it's focusing on success or using structure or celebrating differences, we practice what we preach or intend to sell to someone else. Every technique described in this book has been tested and has proved successful in companies like yours — and the process has been refined based on this experience and the suggestions of clients and experts.

How to Use This Book

Before you use *Cause Analysis Manual*, it would be helpful, but not necessary, for you to attend an approved root cause analysis or incident investigation class. However, by using the manual, you will find out how to achieve the same results without the benefit of formal training.

This text is for reference only — it is not a procedure. The manual provides options on how to satisfy regulatory requirements, license commitments, and business obligations. However, the governing corrective action procedure of your business should specify when the analyses will be performed and other business requirements.

This manual is intended to convey expectations on the manner, methods, and techniques that are acceptable for performing a cause analysis. The actions described in the manual do not need to be performed in the sequence listed. The order given here is a recommendation only. The final sequence of the actions you use should be based on the specific conditions encountered during the investigation. My experience has shown that usually the investigation, root cause analysis, and report writing processes are iterative rather than sequential.

Fred Forck

Jefferson City, Missouri
July 2016

Foreword

I first met Fred Forck around 2001 at an industry conference for practitioners of human performance improvement, root cause analysis, and trending. He impressed me as a soft spoken, personable, clean living fellow, intensely interested in solving problems. We both worked at nuclear power plants at the time, but Fred soon moved on to a successful consulting career.

Several years afterwards, I led a root cause analysis team at a Midwestern nuclear plant. In four days, we created a creditable analysis report with all the constituent parts, causes, extents of cause and condition, corrective actions, etc. — an "accurate, auditable, and defensible record," as Fred would say. Near the end of my last day with the team, as we chatted about our work together, Fred's name came up. Someone remarked, "Yes, Fred came in, put everything on a chart, and the answer just popped out!" His skill at handling the team and applying his process made it all seem easy and straightforward. It was an eye-opener I've never forgotten!

I am writing this foreword because focused, effective cause analysis is rare and *Cause Analysis Manual: Incident Investigation Method and Techniques* can make it less so. In this book, Fred has distilled a lifetime of learning and experience into a cogent, practical manual anyone can use to understand and apply proven methods and techniques to solve problems, improve the enterprise, and prevent similar problems from happening again.

Fred begins with a survey of concepts, objectives, methods, and techniques for cause analysis. Just enough background to help you construct the mindset you need to do the job.

The book employs graphics that beautifully illustrate what to do, why, and how to do it. Fred doesn't stop at conceptual diagrams or process maps. He includes practical tools: checklists and worksheets that guide the user through the process step-by-step. The worksheets are information-mapped to capture the critical information in a logical, assessable format.

For example, instead of a traditional personal statement "form" that is mostly a blank page, Fred gives us a "witness recollection statement" that assembles details about who is making the statement, the witness's job as it related to the event, and a statement of the problem in the subject's own words. The form ends by asking the witness what he or she recommends should be done differently. Every investigator should have this form in his toolkit and use it religiously. Looking at it, I see the distillation of the wisdom of vast knowledge and experience into a finely tuned instrument for evoking and capturing the invisible influences that shape the human side of events. This sort of virtuosity is routine throughout the book.

As the book progresses, each step in the process is dissected and explained with multiple examples, practical tools, and advice. Each fundamental is reinforced in context with each step in the process until the reader becomes committed to the necessity for completing each step in turn – no shortcuts. Warnings and admonitions are strategically placed to help the user avoid pitfalls that could take years to ferret out on your own.

From his straightforward integration of management and investigator responsibilities to his unflinching approach to what to do when the manager is accountable, the book gives you the method and techniques to succeed.

It is clear to me this manual was written by a master of the craft. It is more than a roadmap. Applied conscientiously, it is a vehicle to carry you from your first reaction to a bad outcome to deep understanding of how and why it happened, and a set of actions to keep it from happening again.

Ben Whitmer

Inside Organizational Development Consultant,
Human Performance and Safety Culture SME,
and Event Cause Analyst
STP Nuclear Operating Company
Wadsworth, Texas
July 2016

Foreword

I have been fortunate to have known and worked with Fred Forck for over 30 years. I first encountered Fred when he was the instructor in Quality Assurance. Fred spent a good portion of class explaining why the rules and regulations made good business sense, often reminding the class that "quality" was just a synonym for "good." When I reflect, much of my success can be attributed to this seemingly simple concept! Fred started his career as a teacher — and he is always teaching and learning.

Too often in the arena of cause analysis, you come across either theorists or what I call "checklist" cause analysts. However, in contrast, Fred is a true *craftsman* of root cause analysis. He has successfully applied his craft to many incidents ranging from equipment failures to organizational failures. Although most of his experience has been in the nuclear power generation field, Fred's techniques and tools are basic to any endeavor involving humans, organizations, processes, and machines. Over the years, Fred has taken insights on human behavior and the associated drivers to get the desired behaviors and integrated this with organizations and processes to demonstrate how to get desired results.

Cause Analysis Manual: Incident Investigation Method and Techniques is different and better than other cause analysis material because it incorporates what Fred has learned and *successfully applied* from many other cause analysis practitioners over the past 30 years! This will become apparent as you note the numerous references and suggestions for further reading at the end of each chapter. This book contains Fred's lessons learned from a variety of experiences and molds them into a comprehensive, yet simple, method for cause analysis. He presents a simple seven-step process for performing a cause analysis. But for each step, the book provides multiple tools, techniques, and ideas applicable to different situations. As Fred always does, he provides the reasons when and why a tool or techniques should be used.

One significant difference in Fred's approach to cause analysis is that he starts with success, not failure. You need to be able to clearly define success using objective criteria, not only in results (dollars, product) but also in behaviors. In order to perform a cause analysis, Fred also demonstrates you should understand what tools – knowledge, skills, processes, peer checks, and supervisory oversight – that have been put in place to ensure success. Fred then reinforces this concept in the first step of the process – Scope the Problem. As Yogi Berra said, "If you don't know where you are going, you might wind up someplace else."

This book also offers the added benefit of providing guidance on the management of the cause analysis process. Again, this is based on Fred's extensive experiences and his understanding of the impact this has on the success of the cause analysis effort. This management component includes team formation, roles and responsibilities of cause analyst and team leader, collecting and managing evidence and data, and report writing. Most importantly, Fred describes the critical steps in the cause analysis process in which management's engagement is crucial.

As we have proceeded on separate career paths, I still keep in contact with Fred, not only because I consider him a friend, but because he continues to challenge my thinking and teaches me something new every time we talk. Many times, when encountering a difficult situation, I reach out to Fred, knowing he will be able to provide valuable insights. During a recent interview for a promotion, one of my interviewers commented that I didn't talk and think like an engineer. I smiled, thought of Fred, and responded, "Thank you."

John D. Schnack

Manager, Nuclear Corporate Oversight
Ameren
St. Louis, MO
July 2016

Foreword

I have had the pleasure of both a personal and professional relationship with Fred since 1983. He has a professional passion for solving problems in the workplace, and I have benefitted from Fred's wisdom and expertise to solve problems in a highly technical and potentially high-risk industry — commercial nuclear power.

I recall an early success with a nuclear power company: The use of new inspection assessment tools had caused the Nuclear Regulatory Commission (NRC) to develop concerns with collective radiation dose. As the issue evolved, an urgent need for a root cause analysis emerged. Using Fred's tools and guidance, we identified the drivers of an organization's undesirable behaviors and developed and implemented the necessary corrective action plan. The results spoke for themselves. Collective radiation dose improved dramatically, and the NRC confidence was restored in the licensee performance. Significant collateral benefits were also realized. Because of the improved work planning, refueling outage cost and schedule also improved significantly.

Cause Analysis Manual: Incident Investigation Method and Techniques represents years of applied research in the field of root cause analysis. Because Fred is also an educator, he wants us to benefit from what he has learned. The book presents a positive approach to solving problems by considering "what does *good* look like?" early in the process. Fred recognizes we are running businesses and do not have infinite resources at our disposal, and so he offers tools that managers can apply to make confident decisions to prioritize and focus resources.

A structured approach is a critical aspect of any viable root cause process, keeping you from making assumptions that may not be true or overlooking things that should be factored in. Human performance aspects can be particularly challenging because they seldom result from malicious intent; however, Fred provides the tools to understand what can drive undesirable behaviors and get past the blame game. He reinforces the structured approach further by integrating "line of sight" into the process, ensuring the original problem will be addressed by the solution.

To accelerate practitioners' understanding of concepts, processes, and results, Fred uses graphical presentations extensively. With these graphics, problems that seem to be overwhelming become focused and solvable. Usually, you will see that not all is broken; thus, you can efficiently identify the significant few areas that are driving performance in the wrong direction. Graphical presentations also accelerate the organizational (including management) buy-in and understanding of both the problem and the resulting corrective action plans.

Fred would say that you can't fix everything with a hammer — sometimes you need a wrench or a screwdriver. Because tools appropriate for determining the causes of equipment problems are not always applicable to organizational performance or cultural challenges, Fred provides the range of tools necessary to analyze and correct a problem. For example, a corrective action plan that addresses an equipment problem can be fairly straightforward, whereas changing behaviors typically requires a series of steps, over time, to successfully sustain the change.

The final challenge for the practitioner is, "Did you fix it and how can you tell?" The book recognizes the need to know and integrates the follow-up steps necessary to assess effectiveness and sustainability.

While there are other good root cause processes out there, Fred recognizes some of their limitations, taking them to the next level by offering a state-of-the-art approach. There is substance, without the "bells and whistles" that don't add value. Following his approach will result in an efficient, effective analysis of a problem and a durable result. For example, in that earlier discussion regarding the collective radiation dose, the root cause report with corrective action plans was delivered in less than two weeks due to the use of Fred's method. The results have been sustained for more than 15 years!

Over the years, Fred and I have changed employers, but we continue to collaborate. In my own career, a primary focus for my company is assisting the interaction of clients with the regulators. I am convinced that there is nothing more powerful than a good root cause analysis to manage the resolution of significant regulatory concerns, and applying Fred's approach can get you back on track to address the safety concerns as well as restore the regulators' confidence.

Mark Reidmeyer
Technical Services Director
Certrec Corporation
Fort Worth, TX
July 2016

Table of Contents

Step 5: Validate Underlying Factors 175

Step 6: Plan Corrective Actions 201

Introduction

Getting Started with Cause Analysis

0.1 Defining Cause Analysis

Simply put, *cause analysis* is the process by which you discover the invisible thoughts — mental models, beliefs, values — that influence, and then produce, the visible behaviors/actions. The reasons need to be discovered so actions to prevent recurrence can be initiated to prevent future incidents. The structured search is called *root cause analysis*. The underlying drivers or reasons are called *root causes*. Once your investigation allows you to fully integrate cause analysis techniques into a systematic methodology for analyzing and solving problems, you will be able to take the lead in decision-making and quality control that will be reflected in better and more consistent results for your organization.

0.1.1 Purpose

Why are you learning more about cause analysis? Usually, you need to practice cause analysis because your business has experienced a significant incident. On the surface, it may look like a failure of some piece of equipment. Or perhaps someone had difficulty performing a task as expected. The person made a mistake, slipped up, had a memory lapse, or did not follow instructions. If you follow our formula for successful investigations, you will gain facility at uncovering the answers for why a piece of equipment, a person, or a procedure did not function as intended.

0.1.2 Method

As you move through the exercises and instructions in this book, you will be able to get results by following these steps:

- Step 1: Scope the Problem.
- Step 2: Investigate the Factors.
- Step 3: Reconstruct the Story.
- Step 4: Establish Contributing Factors.
- Step 5: Validate Underlying Factors.
- Step 6: Plan Corrective Actions.
- Step 7: Report Learnings.

Figure 0-1 illustrates the seven basic steps comprising the structured root cause methodology used to identify root and contributing causes and corrective actions to prevent recurrence of significant incidents. You will see this model illustrated again in Figure 0-23 and discussed in more detail in Section 0.6, Investigation Steps.

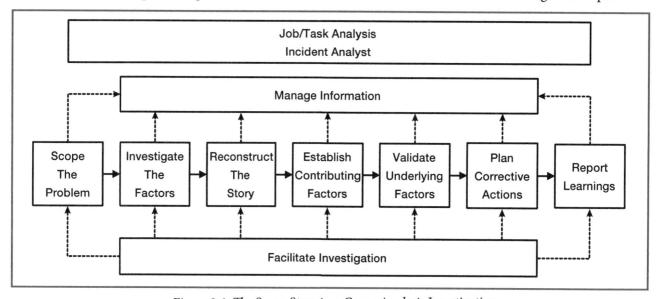

Figure 0-1. The Seven Steps in a Cause Analysis Investigation

Throughout the investigation, as a root cause analyst, you must be able to accomplish two general tasks:

1 Manage information.
2. Facilitate the investigation.

Following a structured process can help you to be prepared to overcome unexpected problems that you may encounter. We will proceed with some background to prepare you for using this seven-step process.

0.2   Successful and Unsuccessful Results

The purpose of this manual is to help you investigate a significant incident which probably involves both equipment and human failure. The seven steps listed above will help you determine and understand the organizational and human factors that influenced or allowed the incident to happen. However, it is important for you to first understand how a business sets up equipment, humans, and organizations to succeed. Once you understand how equipment, humans, and organizations succeed, it will be easier for you to understand the opposite of success; that is, failure. To illustrate this point, student doctors and nurses study anatomy and physiology — how the human body functions when it is healthy — before they study pathophysiology — how the systems of a human body fail. When you are conducting an investigation into a failure, you must first investigate and understand the system the business had in place for ensuring successful performance.

0.2.1 Success (Positive Results)

Let's say that the incident being investigated involves physical hardware. Go back to the time period before the incident occurred, when your business was confident that the material, structure, component, and system were fit for use. You were confident that the equipment would perform reliably in service because of the actions the business had taken in the past to ensure the proper form, fit, and function of the hardware. See Figure 0-2.

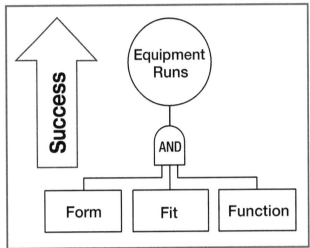

Figure 0-2. Equipment Success

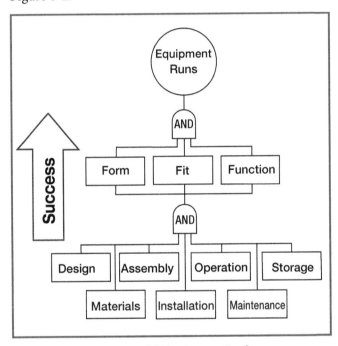

Figure 0-3. Successful Equipment Performance

Your business took systematic actions to ensure proper form, fit, and function through the following types of activities: design control, material selection, assembly, installation, operation, maintenance, and storage (Bloch, 2011). See Figure 0-3. These activities are all performed by humans, and you had a certain degree of confidence in the humans doing the work correctly.

That said, how does your business ensure that the human worker is successful? When humans are hired, they enter your place of business with certain skills, knowledge, and mindsets (e.g., attitude and work ethic). See Figure 0-4.

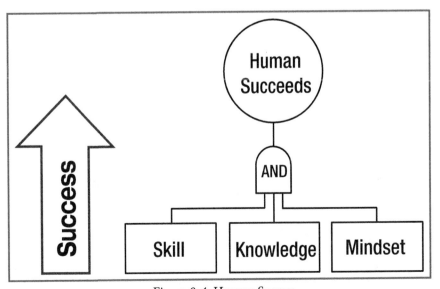

Figure 0-4. Human Success

However, for these workers to be successful in your business, the organization needed to ensure that the skills, knowledge, and mindsets were sufficient to perform within your system. Sometimes, a business will use techniques of *human factors engineering* to ensure the worker is successful when touching company equipment. More often, businesses rely on training, procedures, supervision, peer checks, policies, and communication to ensure the success of workers (Bloch, 2005). See Figure 0-5.

To look at the same concepts from a different angle, Wile (2014) asserts there are factors both internal and external affecting the ability of a human to sense, interpret, and act successfully.

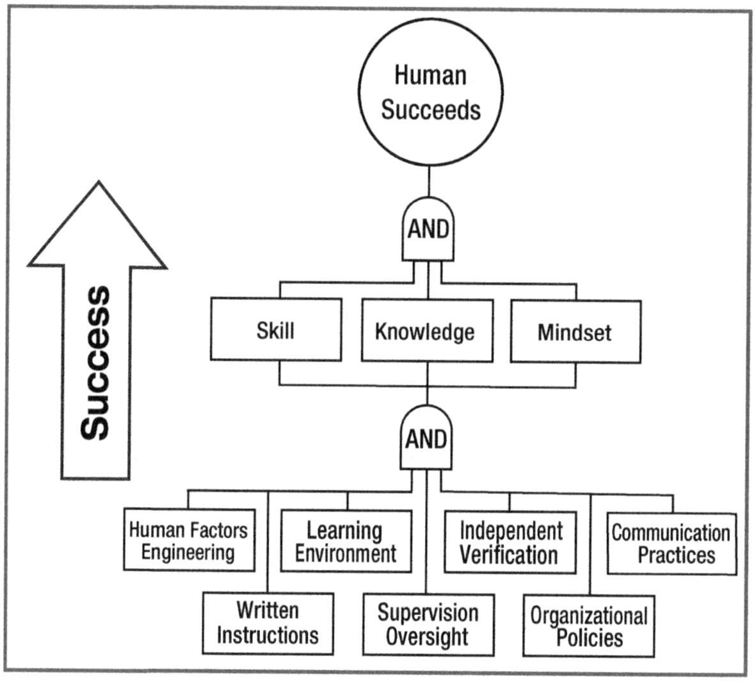

Figure 0-5. Successful Human Performance

See Figure 0-6.

The success models shown in Figures 0-5 and 0-6 graphically depict the forces and factors needed to produce successful results in the general performance of a task or operation. In later chapters, you will find increasingly more detailed graphics showing the expected flow or methodology related to how a job performer, leader, or organization is expected to do well at a given task.

The system your business had in effect prior to the incident is what needs to be investigated.

Once the perceived success path of the business system is laid out, you, as the investigator, will know the paths that need to be scrutinized to find out the ways the equipment or the worker may have been set up to fail.

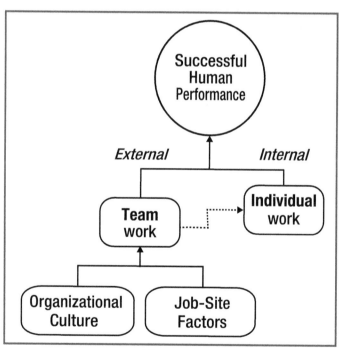

Figure 0-6.
Successful Human Performance Two Prong

0.2.2   Failure (Negative Results)

Conversely, when an incident or failure occurs, the success models can be used in the reverse direction to show the place(s) along the path that broke down and resulted in the adverse consequences. So, in investigations, the model depicts both the success path (usually AND logic) and the failure path (usually OR logic) for a given result. The goal is to look back through the work activity and find the ways the equipment or the job performer may have been set up to fail. See Figure 0-7.

According to Bloch (2011), when equipment fails, the form, fit, or function failure will trace back to possibilities in four areas: force (mechanical or electrical), reactive environment, time, or temperature. To clarify, we have added to the model to provide more detail about these four possible causes for form, fit, and function problems. See Figure 0-8.

On the model in Figure 0-9, the equipment failure cause analysis model represented in Figure 0-8 is combined with the reverse of the human performance success model illustrated in Figure 0-5. The general fault tree is an overall representation of the depth of investigation needed in the root cause analysis of a significant incident. The investigation should identify the physical, human, and latent roots of the incident.

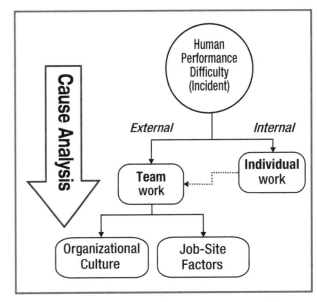

Figure 0-7. Human Performance Cause Analysis

The physical root(s) of the form, fit, or function problem will let you know the specific type of human activities involved (design, operation, maintenance, etc.). Until physical roots are determined, your investigation will not reveal whether the humans involved with the incident were design engineers, operators, maintenance people, or some other group. And, without knowing how humans were involved, you certainly will not be able to uncover programmatic, organizational, or cultural issues (Muschara, 2010).

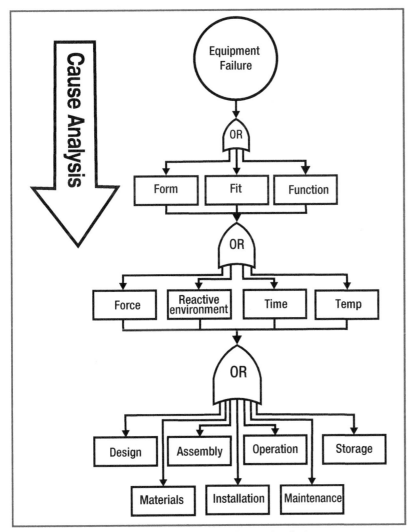

Figure 0-8. Equipment Cause Analysis

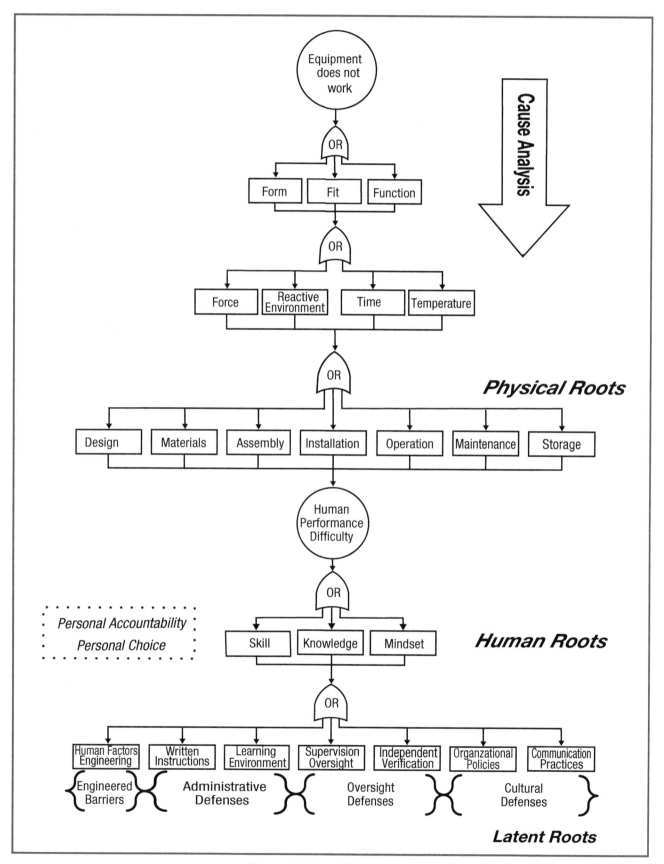

Figure 0-9. General Fault Tree

Businesses that want to survive perform a structured search for the underlying fixable reasons for the incident. The reasons would have to explain the existence of the triggering, aggravating, or exposure factors in the organizational system (Corcoran, 2007). See Figure 0-10. You need to discover the reasons in order to initiate actions to prevent recurrence in order to thwart future incidents. The structured search is called *root cause analysis*. The underlying drivers or reasons are called *root causes*.

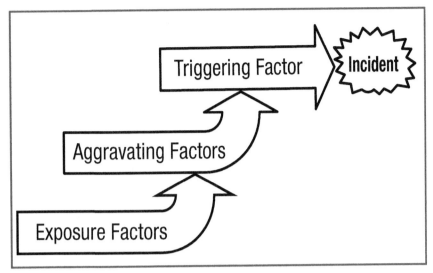

Figure 0-10. Factor Flow

0.3   Human Behavior

It is important that an investigator understands several models of human behavior and performance.

0.3.1   Behavior Model 1

A human behavior is a human action. Behavior is visible. Behaviors produce results. Our invisible thoughts drive our visible behaviors/actions. Thoughts include mental models (vision), beliefs, and values (all invisible). When humans have difficulty performing a task successfully, investigators need to find out what thoughts drove the individual's observable behaviors (actions) for a specific incident. This will tell us something about the individual's knowledge and attitude — factors that influenced this particular incident. See Figure 0-11.

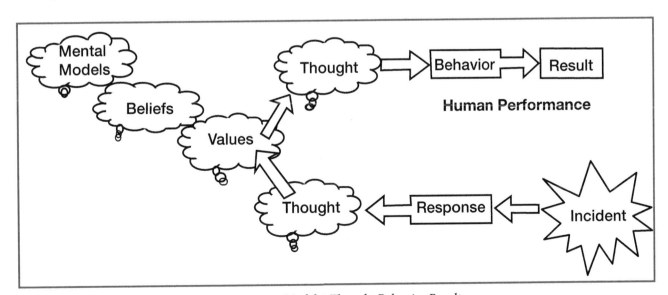

Figure 0-11. Model 1 Thought Behavior Result

Business practices (actions/behaviors/norms) come from the way people think. If you want to change the way people do business, leaders help them change the way they think. This involves changing the material they use in their thinking: their mental models, their beliefs, their values. Changing any or all of these thought processes will change behaviors. When values, beliefs, and mental models change, the corresponding changed behaviors (actions/norms) change cultures. Assuming the original behavior was truly inappropriate, the needed change in behavior becomes a "condition of employment."

Therefore, investigators must focus on discovering the specific underlying thought processes that influenced the decisions to act (behave) inappropriately. The discovery of the factors influencing thoughts — mental models, beliefs, and values — leads to a series of specific corrective actions aimed at changing mental models or beliefs or values. We send people to training to learn the new, expected mental model; then we observe work in the field to see if the behaviors match the new mental model.

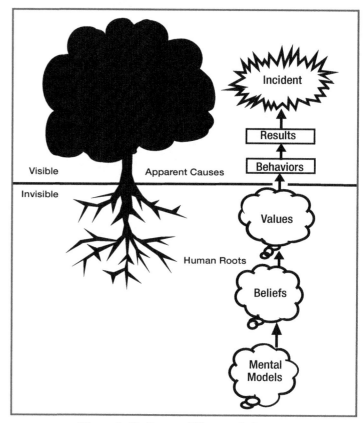

Figure 0-12. Roots of Human Behavior

When there is a match between the (invisible) mental model and the (visible) behavior, we show that we value the changed behavior by positive reinforcement. That helps anchor the belief in and value of the new behavior in the minds of all involved.

Root cause analysis is about discovering the invisible thoughts — mental models, beliefs, and values — that influence, then produce, the visible behaviors/actions. See Figure 0-12. If the visible actions are inappropriate, something about the invisible mental models or beliefs or values is going to have to change. Otherwise, we should expect the inappropriate behavior to recur. The choice is between implementing general corrective actions that will have only minimal effect or specific corrective actions that will produce sustainable positive change.

Investigators are expected to root out the factors that contributed to the incident whether they were a direct or an indirect influence. The direct influences most generally involve the individual — the person who touches the "plant." These are easy to find. The indirect influences involve systems and cultural factors. These are harder to find (generally). The organization is expected to make changes to correct both the direct (readily observable) and the indirect (generally inferred) factors or justify why it was not taking any action.

As analysts, we then have to look into other incidents and areas to see if these same factors have generic implications (some call it extent of condition or extent of cause). If we are able to find situations in which similar factors existed for other individuals in other specific incidents, we begin building a case for a potential problem organizational behavior.

In other words, if a bunch of individuals do the same thing driven by the same thought patterns, we can suspect that there are some flaws in the thinking of the rest of the organization. And we can reasonably expect there to be problems in the future with some other individual or individuals if something in the organizational system is not changed to bring about a better set of behaviors.

Sometimes the system provides education to change the individual's knowledge. Sometimes the incentives or sanctions of the system are changed to change the individual's mindset. Sometimes both.

Investigators often have to infer once the analysis goes deeper than the visible behaviors. Investigators put together a series of individual cases to make a statement about the organization's culture. Then investigators present the culture case to management. Management now has the opportunity to effect changes in the overall organizational thought processes and subsequently behaviors which will give a different look to the culture. If investigators can find no other individual cases driven by the same factors, they tell management that they looked for generic implications and did not find any.

In a court of law, it might be almost impossible to prove the indirect influences (i.e., the case for culture change). However, a learning organization is generally smart enough to figure out that "where there's smoke, there's..." and does not need to take a direct hit to make the necessary changes.

0.3.2   Behavior Model 2

Often one of the first models we learn about human behavior is that behavior involves receiving a stimulus that results in a response (the observed behavior). In root cause analysis, the stimuli are the cues that initiated the responses involved in the incident. A response is a physical action that results in changing the state of a component by manipulation using controls or tools or by informing or directing others through verbal statements. However, between sensing a stimulus and subsequently responding, there is time to process information mentally — to make a decision regarding how to respond to the cue. See Figure 0-13.

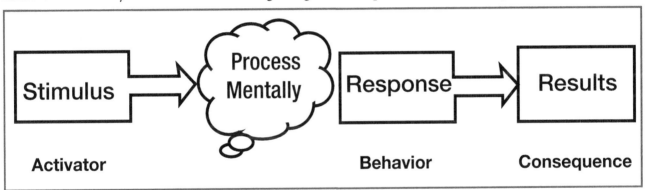

Figure 0-13. Model 2 Stimulus Response Flow

When an incident or failure occurs, the model is used in the reverse direction to show the place(s) along the path that broke down and resulted in the adverse consequences. See Figure 0-14. In this case, the worker's response would be looked at first; then the mental processing followed by the stimuli the worker was receiving. To go to the mental processing before evaluating the nature of the response would be a mistake. And, to go straight to the stimulus before the response and the decision-making thoughts were determined would also be an error on the part of the investigator.

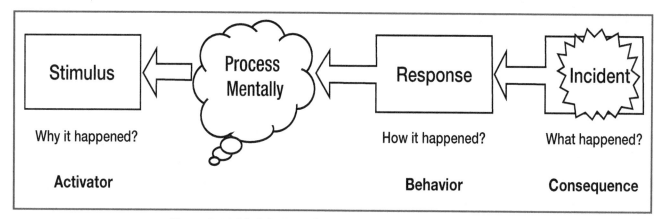

Figure 0-14. Model 2 Stimulus Response Cause Analysis Flow

0.3.3   Behavior Model 3

Daniels, Daniels, and Abernathy (2006) uses an A-B-C depiction of human performance. Since behavior is what business is all about, the A-B-C model is used to help pinpoint at-risk practices and behaviors (Health and Safety Executive, 2012). Why do people act the way they do? Organizations ask this question, especially after an incident.

The investigator identifies and classifies the activators [A] and consequences [C] currently operating for the desired (correct) and undesired (incorrect) behaviors [B]. The activators or antecedents are the stimuli or cues that are sensed at the job site and set the stage for the behavior (response) that follows. Behaviors refer to acts or actions by individuals that can be observed (physically sensed) by others. Job performers behave to achieve or avoid consequences — what happens to a person as a result of the behavior. The worker is the individual with the personal perception of whether the consequence reinforces or punishes the present behavior or future behaviors. See Figure 0-15.

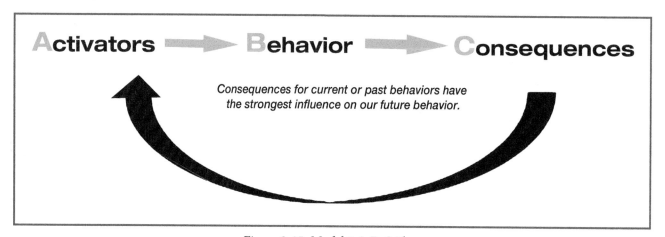

Figure 0-15. Model 3 A-B-C Flow

Table 0-1. Internal and External Behavior Factors

Activator	Behavior	Consequence
External Factor	Internal Factor	External Factor
Examples: ▸ Meetings, training, signs, procedures, supervision. ▸ Visual cues or auditory stimuli. ▸ Anything that sets the stage before a behavior.	Examples: ▸ Something someone says. ▸ Something someone does. ▸ A visible action. ▸ A response to a stimulus.	Examples: ▸ Positive reinforcement. ▸ Negative reinforcement. ▸ Punishment. ▸ Penalty.
Stimulus	**Response**	**[Future] Stimulus/Activator**

Again, the model is used in the reverse direction to show the place(s) along the path that broke down and resulted in the adverse consequences. See Figure 0-16. In this case, the worker's behavior would be looked at first; then the activators/antecedents that preceded the behavior. Also remember to dig back to the previous time the same type of task was performed to determine the consequences for past behaviors. The consequences for past behaviors have a strong influence on current and future behaviors. Daniels, Daniels, & Abernathy (2006) suggests that, in order to understand why people do what they do, beyond asking, "Why did they do that?" ask, "What happens to them when they do that?" When you understand the real or perceived consequences of a behavior, you are able to understand the behavior better.

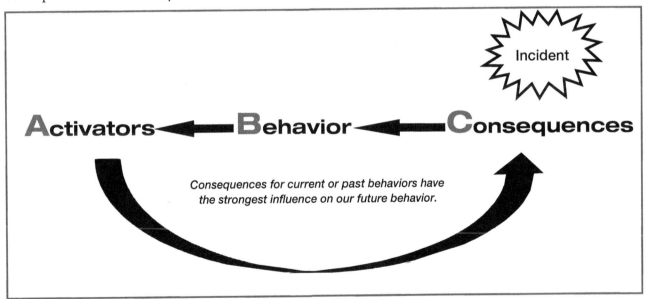

Figure 0-16. Model 3 A-B-C Cause Analysis Flow

0.3.4 Behavior Model 4

The following model shows more detail about both internal and external factors affecting the ability of a human to sense, interpret, and act successfully. On your way to establishing contributors, you should also look into both the human and organizational factors. According to Muschara (2010), these factors can be categorized as engineered, administrative, oversight, or cultural controls or defenses. The human aspect focuses on worker practices, whereas the organizational aspect focuses on the process the worker is expected to use. See Figure 0-17.

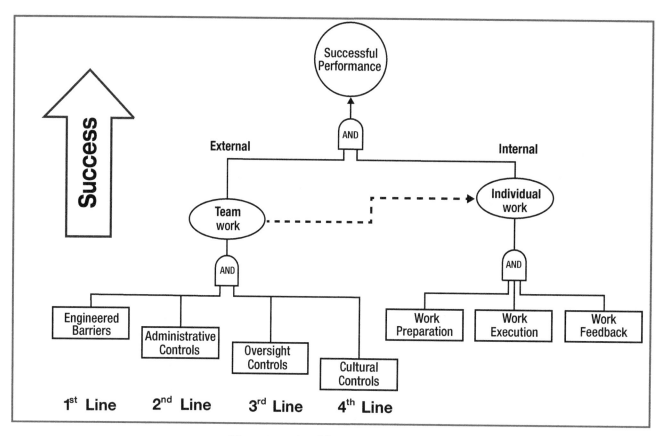

Figure 0-17. Model 4 Two Prongs Flow

The investigator's task is to "root" out the perceptions of the job performer(s) and of the organization regarding the state of the defense-in-depth of the system. See Figures 0-18 and 0-19. And there may be a mismatch between the two sets of mental models (perceptions). The worker may see the job site one way, while the organization perceives the situation differently.

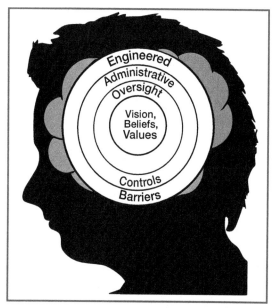

Figure 0-18. Internal Factors: The Worker's Perception (the Human Roots)

Use the model in the reverse direction to show the place(s) along the path that broke down and resulted in the significant incident. See Figure 0-20. If equipment is involved, the first factors the investigator evaluates are the engineered barriers [1] to determine the physical roots of the problem. That should lead the investigator to the individuals [2] associated with the engineered barrier issues. In this phase, the worker's task preparation and execution are evaluated. If the worker has performed this same task previously, determine the nature of the feedback the worker provided the organization about any concerns with the task. The goal is to identify the human root(s) of the incident.

Finally, as investigator, you will look back through the work activity and find the ways the equipment or the job performer may have been set up to fail. The organization should have ensured incident-free operation by installing a variety of overlapping defenses (barriers, controls, and safeguards) and by aggressively monitoring the effectiveness of those defenses.

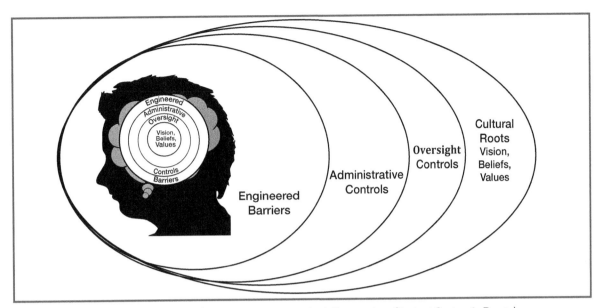

Figure 0-19. External Factors: Organization's Perception (Latent Systemic Roots)

Equipment [1], procedures [3], and oversight [4] processes along with the organization and its culture [5] all contain hidden flaws or latent conditions, which can accumulate without anyone's knowledge. Finding and validating the latent roots of an incident is the most difficult and time-consuming task of an investigation.

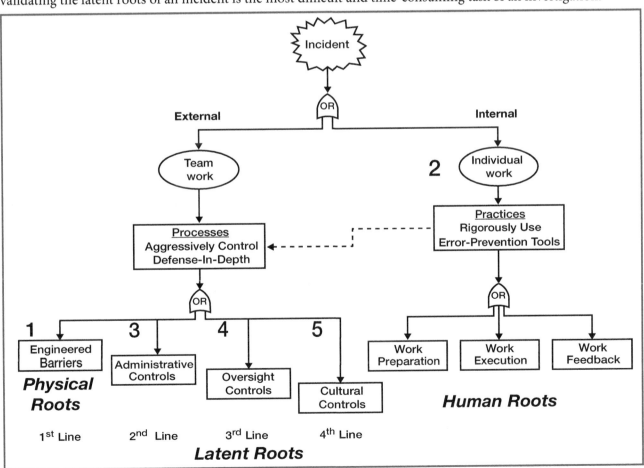

Figure 0-20. Breakdowns on the Path to the Incident

0.4   Accountability

The *American Heritage Dictionary* defines *accountability* as "answerable for performance; liable for being called into account for actions." Accountability has to do with the ability of the members of an organization to clearly identify who is answerable and responsible for a particular outcome.

Whenever there is a possible individual accountability issue at the manager level, there are several angles investigators need to probe. There may be actions by a manager that fall entirely in the realm of a manager's control as an individual (therefore, primarily an individual accountability issue). Often, the organizational culture or processes set up the manager as an individual and make it appear that the manager is personally accountable for items outside the manager's control.

0.4.1   Personal and Organizational Accountability

In root cause analysis, investigators need to do a good job distinguishing between personal accountability and organizational accountability especially when writing about culpability problems at the manager level. The honest truth is that often the person who appears very culpable is just the person in the manager position on the organizational chart at the time an ugly cultural issue manifests itself as an incident.

What happens if an investigator does not do a good job of clearly calling this type of cultural issue an organizational accountability issue? If you are not very clear, managers take it very personally. Why? To the managers, it seems like a personal attack on their abilities and competence. And, honestly, managers are generally very accountable people.

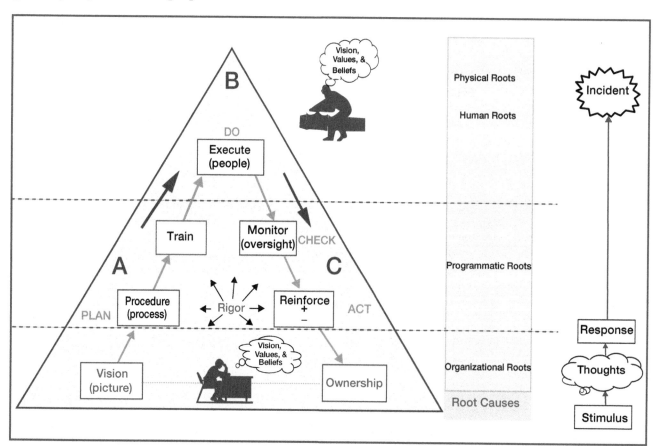

Figure 0-21. Decisions in Relation to Organizational Culture

When there is an individual accountability issue with a manager — such as a poor decision — you need to call that out. However, you also need to clearly call out whenever a manager's seemingly poor decision was set up by the organizational culture. See Figure 0-21.

When planning corrective actions, measures need to be included for institutionalizing fixes involving changes in undesired behavior for latent organizational weaknesses (LOWs). The corrective action plan needs to facilitate the establishment of clear accountability and alignment for future production and protection.

The model in Figure 0-22 illustrates the basic steps to establish clear accountability and alignment for a needed organizational behavior change.

1. Get the "right" mental model.
2. Define standard/expectations. (Find out what "good" looks like by benchmarking, etc.).
3. Communicate standard/expectations (procedures, training, newsletters, etc.).
4. Monitor expected behaviors and results (by observing, by performance indicators [PIs], etc.).
5. Feedback +/- (positively reinforce desired behaviors; correct inappropriate behaviors).

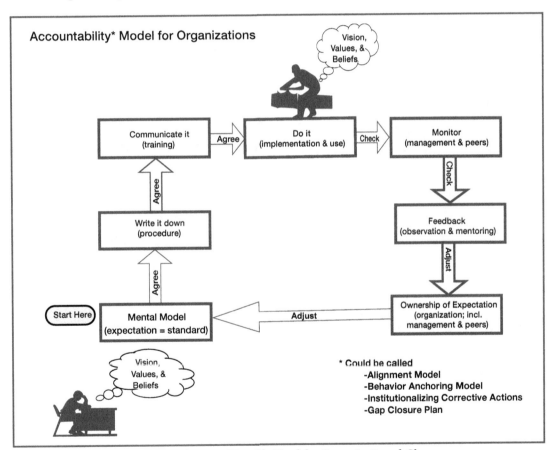

Figure 0-22. Steps to Identify Need for Organizational Change

0.5 Investigator Attitude (Mindset)

As investigators, the fictional characters Sherlock Holmes, Perry Mason, and Dick Tracy solved crimes like murder, blackmail, fraud, and sabotage. These are criminal acts involving general willfulness and malice of forethought or intent. These are not human errors. Human errors like slips, lapses, and mistakes lack general willfulness and malice of intent.

It is true we use a lot of the same logic that a criminal investigator uses when we do root cause analysis. However, our attitude has to be much different toward the humans we encounter in our investigations. If we think we are dealing with a willful or maliciously intentional act, it's time to turn the investigation over to the police or, at the very least, the human resources department.

Our attitude cannot be one of looking for the one bad person to "pin the rap" on. Our attitude is one of looking for how the person got set up. Was there something in the way the person was thinking at the time that set him or her up? Was there something in the system, the process, or the organization that set the person up? We look for holes in the defenses and then make recommendations to plug the gaps. I can't think of a single defense strong enough that I would recommend to an organization that could prevent someone with malicious intent from committing a willful act.

Defenses (a.k.a. barriers or safeguards) are put in place in an organization with the thought that most people are coming to work intending to do a good job, but are also capable of making errors. The defenses are also put in place to keep the person from hurting themselves, others, or the equipment. The defenses also keep the equipment from hurting people.

Criminal investigators work at apprehending the bad guy to prevent that particular bad guy from committing any more crimes. Criminal investigators are generally unsuccessful at preventing future murders. However, we use the learning from a person's human error (not a crime) to prevent that person *and* other people from getting set up by people or the system in the future.

The incident investigator wants the facts, but the investigator must also uncover the underlying factors associated with why humans had performance difficulties. Why did structures, systems, or components fail? Why were work rules broken? Why did humans, while attempting to achieve something positive, instead initiate an incident or an accident?

0.6   Investigation Steps

Investigators need to learn how to use cause analysis techniques such as Pareto Analysis, Fault Tree Analysis, Actions and Factors Charting, Defense (Barrier) Analysis, Difference (Change) Analysis, and the WHY Factor Staircase. But, more importantly, investigators need to be able to fully integrate those techniques (and more) into a systematic methodology for analyzing and solving problems. As an analogy, a person may be able to use a hammer and a saw properly, but still not be able to build a house with those tools without a structured blueprint.

0.6.1   Job Task Analysis

A job task analysis (JTA) was performed so that investigators/root cause analysts would be able to meet the following sets of objectives (derived from Nuclear Regulatory Commission, 2011 and 2013):

A. Problem Identification and Extent of Condition Determinations.

1) Document who identified the issue and under what conditions the issue was identified.
2) Document how long the issue existed and prior opportunities for identification.
3) Document the business-specific risk consequences, as applicable, and compliance concerns associated with the issue.
4) Address the extent of the adverse condition (problem).

B. Root Cause, and Extent of Cause Evaluations.

1) Use a systematic methodology to identify the root and contributing causes.

2) Conduct the evaluation to a level of detail commensurate with the significance of the problem.

3) Study prior occurrences of the problem and knowledge of prior operating experience.

4) Address the extent of the cause(s) of the problem.

5) Determine and address safety culture factors.

C. Corrective Actions.

1) Plan actions to preclude repetition of a similar significant incident.

2) Specify actions for each root and contributing cause so that the business has an adequate evaluation for why no corrective actions are necessary.

3) Prioritize actions with consideration of risk significance and regulatory compliance.

4) Establish a schedule for implementing and completing the corrective actions.

5) Identify quantitative or qualitative measures of success for determining the effectiveness of the corrective actions to prevent recurrence.

6) Address violations of regulations, if applicable.

7) Document actions and report to appropriate levels of management.

0.6.2   The Seven-Step Methodology

The model in Figure 0-23 illustrates the seven basic steps comprising the structured root cause methodology used to identify root and contributing causes and corrective actions to prevent recurrence of significant incidents. (In Table 0-2, the methodology is described.) Throughout the investigation, a root cause analyst also must be able to accomplish two general tasks: manage information and facilitate the investigation. Following a structured process can help an investigator avoid problems that might otherwise be encountered.

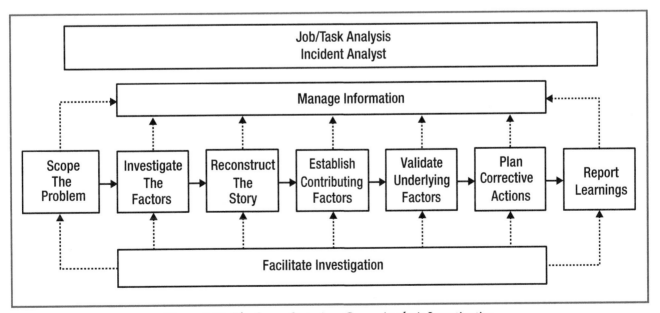

Figure 0-23. The Seven Steps in a Cause Analysis Investigation

Table 0-2. Structured Methodology Steps

Steps	Techniques
SCOPE the Problem (Step 1) Start problem solving by putting a discerning eye on the goals (the requirements, expectations, desires, values — "what should have happened"). Ensure the original performance expectation, requirement, or goal is stated or implied *and* is still valid. Identify the business problem accurately and completely.	▸ Problem Statement ▸ Problem Description ▸ Difference Mapping ▸ Extent of Condition Review
INVESTIGATE the Factors (Step 2) Decide what information to collect and whom to interview. Collect physical evidence, review process and procedures, photograph or video the scene, etc. (the "leg work" of the investigation).	▸ Evidence Preservation ▸ Witness Recollection Statement ▸ Interviewing ▸ Pareto Analysis
RECONSTRUCT the Story (Step 3) Recreate the incident showing a logical sequencing or flow. Develop a detailed timeline to clearly show what happened when. Major incidents are not usually the result of single failures but are the result of complex conditions that have evolved or situations that have drifted over a period of time. Multiple work groups, systems, tasks, and/or components are usually involved.	▸ Fault Tree Analysis ▸ Task Analysis ▸ Critical Activity Chart ▸ Actions and Factors Chart
ESTABLISH Contributing Factors (Step 4) Identify conditions, situations, or actions that triggered, allowed, or influenced the incident. These are causal factors. Usually there is more than one. These factors can be found in the engineered, administrative, oversight, or cultural controls.	▸ Contributing Factor Test ▸ "Five" WHYs ▸ Cause and Effect Trees ▸ Difference Analysis ▸ Defense Analysis ▸ Structure Tree Diagrams ▸ Fishbone (Ishikawa) Diagram ▸ Defense-in-Depth Analysis ▸ MORT Analysis ▸ Production/Protection Strategy Analysis ▸ Safety Culture Analysis
VALIDATE Underlying Factors (Step 5) For each of the incident's contributing factors, find correctable underlying factors — the root causes. In most cases, there will be underlying physical, human, and organizational roots. The extent of the causes must be determined.	▸ Support/Refute Methodology ▸ WHY Factor Staircase ▸ Root Cause Test ▸ Cause Evaluation Matrix ▸ Extent of Cause Review
PLAN Corrective Actions (Step 6) Develop one or more corrective actions to eliminate or control each cause and the extent of cause. Establish a schedule for implementing and completing the corrective actions in a timely manner. Ensure that the long-term effectiveness of the plan to preclude repetition is evaluated.	▸ Action Plan ▸ Change Management ▸ S.M.A.R.T.E.R. ▸ Barriers and Aids Analysis ▸ Solution Selection Tree

	▸ Solution Selection Matrix ▸ Contingency Plan ▸ Communication Plan ▸ Institutionalization/Coaching Plan ▸ Effectiveness Review ▸ Performance Indicator (PI) Development
REPORT Learnings (Step 7) Once your investigation is complete, provide a formal report of your findings. Management may want an oral presentation. The investigation report needs to be a permanent, auditable, defensible record.	▸ Report Template ▸ Grade Cards/Scoresheets

A checklist is provided in Table 0-3. Displayed on a large poster in a team room, the checklist would show everyone involved the general status of the investigation. Following the checklist, the steps are modeled with general acceptance criteria (Figure 0-24), for Equipment Failure Analysis (Figure 0-25), for Common Factor Analysis (Figure 0-26), and as Integrated Tasks of Analysts and Management (Figure 0-27).

To facilitate completion of these steps during a root cause analysis scheduled for 30 days, incident investigation timelines are provided in general in Figure 0-28 and in detail in Tables 0-4 and 0-5. Some investigation deadlines are driven by regulatory requirements; however, other reporting periods are driven by procedures under organizational control.

Table 0-3. Incident Analysis Steps

Initial when completed		Incident Analysis Steps		
	1. SCOPE THE PROBLEM		**Days 0-4**	**"WHAT?"**
		Verify the original performance expectation is stated or implied and is still valid.		
		Determine if a process flowchart exists. If so, use it.		
		Write a problem description (gap, dimensions, consequences, significance).		
		Begin the extent of condition review.		
		Recommend team and scope of the incident evaluation to management sponsor.		
	2. INVESTIGATE THE FACTORS		**Days 3-9**	**"WHO, WHEN, WHERE?"**
		Verify the physical, human, and documentary evidence is protected and collected.		
		Decide what information to collect and whom to interview.		
		Walk down affected area. Take pictures/videos. Interview: Ask RIGHT questions the RIGHT way.		
		Begin review of internal and external operating experience. (A repeat occurrence for _____?)		

	3. RECONSTRUCT THE STORY	Days 3-11	"HOW?"
	Perform trouble shooting or fault tree analysis (for equipment).		
	Reconstruct the incident showing a logical sequencing or flow (progression of the problem).		
	Determine "HOW" the incident happened (i.e., the failure modes, behaviors, visible actions).		
	Integrate all information into actions and factors chart (events and causal factors chart).		

	4. ESTABLISH CONTRIBUTING FACTORS	Days 3-14	"HOW and WHY?"
	Map the cause and effect relationships.		
	Conduct a difference [change] analysis to identify more contributing factors (as applicable).		
	Conduct a defense [barrier] analysis to determine if controls were weak, missing, or not used. Identify all factors that triggered, permitted, or otherwise influenced the incident.		

	5. VALIDATE UNDERLYING FACTORS	Days 15-19	"WHY?"
	For each of the incident's contributing factors, find correctable causes.		
	Determine physical root cause(s) and validate (for equipment).		
	Determine human root cause(s) and validate (for human performance difficulties).		
	Determine organizational root cause(s) and validate (i.e., latent organizational weaknesses).		
	Complete an extent of cause review once root cause(s) have been determined.		
	Document evidence/basis for rejecting possible causes.		

	6. PLAN CORRECTIVE ACTIONS	Days 20-24	"WHAT NEXT?"
	Develop one or more corrective actions to eliminate or control each cause.		
	Establish a schedule for implementing and completing the corrective actions in a timely manner.		
	Validate the proposed intervention plan versus acceptance criteria.		
	Explain the proposed resolution to responsible management and action departments.		
	Generate a trackable activity to evaluate long-term effectiveness in precluding repetition.		

	7. REPORT LEARNINGS	Days 1-30	"COMMUNICATE LESSONS"
	Document as you go. Support conclusions with facts.		
	Show all work in the form of a complete, written analysis.		
	Document findings to provide a permanent, auditable record.		
	Provide retrievable information for subsequent trending, problem solving, and effectiveness review.		

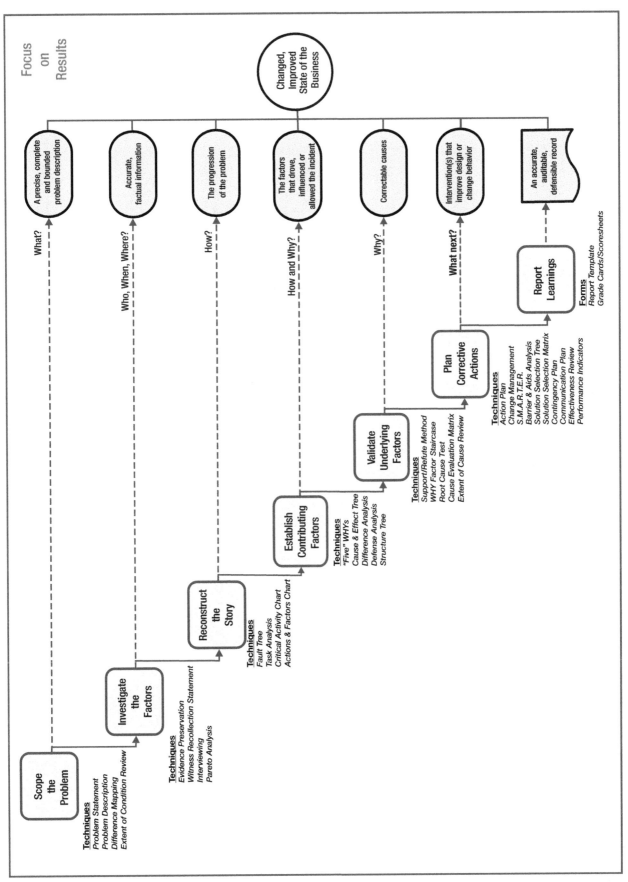

Figure 0-24. Incident Analysis Steps with Techniques

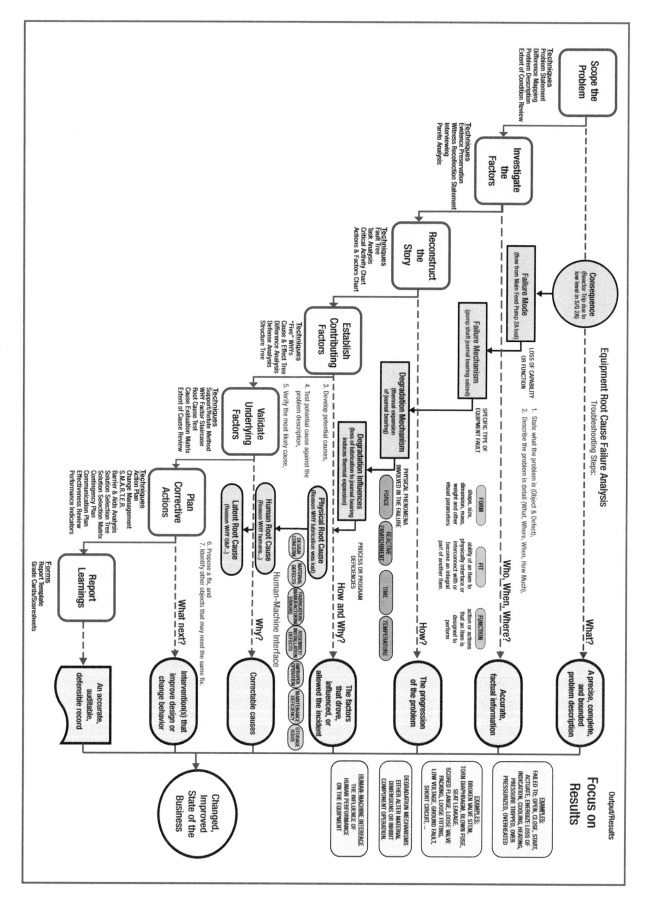

Figure 0-25. Equipment Failure Analysis

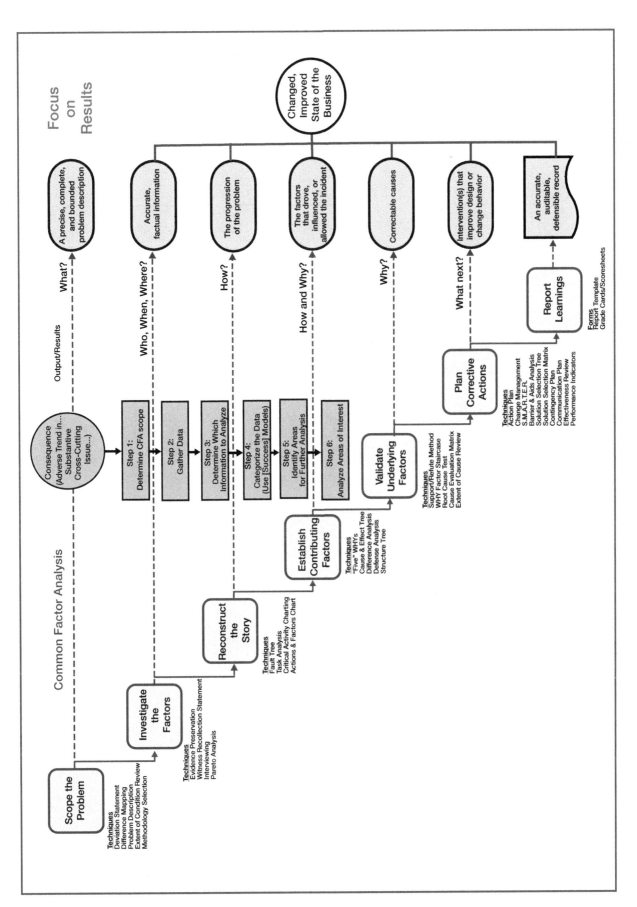

Figure 0-26. Common Factor Analysis

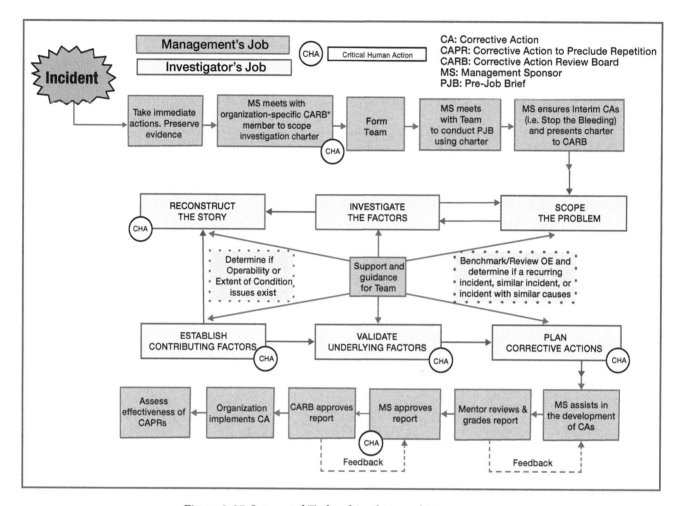

Figure 0-27. Integrated Tasks of Analysts and Management

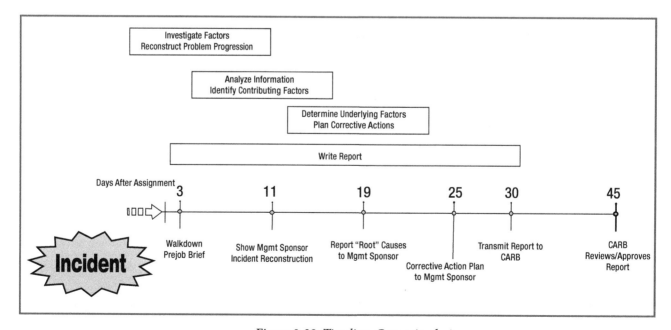

Figure 0-28. Timeline: Cause Analysis

Table 0-4. Base Root Cause Analysis Process Schedule with Key Activities

Day	Screening/Review Activity	Management Sponsor (MS) Or Team Activities	RCA Process Activity	Performance Improvement Team Activity
Zero	A. Flags as "Root Cause" B. Assigns to management sponsor (MS) ▶ "Team Requirement"?	1. **MS:** Initiates Quarantine (If Req'd) [Procedure] Emergent issue response 2. **MS:** Champions required resources	**Scope Problem (Step 1)** ▶ Determine key personnel or groups ▶ Initial extent of condition, applicable operating experience searches	▶ Issues Briefing Action to MS ▶ Designates a Mentor (if needed) May be Cause Analysis Program Sponsor or Lead
1	C. CARB Member Approves Initial Charter	3. Complete Charter & Get Initial CARB Member Approval.		
2		4. Completes Team Leader and Root Cause Analyst Assignments 5. Drafts Problem Description 6. Initial Review With Mentor, Cause Analyst, and Team Leader (as Applicable)	▶ Review Available Incident Information ▶ Begin Interviews, Document & Data Collection ▶ Share Lessons Learned	▶ Mentor/Sponsor Conducts Initial Review with Team Leader and/or Cause Analyst ▶ Coaching on Problem Description, Process Tools, Forms, etc.
3	D. Approve Briefing Content ▶ Set Review Date?	7. **MS:** Briefs review committee — including resources, schedule, support	**Investigate and Reconstruct Phase (Steps 2-4)**	**Mentor Support for Analyst (and/or Team) *Brief Team***
4			▶ Begin writing the report now	
5	E. Charter presented to and approved by CARB	Note: Late date for briefing review committee	▶ Construct Failure Scenario (FTA, E&CF)	
6-12				
13		8. **Team:** Interviews complete; Document & Evidence reviews are in progress		
14			▶ Complete Extent of Condition evaluation	
15	F. CARB updated by Management Owner	9. **MS:** Mid-process update to Review Committee *Confirm Intent to issue OE*	**Determine RC Phase (Step 5)**	
16			▶ Refine Extent of Cause and Previous Occurrence OE Reviews ▶ Begin review for Organizational & Programmatic (O&P) causes	
17			**"Validate RC" Phase (Step 5)**	

Day	Screening/Review Activity	Management Sponsor (MS) or Team Activities	RCA Process Activity	Performance Improvement Team Activity
18			▶ Complete Extent of Cause, O&P issues, and Previous Occurrence OE Review	
19			▶ Provide evidence/basis for rejecting possible root causes (if applicable).	
20	**G. Review & Address Update Content** ▶ *Set/Confirm Review date*		**"Plan Corrective Actions" Phase (Step 6)**	Include CR on Review Committee Agenda
21-24			▶ Address causes and establish Effectiveness Review measures ▶ Validate the Proposed corrective action using the S.M.A.R.T.E.R. technique.	
25		**10. Team: Draft Report to MS and RCA Mentor**	**"Report Learnings" Phase (Step 7)**	Perform Independent Review – Process Standards & Expectations
26-29		11. MS & Team: Reviews & Feedback Complete	▶ Review with Assignees ▶ Obtain concurrence on the Proposed Due Dates	Independent Review Completed
30		12. Team: All Sponsor Review comments addressed	▶ Report is signed by Root Cause Analyst, Team Leader, and Management Sponsor	
31	**H. CARB begin comments**	**13. Team: Report transmitted to CARB for comments**		
32-39				
40	▶ *Department CARB review & Approval (as applicable)*	14. Team: All review comments addressed & ready for Review Committee review.		
45	**I. CARB Review of RCA**	**15. MS: Review comments incorporated; Final Report Approved**	**Complete "Documentation" Phase (Step 7)**	▶ Coordinate release of Lessons To Be Learned to the Organization

CR — Condition Report
MS — Management Sponsor
O&P — Organizational and Programmatic
OE — Operating Experience
RC — Root Cause
RCA — Root Cause Analysis
CARB — Corrective Action Review Board
S.M.A.R.T.E.R. — Specific, Measurable, Attainable, Related, Time-sensitive, Effective, Reviewed

Table 0-5. Potential Schedule Impacts to Base 30 Day RCA Process Milestones

Day	Base Actions	Case #1	Case #2	Case #3	Case #4	Case #5
Zero	**Flags as "Root Cause" Assigns to MS**	**Wednesday**	**Monday**	**Monday**	**Wednesday**	**Friday**
1.		Thursday	Tuesday	Tuesday	Thursday	*Saturday*
2.		*Off-Friday*	Wednesday	Wednesday	Friday	*Sunday*
3.	**Brief Team**	*Saturday*	Thursday	Thursday	*Saturday*	Monday
4.		*Sunday*	*Off-Friday*	Friday	*Sunday*	Tuesday
5.		Monday	*Saturday*	*Saturday*	Monday	Wednesday
6.		Tuesday	*Sunday*	*Sunday*	Tuesday	Thursday
7.		Wednesday	Monday	Monday	Wednesday	*Off-Friday*
8.		Thursday	Tuesday	Tuesday	Thursday	*Saturday*
9.		Friday	Wednesday	Wednesday	*Off-Friday*	*Sunday*
10.		*Saturday*	Thursday	Thursday	*Saturday*	Monday
11.		*Sunday*	Friday	*Off-Friday*	*Sunday*	Tuesday
12.		Monday	*Saturday*	*Saturday*	Monday	Wednesday
13.	**Interviews Completed**	Tuesday	*Sunday*	*Sunday*	Tuesday	Thursday
14.		Wednesday	Monday	Monday	Wednesday	Friday
15.		Thursday	Tuesday	Tuesday	Thursday	*Saturday*
16.	**Mid-Process Review Committee Update**	*Off-Friday*	Wednesday	Wednesday	Friday	*Sunday*
17.		*Saturday*	Thursday	Thursday	*Saturday*	Monday
18.		*Sunday*	*Off-Friday*	Friday	*Sunday*	Tuesday
19.	**Draft Report to MS & CA Mentor/Lead**	Monday	*Saturday*	*Saturday*	Monday	Wednesday
20.		Tuesday	*Sunday*	*Sunday*	Tuesday	Thursday
21.		Wednesday	Monday	Monday	Wednesday	*Off-Friday*
22.		Thursday	Tuesday	Tuesday	Thursday	*Saturday*
23.		Friday	Wednesday	Wednesday	*Off-Friday*	*Sunday*
24.		*Saturday*	Thursday	Thursday	*Saturday*	Monday
25.		*Sunday*	Friday	*Off-Friday*	*Sunday*	Tuesday
26.		Monday	*Saturday*	*Saturday*	Monday	Wednesday
27.		Tuesday	*Sunday*	*Sunday*	Tuesday	Thursday
28.		Wednesday	Monday	Monday	Wednesday	Friday
29.		Thursday	Tuesday	Tuesday	Thursday	*Saturday*
30.	**Report Sent to Review Committee**	*Off-Friday*	Wednesday	Wednesday	Friday	*Sunday*

Questions for Understanding

1. Why is it important early in an incident investigation to understand the success path before an investigator starts looking for the cause(s) of failures?

2. When hardware or equipment is involved, why is it important to find the physical root(s) of the problem before determining the human roots or the organizational roots?

3. Why is it important that an investigator understand models of human behavior?

4. Why is it important that investigators do a good job distinguishing between personal accountability and organizational accountability?

5. What is the difference between a criminal investigation and the investigations being discussed in this manual?

6. What is the purpose of each of the following investigation steps?
   - Scope the problem.
   - Investigate the factors.
   - Reconstruct the story.
   - Establish contributing factors.
   - Validate underlying factors ("root causes").
   - Plan corrective actions.
   - Report learnings.

Questions for Discussion

1. What are the similarities between the A-B-C model of human performance and the stimulus-response model?

2. Why is it important to reach an understanding of an individual's context (work environment and task demands) when performing an investigation?

3. If a problem was found in the training section of the accountability model, how would you work to correct it?

References

Bloch, H.P. (2005, April). Successful failure analysis strategies. *Reliability Advantage: Training Bulletin*. Retrieved from http://www.heinzbloch.com/docs/ReliabilityAdvantage/Reliability_Advantage_Volume_3.pdf

Bloch, H.P. (2011, May). Structured failure analysis strategies solve pump problems. *Machinery Lubrication*. Retrieved from http://www.machinerylubrication.com/Read/28467/pump-failure-analysis

Corcoran, W. R. (2007). *The phoenix handbook: The ultimate event evaluation manual for finding safety and profit improvement in adverse events*. Windsor, CT: NSRC Corporation.

Daniels, A. C., Daniels, J., & Abernathy, B. (2006, May/June). *The leader's role in pay systems and organizational performance*. Retrieved from http://aubreydaniels.com/system/files/Leaders%20Role%20in%20Pay.pdf

Health and Safety Executive (HSE). (2012, March). *Leadership and worker involvement toolkit: The 'ABC' analysis*. Retrieved from http://www.hse.gov.uk/construction/lwit/assets/downloads/abc-analysis.pdf

Muschara, T. (2010). *A risk-based approach to managing the human risk: An unclear and present danger*. Retrieved from http://www.slideshare.net/muschara/managing-human-risk

Nuclear Regulatory Commission (NRC). (2011, February). *Inspection for one degraded cornerstone or any three white inputs in a strategic performance area*. (NRC Inspection Procedure 95002). Washington, DC: US NRC Office of Nuclear Reactor Regulation.

Nuclear Regulatory Commission (NRC). (2013, August). *Problem identification and resolution*. (NRC Inspection Procedure 71152). Washington, DC: US NRC Office of Nuclear Reactor Regulation.

Wile, D. E. (2014, February 19). Why doers do — Part 1: Internal elements of human performance. *Performance Improvement, 53*(2). Retrieved from http://onlinelibrary.wiley.com/doi/10.1002/pfi.21394/pdf

For Further Reading

Daniels, A. C. & Daniels, J. E. (2004). *Performance management: Changing behavior that drives organizational effectiveness*. Atlanta, GA: Performance Management Publications.

Tosti, D. T. (2007, January 8). Aligning the culture and strategy for success. *Performance Improvement, 46*(1). Retrieved from http://onlinelibrary.wiley.com/doi/10.1002/pfi.035/pdf

Step 1

Scope the Problem

If the only tool you have is a hammer, you tend to see every problem as a nail.

— Abraham Maslow, Psychologist

When an incident occurs the first thing you need to do is *scope the problem*. Scoping the problem is the initial information gathering stage of cause analysis. You are going to rely on the material that you acquire during this stage for the rest of your analysis; so be specific.

To properly scope a problem, use the following investigation techniques:

1. Document the *problem statement* which gives a concise reason for the investigation resembling a newspaper headline.
2. Build on the problem statement, using a *problem description* which includes information about the incident's time and location, related equipment, involved personnel, consequences, and significance.
3. Use a *difference map* to illustrate where the problem is and is not.
4. Conduct an *extent of condition review* to determine whether the current problem exists in other activities, processes, programs, organizations, or elsewhere in the business and whether prompt correction is needed.

In this section, you will see why and when you should use each of these tools/techniques. Each technique can enhance your knowledge of what happened, when it happened, where it happened, and who was involved.

Basics of Cause Analysis for Step 1

Many organizations document adverse conditions and incidents on some type of problem or condition report that will be the starting point for your investigation. Sometimes organizational management will provide you with a written charter that defines the investigation and the depth to which your evaluation should go. After you have been assigned to perform an incident investigation, use the condition report and charter (if provided) to start to understand the specific problem and to determine the extent of that problem (see Figure 1-1). Once Step 1, Scope the Problem, has been completed, you should have in writing a precise, complete, and bounded problem description.

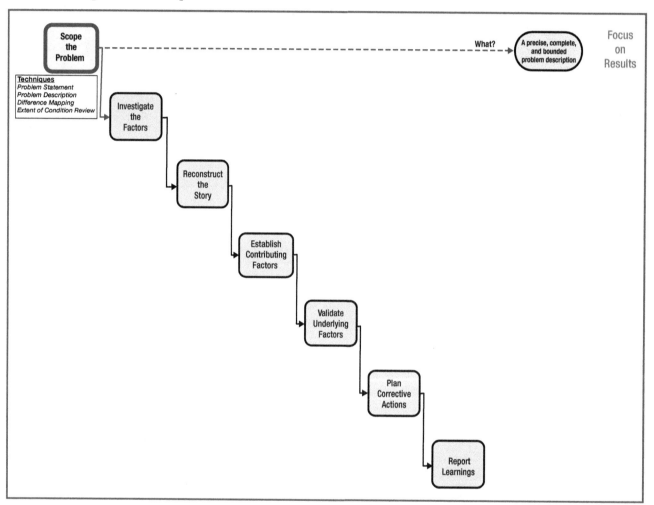

Figure 1-1. Step 1 Scope the Problem

Use Table 1-1 as a checklist to guide you through Step 1 of the investigation. Table 1-1 has two main parts: the *behaviors* (actions/tasks) needed and the *results* that should be achieved by the end of Step 1. Most behaviors listed need to be performed; however, some behaviors may not be appropriate for a particular type of problem. For example, if you are not working on a problem involving a piece of equipment, you would not need to "Verify an equipment performance evaluation has been initiated." For some of the behaviors listed, the following techniques (listed by section number) will help you complete checklist Step 1:

1.1 Problem Statement

1.2 Problem Description

1.3 Difference Map

1.4 Extent of Condition Review

Significant problems are generally put through the most rigorous type of evaluation called *root cause analysis* (RC) and all tasks on the checklist should be completed. This manual is set up so you can complete all the tasks needed to complete the *root cause analysis* of the most significant problems of your business.

However, other business problems are less significant. These problems are still very important to the business and viewed as high value learning opportunities; so the problems are put through a type of evaluation called *apparent cause analysis* (AC). During Step 1 of *root cause analysis* and apparent cause analysis, you should complete all the items on Table 1-1. Minor problems are generally labeled as *adverse* (AD) with only minimal analysis required. Your supervision or management will determine what depth of analysis a problem needs (RC, AC, or AD). Generally, fewer evaluation tasks are required for *apparent cause analysis* (AC) than for *root cause analysis* (RC). Likewise, fewer evaluation tasks are required for minor or *adverse* (AD) conditions than for *apparent cause analysis* (AC).

In Table 1-1, a *required* result is designated with the subscript "R" and needs to be completed. A desired result is designated with the subscript "D" and is generally only completed if the result can be achieved easily (with a minimal amount of effort and in a short time).

Table 1-1. Step 1 Jump Start Checklist

☑ Behaviors [Sub-Tasks]	Tools/Techniques	Required		
☐ Write a short **problem statement** (object/defect or gap) to focus investigation.	*Problem Statement*	RC	AC	AD
☐ Start gathering information/data. (Be cautious handling confidential information).		RC	AC	AD
☐ *Review Condition Report with applicable standard, procedures, training, and drawings*		RC	AC	AD
☐ *Review charter (if applicable)*		RC		
☐ Verify an equipment performance evaluation has been initiated (as needed).		RC	AC	AD
☐ Verify a human performance evaluation has been initiated (as needed).		RC	AC	AD
☐ Verify the original performance expectation is stated or implied and is still valid. (In order to have a problem [adverse condition], there must be a goal.)		RC	AC	
☐ Determine if a process flowchart exists. If so, use it.		RC	AC	
☐ Write a **problem description** (gap, dimensions, consequences, significance).	*Problem Description*	RC	AC	
☐ *Express the gap between the way things are and the way they ought to be (an ideal or an expectation) This should include specific citation of any applicable requirement not met. (GAP)*		RC	AC	
☐ **Map differences** *to explicitly state WHO (by position not by name), WHEN, and WHERE the failure or inappropriate action occurred. (DIMENSIONS)*	*Difference Mapping*	RC	AC	
☐ *Emphasize WHAT is wrong,* **not** *WHY it is wrong. (CONSEQUENCES: Actual and Potential) Define so that everyone involved in its solution can understand it.*		RC	AC	
☐ *State undesirable or unacceptable circumstances, conditions, risks, occurrences, methods, or results. Explain how the problem affects the plant or personnel. (SIGNIFICANCE)*		RC	AC	
☐ Begin determination of the **extent** of the adverse **condition** – other pieces of equipment or processes or organizations that could be affected.	*Extent of Condition Review*	RC	AC	AD
☐ Recommend team and scope of the incident evaluation to Management Sponsor.		RC	AC	
☐ Obtain Management Sponsor approval on the problem description and scope.		RC	AC	
☐ Recommend prompt remedial, interim, or compensatory actions for the problem.		RC	AC	

RC = Root Cause Analysis; **AC** = Apparent Cause Analysis; **AD** = Adverse

☑ **Results** Required [R] / Desired [D]			
☐ A simple **problem statement**. *KISS – "Keep It Simple" and to the point.*	RC$_R$	AC$_R$	
☐ A specific, concise, objective, observable, and measurable **problem description** that meets the following criteria:	RC$_R$	AC$_R$	
☐ *States WHAT, WHEN, WHERE, and WHO. (DIMENSIONS)*	RC$_R$	AC$_R$	
☐ *Describes the GAP between the way things are and the way they ought to be.*	RC$_R$	AC$_R$	
☐ *Focuses on the problem; not the symptoms or causes of the problem.*	RC$_R$	AC$_R$	
☐ *Explains the undesirable or unacceptable CONSEQUENCES, conditions, methods, or results. A statement of the safety SIGNIFICANCE must be in the report.*	RC$_R$	AC$_R$	
☐ The **extent** of the adverse **condition** (actual and potential).	RC$_R$	AC$_R$	AD$_D$
☐ The scope of the evaluation with spatial, chronological, and organizational boundaries.	RC$_R$	AC$_R$	

1.1   Problem Statement

What is it?

A *problem statement* concisely describes the item you are concerned about and the item's deviation or malfunction for which you want to find the cause. A problem statement provides factual information to identify what has gone wrong (*defect/deviation*) with what (*object*). A good problem statement is brief, precise, and based on what can be observed.

Why is it useful?

The problem statement provides a starting point for problem-solving by identifying the specific person, place, or thing observed and what is substandard about the observed performance. Later, it helps all readers and listeners concentrate on the core problem – the reason for this investigation.

When is it used?

When a problem is discovered, it is used to provide initial focus on the concern. Many organizations will ask the lead investigator for help in developing the investigation charter. You can use the problem statement technique to help management develop the team charter. The problem statement is also needed to build a *difference map* (presented in section 1.3). In Step 3, Reconstruct the Story, you put the problem statement in the circle symbol on an *actions and factors chart* (as shown in Figure 1-2).

Figure 1-2. Problem Symbol

How is it done?

There are two parts to the problem statement: the *object* and the *defect* (deviation/malfunction).

1. **STATE** the object (person, place, or thing) affected.
2. **STATE** the defect or deviation (gap, equipment malfunction, human failing, programmatic deficiency, systemic flaw, or organizational weakness).

1.1.1   Problem Statement Examples

At the start of your investigation, write a short *problem statement* that will be the reason and the focal point of your investigation. Use the following for examples:

1. ACME **staff member** (object) **injured back** slipping on paperwork (deviation).
2. Three AJAX **personnel** (object) received **acid burns** (deviation) on their faces, extremities, and torsos.
3. An **electrician** (object) received a **puncture wound in a high contamination area** (deviation).
4. Florida hospital **surgeons amputated wrong leg** (deviation) of **patient** (object).
5. **Bearings** (object) with chromium content outside acceptance criteria were accepted by procurement engineering (deviation).
6. Residual heat removal suction relief **valve** (object) failed surveillance test (defect).
7. Unit 3 **reactor** (object) tripped on low "B" steam generator level (deviation).
8. Unit 2 "A" containment spray **header** (object) had a void condition (defect).
9. A substantive cross-cutting issue (deviation) exists in the Nuclear Regulatory Commission (NRC) **Safety Culture Area** of Problem Identification and Resolution (object).
10. Vortex prevention was not properly accounted for (deviation) in the **calculation** of the usable volume in the emergency diesel generator fuel oil storage tanks (object).
11. Groundwater **samples** from discharge line manholes (object) were radioactively contaminated above normal background levels (deviation).

1.2   Problem Description

What is it?

The *problem description* identifies the business issue being evaluated. It describes what happened and the consequence to the business. The condition description in the corrective action document is not necessarily the problem description. The elements of an effective problem description are illustrated in Figure 1-3.

Why is it useful?

A problem description provides appropriate bounds for the scope of an investigation. The problem description helps focus and scope the evaluation because it clarifies the undesirable or unacceptable results and consequences for readers and decision-makers.

When is it used?

A problem description is generated in Step 1 (Scope the Problem) of the problem identification and resolution process and is used throughout the remainder of the investigation. As more information becomes available, the problem description may be modified.

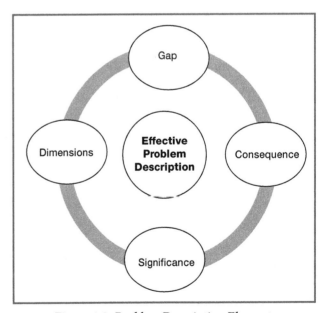

Figure 1-3. Problem Description Elements

How is it done?

> ### Prerequisite
>
> Before describing the problem, first investigate the facts about what occurred, when and where the incident occurred, who was involved, and the consequences. Obtain preliminary information by discussing the incident with cognizant personnel to clarify the perceived **PROBLEM** and the resulting **CONSEQUENCE**(s) caused by the problem. The perceived problem may not always reflect the actual problem but may be a symptom of the actual problem. Use the information available from the corrective action document and other sources.

1. Identify the **GAP** (the difference between "what should be" and "what is"). You may use one of two methods, defined below:

    Method A: Write a problem statement (noun/verb).

    1. **OBJECT**: What is the item (person, place, or thing) that is affected?
    2. **DEFECT**: What is the deviation from the expected or required standard of performance?

    Example: A student (object: person) conducting electrical measurements on a microwave oven received a 4000 volt shock (defect: deviation).

    Method B: Expected vs. actual statement.

    1. Compare "what should be": Requirement, standard, norm, or expectation.
    2. With "what is": The existing, as-found condition. Define so that everyone involved in the problem's solution can understand it. Emphasize what is wrong, not why it is wrong (effect).

    Example 1: The department's goal is to complete root cause investigations within 30 days. In the past year, only one of ten investigations was completed within 30 days.

    Example 2: Section 4.2.1 of procedure HTP-033, *Access Control*, states that workers read and understand the radiation work permit (RWP) and review work area radiological survey data to ensure awareness of radiological conditions prior to entering the radiological controlled area (RCA).

    On March 29, 2013, an NRC inspector identified that seven radiation workers failed to understand the restrictions/limitations of their RWPs and were not aware of the radiological conditions in their work area prior to entering the RCA.

2. Detail the **DIMENSIONS**.
    - *When* did it happen? (Time)
    - *Where* did it happen? (Location)
    - *Who* (by position) was involved? (Personnel)

3. Document the **CONSEQUENCE** (actual or potential). Describe "What is the effect on the enterprise?"
    - The adverse result of the incident.
    - Adverse business, regulatory, or personnel outcome created by the issue.

4. Assess the **SIGNIFICANCE** of the actual or potential consequences. Describe any challenges to nuclear, radiological, and industrial safety that required interim actions to be implemented. Address safety challenges at the time of the incident and interim actions needed to reduce the challenge. Use Table 1-2 to help establish the significance of the problem.

Table 1-2. Significance Assessment

Risk	▸ Impact on the safe operation of the business (e.g., nuclear plant safety significance)
	▸ Impact on the reliable operation of the enterprise (revenue and cost)
	▸ Impact on the environment
	▸ Personnel radiation safety threat
	▸ Personnel industrial safety hazard
Recurrence	▸ Repeat incidents (known frequency)
	▸ Adverse trends (known frequency)
	▸ Acceptability of the potential for recurrence (likelihood of occurrence)
Precursors and Defenses	▸ Precursor to a much more serious incident
	▸ Potential to be more severe if different conditions, that could be reasonably expected, had been present
	▸ Defenses penetrated (number and dependability)
	▸ Defenses remaining (number and dependability)
Exposure	▸ Regulatory margin
	▸ Public impact
	▸ Safety culture component contribution

1.2.1   Problem Description Examples

From your problem statement, build a *problem description* by adding information about the people involved, the location of the incident, and the time of the incident. Include the actual or potential consequences of the problem so readers understand why they should care about solving this problem. The following example problem descriptions relate incident details, and the four parts of a problem description are labeled in the first example:

1. On the morning of June 13, 2013 [*Dimension – When*], an ACME staff member, who was carrying a few items into work [*Dimension – Who*], opened the door to enter an office [*Dimension – Where*]. The staff member slipped on some paperwork [*Gap*] that a co-worker had previously slid under the door on the tile floor. Reacting quickly to maintain balance, the first staff member sustained a recordable [*Significance*] back injury [*Consequence*].

2. On July 1, 2013, three AJAX National Security personnel working to a procedure titled "Synthesis of Energetic Materials" were exposed to strong acids ejected from a reactor vessel. The acid exposure resulted from an exothermic reaction initiated by the rapid addition of fuming sulfuric acid to the reactor vessel's contents. The personnel experienced acid burns on their faces, extremities, and torsos that resulted in hospitalization.

3. On March 2, 2013, while changing out hydraulic lines on remotely operated equipment in a high contamination area, a Montana treatment plant employee received a puncture wound. A small support wire protruding from a frayed hydraulic hose punctured the employee's personal protective equipment (PPE) while the employee was attempting to disengage the hose. Survey results indicated no radiological contamination of the employee.

4. On February 20, 1995, a 51-year-old man underwent surgery to have his right foot amputated below the knee, but surgeons at the University Community Hospital in Tampa, Florida, amputated the left leg below the knee instead.

5. At approximately 10:30 a.m., on Wednesday, June 8, 2011, a student intern conducting electrical measurements on a microwave oven received a 4000 volt shock. At the time the student was working alone in building 123 of the Atlantic Northwest Regional Laboratory. The injured student was transferred to the Hillsdale Medical Center and underwent eight days of inpatient treatment.

6. At 4:00:36 a.m., Wednesday, March 28, 1979, the feedwater pumps and main turbine at Three Mile Island, Unit 2, tripped off-line while the reactor was operating at full power. The power-operated relief valve (PORV) opened at 2255 psig and the reactor tripped (control rods dropped) five seconds later at 2355 psig. The PORV failed to reclose when the primary pressure decreased to 2205 psig resulting in a continuous loss of reactor coolant for 2½ hours. Highly contaminated water was spilled into the containment and auxiliary buildings. The auxiliary feedwater system failed to send water to the steam generators that remove heat from the reactor core so steam generators A and B boiled dry. High pressure injection, which initiated automatically, was throttled back by the operations crew. Pressurizer function was lost, and steam formed in the reactor. When the reactor coolant pumps were stopped and the PORV was blocked, all effective cooling of the core ceased. The core overheated, zirconium alloy cladding reacted with steam forming a hydrogen bubble, and fuel melted.

7. At 12:20 p.m., on March 22, 1975, Unit 1 of the Browns Ferry Nuclear Power Plant experienced a serious in-plant cable tray fire. The fire was started by an engineer who was using a candle to check for air leaks through a fire wall penetration seal. The flame ignited a temporary polyurethane cable penetration seal. The fire spread into the polyurethane seal and cables. The fire was fought on both sides of the reactor building and cable spreading room wall by plant and local community fire-fighting personnel. All Unit 1 emergency core cooling systems were lost, as well as the capability to monitor core power. There was no release of radioactivity.

8. At 2:46 p.m. (Japanese Standard Time) on Friday March 11, 2011, a 9.0-magnitude earthquake struck Japan about 231 miles (372 kilometers) northeast of Tokyo off the coast of Honshu Island. The earthquake led to the automatic shutdown of 11 reactors at four sites (Onagawa, Fukushima Dai-ichi, Fukushima Dai-ni, and Tokai) along the northeast coast. Diesel generators provided power until about 40 minutes later, when a tsunami, estimated to have exceeded 45 feet (14 meters) in height, appeared to have caused the loss of all power to the six Fukushima Dai-ichi reactors. The tsunami inundated the area, surrounding units 1 to 4 to a depth of 13 to 16 feet above grade (4 to 5 meters), causing extensive damage to site buildings and flooding of the turbine and reactor buildings.

1.3   Difference Mapping

What is it?

To properly describe a problem, you need to put a boundary around the problem. Setting this boundary has two aspects. First, describe the major dimensions of the problem: WHAT occurs, WHERE, WHEN, and involving WHOM (Kepner & Tregoe, 1981). These are the *positive indicators* of the problem (Table 1-3). Second, describe what does not occur, where it does not occur, when it does not occur, and who it does not involve. These are the *negative indicators* of the problem (Table 1-4).

Table 1-3. Positive Indicators

WHAT is involved?	
WHEN does it occur?	
WHERE does it occur?	
WHO is involved?	

Table 1-4. Negative Indicators

What is not involved?	
When does it not occur?	
Where does it not occur?	
Who is not involved?	

Why is it useful?

This technique helps you determine exactly WHAT IS and WHAT IS NOT a part of the problem. It is an excellent feeder for your *extent of condition review*. The positive and negative indicators allow you to readily communicate the exact nature of the problem with decision-makers. They also help remind your investigation team of precisely what the team is attempting to change or solve. Additionally, mapping a problem's differences may often assist teams in pinpointing the cause(s) of an incident.

When is it used?

Difference mapping is used in Step 1 (Scope the Problem) – especially in determining a problem's extent or boundaries. The difference map may be useful at other steps of the problem solving process. Save difference maps for further reference during your *difference analysis* (in Step 4) and *extent of cause review* (in Step 5).

How is it done?

1. Using the tables, RECORD the current problem statement or the main focus of the investigation. If known, document numbers and percentages. Then record all things known or believed about the issue. If preliminary information or data have been collected, document the results. Enter the positive indicators first; then follow with all of the negative indicators. Another way is to record one set of positive indicators followed by the corresponding negative indicators (e.g., WHAT IS involved followed by WHAT IS NOT involved).

Positive Indicators

WHAT is involved?	Which equipment, machines, or tools; what materials or supplies; which procedures?
WHEN does it occur?	At what times – is it periodic or random; which shifts?
WHERE does it occur?	Which areas or locations?
WHO is involved?	Which workers; departments; vendors; customers or clients; or other individuals?

2. GENERATE negative indicators that are closely related to the problem – not completely unconnected or "off-the-wall." Negative indicators should help decision makers understand the problem, not confuse the reader. They should help set apart the problem effectively so that the problem is more effective to work with and eventually solve.

Negative Indicators

What is not involved?	Which equipment, machines, or tools; what materials or supplies; which procedures?
When does it not occur?	At what times – is it periodic or random; which shifts?
Where does it not occur?	Which areas or locations?
Who is not involved?	Which workers; departments; vendors; customers or clients; or other individuals?

3. For any unconfirmed positive or negative indicators, COLLECT information to verify that the indicators actually exist or are true. Using the complete listing of both the positive and negative indicators, modify the problem description with the new boundaries. Begin with what occurs (the problem description) and modify it with the indicators. See examples below.

4. MODIFY the original problem statement and KEEP the (new) description, with boundaries, for further development.

1.3.1   Difference Mapping Examples

You also need to find out how big of a problem you have to solve. By mapping an incident's differences, you put a boundary around the problem. You can say this person is having difficulty with this task, but these people doing the same task are not. You can determine when the problem is occurring and when else it could be occurring, but is not. You can isolate where the problem is happening and other places where else it could be happening, but is not. The following examples of difference mapping start out with a very general problem and end up with a problem that has very specific boundaries.

Problem Statement 1: *A worker complained of arm pain*

Positive Indicators

WHAT is involved?	Sharp pain
WHEN does it occur?	Constantly
WHERE does it occur?	Left elbow

Negative Indicators

What is not involved?	Dull pain
When does it not occur?	Sporadic, periodic
Where does it not occur?	Left forearm, upper arm, hand

Modified Statement 1 with Boundaries: A worker reported pain in the left elbow. There was no pain in the left forearm, upper arm, or hand. The pain was sharp, not dull. The pain was constant, not sporadic or periodic.

Problem Statement 2: *ACME Company is getting inappropriate requests for laboratory analyses.*

Positive Indicators		**Negative Indicators**	
WHAT is involved?	Blood/urine analysis requests (20%)	*What is not* involved?	Other requests for analyses (80%)
WHEN does it occur?	Nights (70%) Weekends (25%)	*When does it not* occur?	Days (30%)
WHO is involved?	Workers with less than two years of experience	*Who is not* involved?	Workers with two years of experience or more.

Modified Statement 2 with Boundaries: Twenty percent of the requests to ACME Company for blood and urine analyses are inappropriate. Seventy percent of these requests are from the night shifts and 25% are from weekend shifts. Night and weekend shifts are primarily staffed by people with less than two years of experience.

Problem Statement 3: *Objects falling off scaffolds present safety hazards.*

Positive Indicators		**Negative Indicators**	
WHAT is involved?	Small tools (8), small scaffold pieces (6)	*What is not* involved?	Small instruments (0), large scaffolding (0)
WHEN does it occur?	Nights (11) 0200-0500 (7), Weekends (9)	*When does it not* occur?	Days (3)
WHERE does it occur?	Containment (14)	*Where does it not* occur?	Auxiliary Building (0)
WHO is involved?	Generator Crew (14)	*Who is not* involved?	Turbine Crew (0)

Modified Statement 3 with Boundaries: In the past twenty days, Prince Nuclear Station had 14 separate documented instances of objects dropped from scaffolding during the outage. The objects were small hand tools or small scaffold pieces (knuckles), not small instruments or big pieces of scaffold. Of the 14 incidents, 11 happened on night shift with 7 of the 11 happening between 2 a.m. and 5 a.m. (0200-0500). Of the 14 incidents, 9 happened on weekends. All of the incidents involved the steam generator replacement crew and occurred in the containment building, while the turbine crew in the auxiliary building experienced no incidents involving objects falling off scaffolds.

1.4 Extent of Condition Review

What is it?
An *extent of condition review* determines whether the current problem being investigated has occurred in other activities, processes, programs, organizations, or elsewhere in the business. The review process involves putting a reasonable boundary around the population of other susceptible business processes, equipment, or human performance jobs. Tasks with the potential to exhibit the same undesired symptoms, circumstances, or effects as the current issue are investigated. Peer reviews are used to ensure the extent of the investigation is reasonable.

Why is it useful?

High reliability organizations seldom rely on a single component or single activity for successful operation. If there is a problem with one piece of equipment, there is a good chance there are problems with the same or similar redundant pieces of equipment. You should clearly define how wide the scope of the problems may be and what actions would be appropriate to resolve any additional problems identified. The level of effort in determining and documenting the extent of condition should be commensurate with the level of investigation and significance of the incident.

When is it used?

The extent of condition review begins "promptly" in Step 1 (Scope the Problem) of the problem solving process. For a significant adverse condition, "promptly" should be measured in hours – not days. As more information is found or more issues arise, the extent of condition review may be modified or expanded. The review is generally finalized by Step 5 (Validate Underlying Factors).

How is it done?

Evaluate from the adverse condition or the direct cause perspective or both. Use Table 1-5 for the first three steps.

1. RESTATE the *object* (from problem statement).
2. RESTATE the *defect* or *deviation* (from problem statement).
3. STATE the *application*.

	Object (Person, Place, Thing)	**Application** (Activity, Form, Fit, Function)	**Defect** (Flaw, Failing, Deficiency)
Problem Statement	1	3	2

Table 1-5. Problem Statement Table

4. Then EVALUATE various combinations. (See Table 1-6 as an example.)

   ▸ Same → Same → Same
   ▸ Same → Same → Similar
   ▸ Similar → Same → Same
   ▸ Similar → Similar → Same
   ▸ Other combinations…

5. DOCUMENT a reasonable and conservative boundary (i.e., extent) for the adverse condition and the basis for the chosen extent (considering associated risks and consequences).
6. DETERMINE additional actions needed to pursue the extent of the adverse condition.

1.4.1   Extent of Condition Review Examples

When you have a problem with one piece of equipment, there is a good possibility a similar piece of equipment has the same problem. The same goes for people. If one person has difficulty doing a job, other workers may have the same type of difficulty. The *extent of condition review* gives your business the opportunity to solve systemic problems.

Table 1-6. Extent of Condition Review Template

Extent of Condition Review Criteria	Object (Person, Place, Thing)	Application (Activity, Form, Fit, Function)	Defect (Flaw, Failing, Deficiency)	Scenario Pursue?
Problem Statement				
Same-Same-Same An identical object in an equivalent application with a matching defect				
Same-Same-Similar An identical object in an equivalent application with a related defect.				
Similar-Same-Same A comparable object in an equivalent application with a matching defect.				
Similar-Same-Similar A comparable object in an equivalent application with a related defect.				
Same-Similar-Same An identical object in a corresponding application with a matching defect.				
Similar-Similar-Same A comparable object in a corresponding application with a matching defect.				
Same-Similar-Similar An identical object in a corresponding application with a related defect.				

Example 1: Flat tire (Heavier black line shows recommended extent (boundary) to pursue for the problem based on its significance.)

Extent of Condition Review Criteria	Object (Person, Place, Thing)	Application (Activity, Form, Fit, Function)	Defect (Flaw, Failing, Deficiency)	Scenario Pursue?
Problem Statement	*Rental car driver's side front tire*	*parked in my driveway*	*is flat*	
Same-Same-Same An identical object in an equivalent application with a matching defect.	1. Other tires on rental car 2. Tires on pickup truck	1. Parked in my driveway 2. Parked in my driveway	1. Flat 2. Flat	**Pursue**
Same-Same-Similar An identical object in an equivalent application with a related defect.	1. Other tires on rental car 2. Tires on pickup truck	1. Parked in my driveway 2. Parked in my driveway	1. Low on air 2. Low on air	**Pursue**
Similar-Same-Same A comparable object in an equivalent application with a matching defect.	1. Tires on boat trailer 2. Tires on bicycle	1. Parked in my driveway 2. Parked in my driveway	1. Flat 2. Flat	Do not pursue
Similar-Same-Similar A comparable object in an equivalent application with a related defect.	1. Tires on boat trailer 2. Tires on bicycle	1. Parked in my driveway 2. Parked in my driveway	1. Low on air 2. Low on air	Do not pursue
Same-Similar-Same An identical object in a corresponding application with a matching defect.	1. Car spare tire 2. Tires on son's vehicle 3. Tires on spouse's vehicle	1. In trunk as a spare 2. Parked on the street 3. Parked in the garage	1. Flat 2. Flat 3. Flat	Do not pursue
Same-Similar-Similar An identical object in a corresponding application with a related defect.	1. Car spare tire 2. Tires on son's vehicle 3. Tires on spouse's vehicle	1. In trunk as a spare 2. Parked on the street 3. Parked in the garage	1. Low on air 2. Low on air 3. Low on air	Do not pursue

Example 2: During a fire, isolation valve 3-FCV-04 cannot be closed from the main control room as required by safe shutdown instruction SSI-3 (which is based on design calculation Q037).

Extent of Condition Review Criteria	Object (Person, Place, Thing)	Application (Activity, Form, Fit, Function)	Defect (Flaw, Failing, Deficiency)	Scenario Pursue?
Problem Statement	*Isolation valve 3-FCV-04*	*as required by safe shutdown instruction SSI-3 during a fire (based on design calculation Q037)*	*cannot be closed from the main control room*	
Same-Same-Same An identical object in an equivalent application with a matching defect.	Isolation valve 1-FCV-04	as required by safe shutdown instruction SSI-3 during a fire	cannot be closed from the main control room	A **Pursue**
	Isolation valve 2-FCV-04	as required by safe shutdown instruction SSI-3 during a fire	cannot be closed from the main control room	B **Pursue**
Same-Same-Similar An identical object in an equivalent application with a related defect.	Isolation valve 1-FCV-04	as required by safe shutdown instruction SSI-3 during a fire	will not function upon other demands from the main control room (e.g., open)	C **Pursue**
	Isolation valve 2-FCV-04	as required by safe shutdown instruction SSI-3 during a fire	will not function upon other demands from the main control room (e.g., open)	D **Pursue**
	Other equipment listed in design calculation Q037	as required by safe shutdown instruction SSI-3 during a fire	cannot be closed from the main control room	E Do not Pursue
	Other equipment listed in other calculations used as inputs to instruction SSI-3	as required by safe shutdown instruction SSI-3 during a fire	cannot be closed from the main control room`	F Do not Pursue
Similar-Same-Same A comparable object in an equivalent application with a matching defect.	Other equipment listed in the following calculations cross-referenced in calculation Q037: • Q017 • Q027 • QN01	as required by safe shutdown instruction SSI-3 during a fire	cannot be closed from the main control room	G Do not Pursue

Extent of Condition Review Criteria	Object (Person, Place, Thing)	Application (Activity, Form, Fit, Function)	Defect (Flaw, Failing, Deficiency)	Scenario Pursue?
Similar-Same-Similar — A comparable object in an equivalent application with a related defect.	Other equipment listed in design instruction Q037	as required by safe shutdown instruction SSI-3 during a fire	will not function upon other demands from the main control room (e.g., open)	H Do not pursue
	Other equipment listed in other calculations used as inputs to Instruction SSI-3	as required by safe shutdown instruction SSI-3 during a fire	will not function upon other demands from the main control room (e.g., open)	I Do not pursue
	Other equipment listed in the following calculations cross-referenced in calculation Q037 ▸ Q017 ▸ Q027 ▸ QN01	as required by safe shutdown instruction SSI-3 during a fire	will not function upon other demands from the main control room (e.g., open)	J Do not pursue
Same-Similar-Same — An identical object in a corresponding application with a matching defect.	Isolation valve 3-FCV-04	as required by other safe shutdown instructions	cannot be closed from the main control room	K **Pursue**
	Isolation valve 1-FCV-04	as required by other safe shutdown instructions	cannot be closed from the main control room	L **Pursue**
	Isolation valve 2-FCV-04	as required by other safe shutdown instructions	cannot be closed from the main control room	M **Pursue**
Similar-Similar-Same — A comparable object in a corresponding application with a matching defect.	Other equipment listed in design calculation Q037	as required by other safe shutdown instructions	cannot be closed from the main control room	N Do not pursue
	Other equipment listed in other calculations used as inputs to Instruction SSI-3	as required by other safe shutdown instructions	cannot be closed from the main control room	O Do not pursue
	Other equipment listed in the following calculations cross-referenced in calculation Q037 ▸ Q017 ▸ Q027 ▸ QN01	as required by other safe shutdown instructions	cannot be closed from the main control room	P Do not pursue

Extent of Condition Review Criteria	Object (Person, Place, Thing)	Application (Activity, Form, Fit, Function)	Defect (Flaw, Failing, Deficiency)	Scenario Pursue?
Same-Similar-Similar An identical object in a corresponding application with a related defect.	Isolation valve 3-FCV-04	as required by other safe shutdown instructions	will not function upon other demands from the main control room (e.g., open)	Q **Pursue**
	Isolation valve 1-FCV-04	as required by other safe shutdown instructions	will not function upon other demands from the main control room (e.g., open)	R **Pursue**
	Isolation valve 2-FCV-04	as required by other safe shutdown instructions	will not function upon other demands from the main control room (e.g., open)	S **Pursue**
	Other equipment listed in design calculation Q037	as required by other safe shutdown instructions	will not function upon other demands from the main control room (e.g., open)	T Do not pursue
Similar-Similar-Similar A comparable object in a corresponding application with a related defect.	Other equipment listed in other calculations used as inputs to Instruction SSI-3	as required by other safe shutdown instructions	will not function upon other demands from the main control room (e.g., open)	U Do not pursue
	Other equipment listed in the following calculations cross-referenced in calculation Q037 • Q017 • Q027 • QN01	as required by other safe shutdown instructions	will not function upon other demands from the main control room (e.g., open)	V Do not pursue

Extent of Condition Follow Up Action Plan Checklist. (Check for the existence of any of the following scenarios at Prince Station.)

☐ **A.** Verify valve 1-FCV-04 can be closed from the main control room as required by safe shutdown instruction SSI-3 during a fire (based on design calculation Q037).

☐ **B.** Verify valve 2-FCV-04 can be closed from the main control room as required by safe shutdown instruction SSI-3 during a fire (based on design calculation Q037).

☐ **C.** Verify valve 1-FCV-04 will function upon other demands from the main control room (e.g., open) as required by safe shutdown instruction SSI-3 during a fire (based on design calculation Q037).

☐ **D.** Verify valve 2-FCV-04 will function upon other demands from the main control room (e.g., open) as required by safe shutdown instruction SSI-3 during a fire (based on design calculation Q037).

☐ **K.** Verify valve 3-FCV-04 can be closed from the main control room as required by other safe shutdown instructions.

☐ L. Verify valve 1-FCV-04 can be closed from the main control room as required by other safe shutdown instructions.

☐ M. Verify valve 2-FCV-04 can be closed from the main control room as required by other safe shutdown instructions.

☐ Q. Verify valve 3-FCV-04 will function upon other demands from the main control room (e.g., open) as required by other safe shutdown instructions.

☐ R. Verify valve 1-FCV-04 will function upon other demands from the main control room (e.g., open) as required by other safe shutdown instructions.

☐ S. Verify valve 2-FCV-04 will function upon other demands from the main control room (e.g., open) as required by other safe shutdown instruction.

Looking Forward

By this time in the investigation, you should have a very precise idea of the problem you need to solve. The gap between the way things are and the way they ought to be should be clear to all interested parties. You should also check with the key decision-makers in your organization (like your supervisor and management sponsor) to make sure the problem you believe you are solving is the problem they need you to solve. The *problem statement* technique ensures you have pinpointed the specific reason for the investigation and related WHAT happened.

Your problem statement should have been fleshed out into a more detailed *problem description* of the business issue you are investigating. Your description should now relate WHEN and WHERE the incident occurred and WHO was directly involved with the incident. In some organizations, you may be required to present your problem description to an upper management review committee for concurrence.

You may have needed to use *difference mapping* to determine exactly WHAT IS and WHAT IS NOT a part of the problem. This technique should also have helped to consider WHERE else and WHEN else the problem could occur and WHO else could be having the same issue.

By using a combination of the problem statement and difference map you have developed, you should have established the actual and potential *extent of* the adverse *condition* you are investigating. By establishing the space, time, and organizational boundaries of the problem, you have enabled the business to not only correct the problem that occurred but also the opportunity to prevent a same or similar incident elsewhere.

In Step 2, Investigate the Factors, you will be gathering more facts to establish the actions and conditions that led up to the problem. You will be looking for factors that were direct causes of the incident and indirect influences that allowed the incident to occur.

Questions for Understanding

1. Why should you develop a short problem statement early in an investigation?
2. What are the parts of a problem description? Describe each one.
3. Why is it necessary to put a boundary around a problem?
4. Why is it necessary to find out the extent of an adverse condition?

Questions for Discussion

1. If your problem description is poorly conceived, what might the consequence(s) be of having an inadequate problem description?
2. What are some of the challenges you could encounter when determining an extent of condition that is too narrow?
3. What are some of the challenges you could encounter when determining an extent of condition that is too wide?

References

Kepner, C. H. & Tregoe, B. B. (1981). *The new rational manager*. New York, NY: McGraw-Hill, p. 41.

For Further Reading

Addison, R., & Kaufman, R. (2013, June 3). The performance village — A fable. *Performance Xpress.* Available from http://www.performancexpress.org/2013/06/the-performance-village-a-fable/

Buchen, I. H. (2014, December). The new species of boxes — Think yourself out of those! *Performance Xpress.* Available from http://www.performancexpress.org/2014/12/the-new-species-of-boxes-think-yourself-out-of-those/

Clark, S., Collins, A., Kwan, J., & Sesnon, A. (2012, August 1). Tales from the field: Making service standards real for families in need. *Performance Xpress.* Available from http://www.performancexpress.org/2012/08/tales-from-the-field-making-service-standards-real-for-families-in-need/

Swan, E. (2012, August 22). *Lean six sigma glossary: Project charter.* Available from https://goleansixsigma.com/project-charter/

Step 2

Investigate the Factors

Sit down before fact as a little child, be prepared to give up every preconceived notion, follow humbly wherever and to whatever abysses nature leads, *or you shall learn nothing*.

— Thomas Huxley, Biologist

As a result of Step 1 (Scope the Problem) you should have a fairly clear definition of the problem you are investigating. Now you need a good information gathering strategy to ensure you consider all possible scenarios in the conduct of your investigation.

> **Caution:** One of the biggest mistakes you can make as an investigator is to seize upon a possible failure scenario and then go looking for information that supports that scenario.

To thoroughly *investigate the factors* associated with an incident, use the following investigation techniques.

1. Practice *evidence preservation* to ensure objects, locations, and information are not changed, contaminated, or lost during the process of gathering facts and data.
2. Use *witness recollection statements* to record facts observers can recall about an incident.
3. Gather more facts by directly *interviewing* witnesses.
4. Make more sense of the facts you have gathered by performing *Pareto analysis*.

In this section, you will learn when and how to use each of these tools and techniques. They will help you accumulate the pieces of the puzzle needed to reconstruct an accurate story about an incident.

Basics of Cause Analysis for Step 2

Gather information about the factors associated with the incident as quickly as possible. Make sure to establish "what did happen" *before* chasing missed opportunities, that is, "what did not happen." Examples of missed opportunities would be *did not pay attention to detail* or *did not follow procedures*. Instead of pursuing what did not happen, it is more important initially for you to find out specifically what did happen.

If the worker was not paying attention to something, find out what the worker was paying attention to — what the worker was focused on. This means finding out exactly what they did do (instead of following the procedure), what they were thinking, what they were feeling, and what they were sensing. You can concentrate on "facts" related to finding out the underlying factors of the incident rather than dwelling on a symptom such as "noncompliance." As Dr. Sidney Dekker states, "The reconstruction of mindset begins not with the mind; it begins with the circumstances in which the mind found itself" (Dekker, 2002).

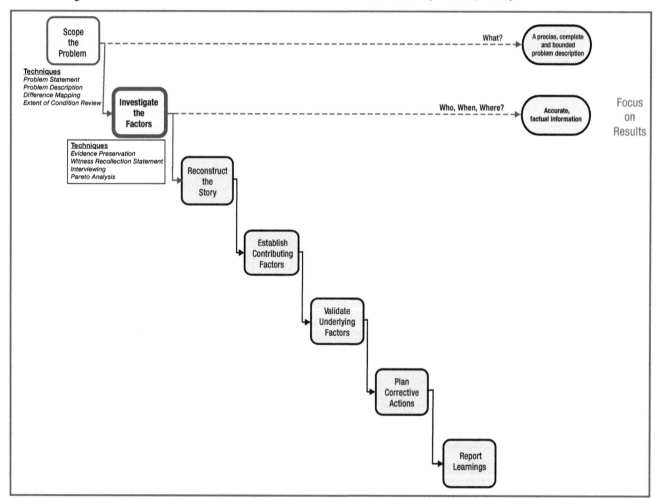

Figure 2-1. Step 2 Investigate the Factors

Below are some basic questions that should have been answered by the time you get to Step 2. However, if they have not, the following would be your initial line of inquiry:

- What happened? Specific actions that occurred?
- What did not happen? Inactions (actions should have occurred)?
- Conditions under which the actions occurred?
- Circumstances surrounding the inaction?

- Work activities, if any, going on at the time of the error?
- Work activities linked to the human performance problem?
- What systems or equipment were involved? Affected by the actions?
- When did the problem occur? Where?
- Who was involved in the work activity? Supervising?

For minor problems (low consequence/low risk issues), the answers to these questions may be all you need to establish a cause and recommend some action to address the cause. Not all problems deserve the same depth of cause analysis.

For more significant incidents and adverse conditions, you will generally be required to do a deeper cause analysis. As such, you will need to pursue lines of inquiry (questions) that ensure you systematically consider all possible scenarios that may have produced the problem. You could use what you already have in your mind which may be very thoughtful and logical. However, to show you have used a structured approach, consider using models that show how positive results are achieved.

The model depicted in Figure 2-2 shows three general drivers for equipment to perform successfully. If you are investigating an equipment failure, your first line of inquiry will be aimed at determining any form or

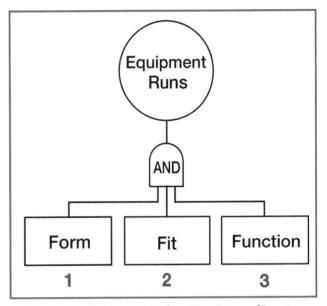

Figure 2-2. Equipment Failure First Lines of Inquiry

fit or function concerns. Be aware that a specific form, fit, or function concern may be triggered by another set of form, fit, or function concerns. Pursue your questions until you pinpoint the specific form, fit, or function issue. With equipment, you will be able to narrow it down to a form, fit, or function problem that needs to be fixed. For minor equipment problems, this may be all the deeper you need to go in your cause analysis. Check with your supervisors to make sure they agree this is all the deeper you need to go.

For more significant equipment failures, you will be expected to get to the *physical root* of the problem. The model depicted in Figure 2-3 shows the general lines of inquiry you should pursue. Once your first set of questions finds the specific form or fit or function failure, your next set of questions will be looking for the four possible degradation mechanisms: force, reactive environment, time (aging), and temperature (Bloch, 2005). One or possibly more of the degradation mechanisms will be considered the *physical root(s)* that induced the equipment failure.

The third set of questions will lead you to the tasks involving humans who influenced or allowed the physical phenomena to exist. These tasks are generally design control, material selection or identification, hardware assembly or installation, equipment operation or maintenance, and storage of parts or components (Bloch, 2011). These are the primary human-machine interfaces you will evaluate. This is the start of your pursuit of the *human root(s)* of the incident.

The model depicted in Figure 2-4 shows two general drivers for humans to perform successfully. If the incident you are investigating involves a person who had difficulty performing a task, you have two primary lines of inquiry in this sequence:

1. What did the individual do and how?
2. What is there about the work process that set up the worker?

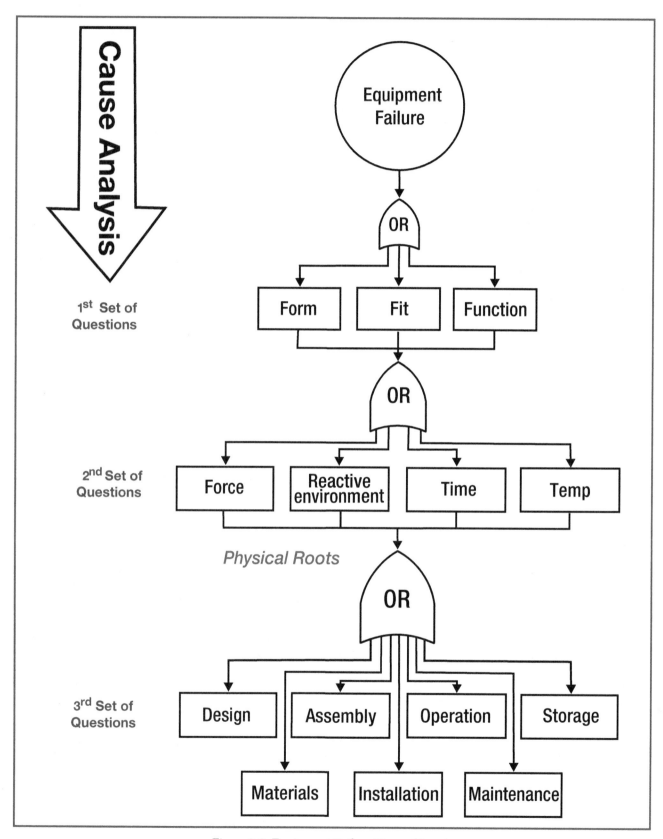

Figure 2-3. Equipment Failure Lines of Inquiry

To establish what the individual did and how they did it, you should get the individual's perspective from three different angles: 1) the task the worker was performing; 2) the worker's potential to succeed at the task; and 3) processing of job related information.

Figure 2-5 illustrates the need to gather information about how the worker prepared for the task, how the worker executed the task, and what feedback the worker provided after the task was completed.

Figure 2-6 shows the individual's potential to succeed at a task depends on skill, knowledge, and mindset at the time of the task.

Figure 2-7 depicts the general sequence of the need to gather information about how the worker prepared for

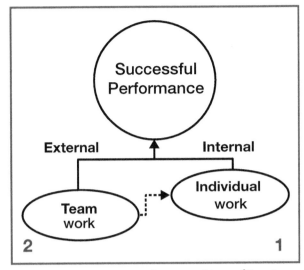

Figure 2-4. Human Performance Lines of Inquiry

the task, how the worker executed the task, and what feedback the worker provided the organization after the task was completed.

Since humans make errors and humans work in organizations, an organization will set up controls to protect the business from the people and to protect people from the physical plant while ensuring maximum production. These management controls are also called barriers or defenses. See Figure 2-8. The primary lines of defense against human error and its consequences are the next lines of inquiry you

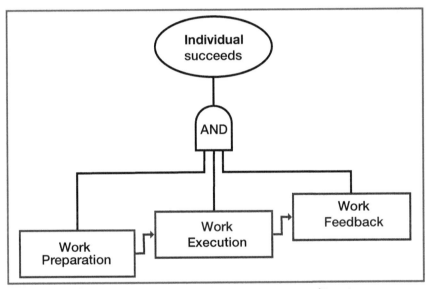

Figure 2-5. Human Task Performance Lines of Inquiry

should pursue: 1) engineered barriers, 2) administrative defenses, 3) oversight defenses, and 4) cultural defenses (Muschara, 2007).

In the area of engineered defenses, you will need to observe the environment the work was done in as well as the workplace layout. The administrative controls generally examined are the quality of the written instructions governing the task, the training provided by the organization to do the job, and the programs associated with the work activity. Oversight includes

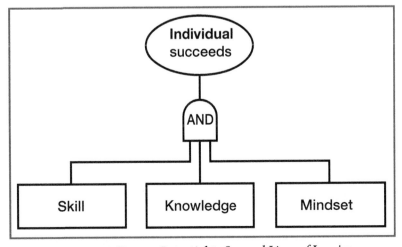

Figure 2-6. Human Potential to Succeed Lines of Inquiry

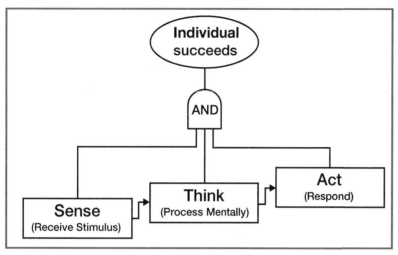

Figure 2-7. Human Information Processing Lines of Inquiry

looking into supervision's presence in the field and verification activities such as peer checks, quality control, and audits or surveillances. In the realm of cultural controls, you will start with the visible normal behavior of the worker to establish the norms of the business. From the norms, you will work at determining whether any flawed mental models, misguided beliefs, or misplaced values influenced the worker's thought processes during this incident. But more importantly, you will determine whether any cultural norms are setting up the business for future incidents.

Figure 2-8 shows that the *human roots* of an incident will have deeper *latent roots* in the business system. All of this information gathering is aimed at not only finding out what humans did that led up to the incident but also to finding out the circumstances in which the humans' minds found themselves (Dekker, 2002).

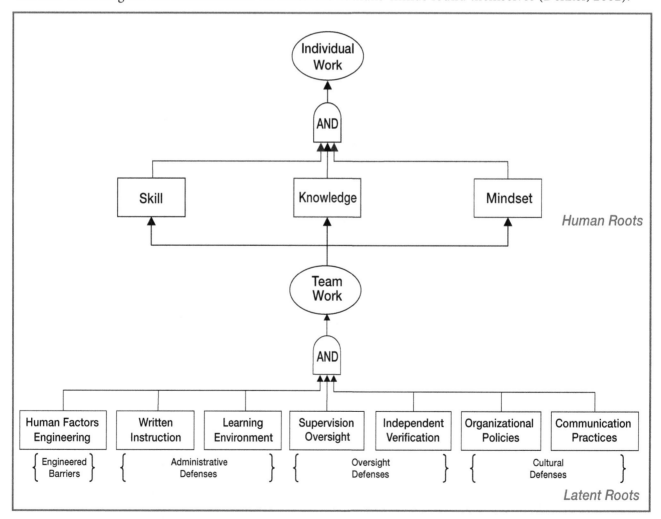

Figure 2-8. Organizational Drivers of Individual Success Lines of Inquiry

Use Table 2-1 as a checklist to guide you through Step 2 of the investigation. The following techniques and tools in the following sections will help you complete checklist Step 2:

  2.1 Evidence Preservation

  2.2 Witness Recollection Statement

  2.3 Interviewing

  2.4 Pareto Analysis

Table 2-1. Step 2 Jump Start Checklist

☑ Behaviors [Sub-Tasks]	Tools/Techniques	Required		
☐ Document as you go. Begin writing the report now.	*Witness Recollection Statement*	RC	AC	AD
☐ Verify that the three types of evidence are protected and collected.	*Evidence Preservation*	RC	AC	AD
☐ Walk down affected area. Take pictures or videos of the equipment, component, investigation area, etc., to document the incident.		RC	AC	
☐ Decide what information to collect and whom to interview, what equipment analysis to get, etc.		RC	AC	AD
☐ Perform individual interviews (within 24 hours). Ask "right questions." Suspend judgment. This leads to appreciative understanding.	*Interviewing*	RC	AC	
☐ Review equipment performance evaluations (if applicable).		RC	AC	AD
☐ Review prompt human performance evaluations (if applicable).		RC	AC	AD
☐ Corroborate critical information with an independent source of data.		RC	AC	
☐ Evaluate to level of detail commensurate with incident's significance.		RC	AC	AD
☐ *Identify the equipment failure and degradation mechanisms (if applicable).*		RC	AC	
☐ *Identify initiating actions, inappropriate actions, any error precursors.*		RC	AC	
☐ *Identify flawed defenses.*		RC	AC	
☐ *Identify the latent organizational weaknesses.*		RC		
☐ Make systematic method(s) used to identify root cause(s) and contributing cause(s) visible. Show on-lookers that structured investigative tools and techniques are being used with quantitative information on team's actions and factors chart, Pareto chart, etc.	*Pareto Analysis*	RC		
☐ Start review of internal operating experience (OE).		RC	AC	
☐ *Consider prior occurrences of problem. (Only applies to a recurring problem/repeat occurrence)*		RC	AC	
☐ *Evaluate failure of original corrective actions. Use as contributing factor?*		RC	AC	

☑ Behaviors [Sub-Tasks] (continued)				
☐ *Provide feedback to strengthen previous ineffective corrective actions.*		RC	AC	
☐ Start review of external OE. Consider knowledge of prior OE.		RC	AC	
☐ Incorporate lessons to be learned into corrective action plan.		RC	AC	
☐ Share lessons learned with other departments and industry.		RC	AC	

RC = Root Cause Analysis; **AC** = Apparent Cause Analysis; **AD** = Adverse

☑ Results Required [R]/Desired [D]			
☐ The beginning of a "**story**" — a reconstructed incident in chronological sequence.	RC_R	AC_R	
☐ Accurate, factual information about triggering, aggravating, and exposure **factors**.	RC_R	AC_R	AD_D
☐ **A**ntecedents (RC/AC), **B**ehaviors (RC/AC/AD), and **C**onsequences (RC).	RC_R	AC_R	AD_D
☐ A **foundation** for the investigation, including analyses performed and their conclusions.	RC_R	AC_R	

2.1   Evidence Preservation

What is it?

This tool addresses actions to be taken immediately following an incident or accident. Instructions for successfully preserving, collecting, and documenting evidence are provided so the incident or accident can be effectively investigated.

Why is it useful?

Preserving and controlling evidence are essential to the integrity and credibility of the investigation. Security and custody of evidence are necessary to prevent the alteration or loss of evidence. It establishes the accuracy and validity of all evidence collected.

When is it done?

The effectiveness of an incident investigation depends on immediate preservation of the incident scene and the physical, human, and documentary evidence related to the incident. Initiate the investigation with minimal delay to avoid the following problems:

- Loss, movement or misplacement of physical and/or documentary evidence. This includes failed/broken hardware, strip charts, business computer information, etc.
- Changes in first-hand reports of incident from participants and witnesses, which may alter with time due to stress, rationalization, poor or inaccurate memory, etc.
- Recurrence of a similar incident.

How is it done?

> **Caution:** Follow precautions when handling potentially infectious materials such as: 1) blood; 2) all body fluids, secretions, and excretions (except sweat) regardless of whether or not they contain visible blood; 3) non-intact skin; and 4) mucous membranes.

2.1.1   Preserve and Control Evidence

1. STORE evidence so its integrity is maintained after collection. This may require quarantining the incident scene and/or certain pieces of documentary or physical evidence.

   ▸ STORE evidence in a secure location to reduce the opportunity for unauthorized or unintended removal.
   ▸ ESTABLISH the chain of custody for all evidence and ensure it is strictly maintained throughout the investigation.
   ▸ REQUEST that security personnel establish boundaries for preservation of the scene and control access to incident scene.

2. MEET with person(s) who reported the incident to collect information about:

   ▸ Conditions before, during, and after the incident.
   ▸ Personnel involvement (including actions taken).
   ▸ Environmental conditions.
   ▸ Other items having relevance to the incident.

2.1.2   Collect Physical Evidence

1. RECORD incident/accident scene as follows:

   ▸ PHOTOGRAPH, VIDEOTAPE, and/or SKETCH scene in its original location, provided it does not interfere with rescue or mitigation activities.
   ▸ LOG the location, date, and time photos and videos are taken.
   ▸ RECORD, as-found, locations of significant incident-related materials.
   ▸ RECORD names and badge numbers of individuals who observed or participated in the incident.
   ▸ TAKE pre-tear down photos showing scale and orientation.
   ▸ RECORD investigator impressions of the accident scene (e.g., cleanliness, lighting, and/or marks on equipment).

2. COLLECT and LABEL physical evidence as follows:

   ▸ MARK each piece of evidence for future identification without contaminating or damaging the evidence; then LOG in an evidence ledger. See Table 2-2.
   ▸ PHOTOGRAPH successive stages of tear down, noting scratches, stains, dimensions, orientation, etc.
   ▸ ENSURE symmetric failed components are marked to preserve orientation for analysis.
   ▸ BAG failed parts separately and IDENTIFY the component name, number, date, etc.
   ▸ MOVE items to an area under your personal control to prevent tampering or loss.
   ▸ AVOID any alteration of the fracture surfaces, coatings, lubricants, etc. (Do NOT unnecessarily decontaminate or otherwise clean failed components. Wear clean gloves if chemical analysis of the sample surfaces will be desired.)

Table 2-2. Evidence Ledger

Tag/ Item Number	Article/ Property Description	Location from Where Obtained	Storage Location	Inventoried & Tagged by: Name/Signature/ Date/Time	Released by: Name/Signature/ Date/Time	Received by: Name/Signature/ Date/Time	Purpose of Change of Custody

Acknowledgements of Transfer of Custody

- ▸ OBTAIN any perishable data such as temperatures, pressures, radiation levels, and water levels.
- ▸ COLLECT chemical samples such as:
    - ✓ Lubricants and coolants.
    - ✓ Paint and other coatings.
    - ✓ Ash or other degraded material.
    - ✓ Transferred material, such as smeared metal.

3. Using judgment to assess cost vs. gain, CONSIDER the need for laboratory tests to obtain destructive/non-destructive failure analysis and the use of onsite/offsite experts.

4. IF the use of an unauthorized substance or fatigue is suspected, CONSULT fitness for duty (FFD) procedures for guidance.

2.1.3   Collect Documentary Evidence

1. Immediately COPY potentially relevant documents such as:
    - ▸ Copies of work packages with signoffs.
    - ▸ Log books (operations, maintenance, engineering, management).
    - ▸ Printouts of relevant sources of information from business computer, strip charts, etc.

2. EXAMINE the policies, standards, and specifications that shaped the work environment in which the incident occurred. Look for:
    - ▸ Indications of the attitudes and actions of people involved in the incident.
    - ▸ Revealing evidence that generally is not established in verbal testimony.

3. SEARCH previous operating experience (OE) to determine whether:
    - ▸ The same or similar conditions have occurred either at this site or within the industry.
    - ▸ If so, why any associated corrective actions for the condition were unsuccessful at preventing recurrence of the incident.

2.1.4   Collect Human Evidence

> **Caution:** The human memory is the most unreliable form of evidence. Failure to obtain statements within the first few hours of the incident may cause error precursors OR important human factors to be overlooked in the investigation.

1. IDENTIFY witnesses as soon as possible after the incident to obtain witness recollection statements and interviews. The following are several types of witnesses who should provide preliminary statements:

    - ▸ Principal witnesses (directly involved in incident or sustained injury from the accident).
    - ▸ Eyewitnesses (participants/observers who actually saw the incident or the events immediately preceding, during, or following incident).
    - ▸ Emergency response personnel and investigators.
    - ▸ People in the vicinity of the incident/accident.
    - ▸ People with knowledge of preceding actions or conditions, such as shift workers on duty prior to the shift during which the incident occurred.
    - ▸ Security personnel who may have conducted a recent walkthrough.

> **Note:** The Witness Recollection Statement will be covered under a separate technique in this chapter.

2. PREPARE for the interviews by doing the following:

- ▶ Discuss interviewing objectives and plan strategies for consistent questioning.
- ▶ Develop a standardized set of interview questions or themes.
- ▶ Identify all interviewees. Use Table 2-3. Ensure these are the right people.
- ▶ Schedule an appointment with each witness at an appropriate location.
- ▶ Assign a lead interviewer for each interviewee.
- ▶ Have required reference documents at hand.
- ▶ Develop sketches and diagrams to pinpoint locations.
- ▶ Determine the best way of recording information.

Table 2-3. Incident Investigation Interviewee List

Interviewee/ Position	Reason for Interview	Group/Shift/Location	Phone Number	Notes (Interviewer/ References)

3. INTERVIEW the witness using the following general steps:

> ▸ OPEN by introducing yourself and explaining the purpose of the interview.
> ▸ ASK questions to seek to understand WHY not just WHAT.
> ▸ NOTE crucial information immediately in order to ask meaningful follow-up questions.
> ▸ CLOSE the interview by summarizing and thanking the interviewee for his or her time.

Note: Interviewing techniques will be covered in more detail later in this chapter.

2.2   Witness Recollection Statement

What is it?

A *Witness Recollection Statement* is a document recording the recollections of a person involved with an incident regarding what happened before, during, and after the incident. The statement is signed by that person to confirm that the contents of the statement are true. In general, the statement should only contain information on what the individual saw, and not what others have said to him or her. However, it is important to record anything that may open up a new line of inquiry or help in corroborating other information.

Why is it useful?

This account will help determine the time and sequence of incidents. Since the persons providing the information have some knowledge or involvement relative to what occurred, their input is crucial to determining the root cause(s) of the incident.

When is it used?

It is used early in the investigation before memories fade. Follow-up interviews may occur throughout the process (Steps 1 to 5). Witnesses should provide written input prior to leaving their shift on the day the incident is identified.

How is it done?

Caution: It is improper for an individual to be coached or trained about the evidence or information to be provided. An individual can, however, seek general information on the procedure for submitting a Witness Recollection Statement.

---

1. REQUEST written statements as soon as possible after the incident from all personnel involved. Have them use the Witness Recollection Statement. See Table 2-4.
2. START obtaining statements and interviews with individuals who were involved with the incident.
3. ASK witnesses to list or recall others at the scene.
4. Then COLLECT statements from other personnel with knowledge of the incident. Be sensitive to any fact-finding and resulting disciplinary action that may have occurred.

Table 2-4. Witness Recollection Statement

Name:		Job Responsibility (related to incident):	
Phone:	Supervisor:	Group/Work Location:	
Location of Incident/Accident:		Incident Date:	Incident Time:

Problem Description (Why is this an incident? Give the reason for this investigation.)

Please fully describe the task in progress and working conditions leading up to the incident.

Please fully describe the incident sequence from start to finish. Include your answer to these questions:
- ☐ What happened?
- ☐ What was expected?
- ☐ Anything unusual you observed during the incident (sights, sounds, odors, alarms, individual actions or behaviors, etc.).
- ☐ Conditions that may have influenced the incident (equipment malfunction or position, weather, inexperience, etc.).
- ☐ Any ideas about the cause?
- ☐ Other possible witnesses?
- ☐ How was the problem discovered?
- ☐ What you saw? What you did?
- ☐ Other information?
- ☐ Additional comments?

Knowing what happened, what would you recommend be done differently?

Signed:	Date/Time of Statement:

General Instructions: In your own words, describe your involvement in the incident before, during, and after the final outcome. Include any pertinent verbal communications you had and specify with whom you had the communications (by name and/or position). Indicate the format of the communications (pre-job brief, direct assignment, interdepartmental interfaces, etc.), and specify with whom you had them. List any pertinent procedural or equipment conditions relating to the incident. A sketch or diagram may help. Use additional sheets as necessary.

2.3   Interviewing

What is it?
Interviewing is a technique to help get information, ideas, and themes by talking with others.

Why is it useful?
Knowledge based on the accumulated experience of people is a powerful source of information and understanding. To seek what others know helps to expand our knowledge. Interviews are an excellent way of understanding what problems others are having with a process, product, or service.

When is it used?
Interviews may occur throughout the problem-solving process (Steps 1 to 5). Some applications of interviewing include:

- Analyzing an incident's causes.
- Discovering other solutions/corrective actions.
- Recommending approaches to implementations.

How is it done?
Discuss what information is needed, who might have it, and questions to be asked. List whom to interview, determine what questions to ask, and establish a deadline for completion of the interviews. WHAT is asked is *important*; but HOW the questions are asked is *critical*.

A. **Concerning WHAT:** Use standard questions; then follow your hunches. The following questions should be asked in most interviews of principal witnesses and co-workers to build the context of the task and the work environment:

- What were they trying to accomplish? (goals)
- What were they paying attention to? (focus)
- What did each person know at critical points in the sequence of actions? (knowledge and situation awareness)

B. **Concerning HOW:**

- Make the interviewee feel **trusted**. Assume the person is responsible, dependable, and accountable.
- Make the interviewee feel WE (interviewer and interviewee) are here to **discover** how he or she got set up.
- Use a funnel approach — broad questions leading to specific questions.
- Seek to understand WHY, not just WHAT.
- Lead the interview.
- Keep questions simple and focused.
- Focus on facts.
- Anticipate unsatisfactory replies and have a means to deal with them.
- **DO NOT** accept admissions of guilt. Person may be feeling hopeless, defensive, or doomed. Additionally, you may never get to the true cause.
- **DO NOT** impugn motives — stay with objective, observable information.
- Avoid jargon.
- Avoid devious or trick questions.
- Be aware that interviewing is *not* interrogating.

Table 2-5. Individual Interviews vs. Group Interviews

	Individual Interviews	Group Interviews
Advantages	▸ Obtain independent stories ▸ Obtain individual perceptions ▸ Establish one-to-one rapport	▸ More efficient use of time ▸ May get more complete picture as interviewees supplement story ▸ Other witnesses serve as "memory joggers"
Disadvantages	▸ Consume more time ▸ Possibly more difficult to schedule all interviewees	▸ Interviewees will not have independent stories. ▸ "Group think" may develop. ▸ Some individual details may get lost. ▸ More vocal members will say more and thus may influence those who are quieter. ▸ Interviewees may state as fact details that they could not have possibly seen from their vantage point. ▸ Contradictions in accounts may not be revealed.

1. PREPARE for the interview.

   ▸ Set interviewing objectives. Determine what information should be gained from the interview.
   ▸ Outline areas to be covered and major questions to be asked. Gather background information on the topic.
   ▸ Plan strategies for consistent questioning. Develop a standardized set of interview questions or themes in advance.
   ▸ Generate open-ended questions to encourage volunteering of ideas. (Open-ended questions are ones that cannot be answered with "yes" or "no.")
   ▸ Identify all interviewees. Ensure you are interviewing the right people in the right sequence.
   ▸ Schedule the appointments. Tell interviewees the purpose and proposed length of the interview.
   ▸ Assign a lead interviewer for each interviewee. Gather background information on each interviewee.
   ▸ Select a convenient meeting place, preferably a "neutral" location not associated with the incident.
   ▸ Have required reference documents at hand.
   ▸ Anticipate interviewee questions.
   ▸ Be mentally prepared and focused.
   ▸ Develop sketches and diagrams to pinpoint locations.
   ▸ Determine the best way of recording information.

> **Note:** Learn the advantages and disadvantages of the following types of questions.

☐ *Open-Ended*: A question or statement that invites a wide-ranging response, often asks for ideas, opinions or views. Broad and allows freedom in answering.

Advantages	**Disadvantages**
✓ Allows the interviewee to do the talking.	✄ Time.
✓ Easy to answer.	✄ Difficult to record complete answers.
✓ Interviewee may volunteer information.	✄ May not get at the needed information.

☐ *Closed-Ended* (Fact Finding): A question that limits the answer by requesting specific facts or a yes/no answer. Narrow and limits answer options.

Advantages	**Disadvantages**
✓ Interviewer retains control.	✄ Too little information.
✓ Takes less time and easy to record.	✄ Restrictive and could have negative impact.
✓ Less effort of the interviewee to respond.	

☐ *Primary*: Introduces a topic. Stands alone out of context.
   Example: "What takes up most of your time?"

☐ *Secondary*: Follows up on other questions. Pulls more information on same subject.
   Example: "Tell me more about … ?" "What do you mean by … ?"

☐ *Leading*: Suggests a preferred answer.
   Example: "You think you need more engineers, don't you?"

☐ *Neutral*: Interviewee chooses answer freely.
   Example: "How do you feel about the number of engineers on the staff?"

☐ *Reflective*: A statement that describes and reflects a feeling or emotion (without implying agreement or disagreement).

☐ *Summary*: A brief restatement, in your own words, of the content of what was said.

☐ *Pause* (Silence): An intentional, purposeful period of silence.

2. OPEN the interview by creating a relaxed atmosphere.
   ⁃ Introduce yourself. Shake hands, if culturally appropriate.
   ⁃ Set the tone for the rest of interview. Be polite, patient, and friendly.
   ⁃ Explain the purpose of the interview:
     ☐ "Fact Finding" not "Fault Finding"
     ☐ "Prevent Accidents" not "Assign Blame"
     ☐ Goal is improving the organization.
   ⁃ Provide overview of the material to be covered.
   ⁃ Give direct answers to interviewee questions. Treat witnesses with respect.
   ⁃ Take control and maintain it.
   ⁃ Explain that there may be more than one interview.

3. ASK questions; then LISTEN.

- Ask the witness to describe the incident or accident in full before asking a structured set of questions. Let witnesses tell things in their own way. Start the interview with a statement such as "Would you please tell me about...?"

- Ask questions using the words:

  □ **How?**

  "How did you perform the task?"

  "How do you think the incident happened?"

  □ **What?**

  "What happened?"

  "What happens to a worker when they do it that way?"

- Ask the questions which have been developed. Stay on track. Use follow-up questions to gain more information or if you didn't understand the answer.

- Ask open-ended questions that generally require more than a "yes" or "no" answer.

- Aid the interviewee with reference points; e.g., "How did the lighting compare to the lighting in this room?"

- Use visual aids, such as photos, drawings, maps, and graphs to assist witnesses.

- Keep an open mind; ask questions that explore what has already been stated by others in addition to probing for missing information.

- Be an active listener, and give the witness feedback. Restate and rephrase key points.

  □ Suspend your frame of reference.

  □ Suspend judgment; provide appreciative understanding.

  □ Listen to an answer before asking next question.

  □ Be relaxed, friendly.

  □ Do not let note-taking interfere with listening.

- Help interviewees feel comfortable by answering any question from them.

- Avoid asking "why" questions because this tends to put people on the defensive. Often a non-judgmental question such as asking the interviewee to state "in your own words" can put the interviewee at ease.

- Do not try to influence the answers by offering your opinions.

- Take brief notes while listening. Note crucial information immediately in order to ask meaningful follow-up questions.

  □ Add more detail as soon as possible from memory.

  □ If you do not understand, ask for clarification.

  □ Do not wait until next day.

  □ Discuss with counterparts.

  □ Request copies of documents for later study.

  □ Carefully consider use of electronic recording devices.

4. CLOSE the Interview.

- Provide a preview. Example: "...only a few more questions...."

> ▸ Ask the last key questions.
>   > ☐ "What would you suggest to fix this problem?"
>   > ☐ "What would you suggest to prevent it from happening again?"
>
> ▸ Summarize what you heard during the interview.
> ▸ Allow the witness to read the interview transcript and comment if necessary.
> ▸ Set up potential for asking follow-up questions and for interviewee to provide follow-up information.
> ▸ End on a positive note; thank the interviewee for his or her time and effort.
> ▸ Review and interpret data as soon as possible after the interview.

2.3.1   Lines of Inquiry: Question Generators

The following are three additional sets of questions — covered in more detail in later sections of this chapter — to help interviewers generate the right questions.

1. Ability and Mindset Questions (directed primarily at the *mindset of the job performer* while probing for a minimal amount of organizational insight) Table 2-6.
2. Accountability Decision Tree Questions (directed at both getting the mindset of the job performer while probing for more organizational insight) Table 2-7.
3. Management Control Questions (directed primarily at *getting organizational insight* derived from the behavior of the job performer) Tables 2-8 and 2-9.

2.3.2   Question Generator: Individual Mindset

Figure 2-9 illustrates three areas to investigate when a worker has difficulty performing as expected. If you are investigating an error (slip, lapse, mistake) or a violation, use the questions in Table 2-6 to pinpoint the performance gaps in manual or mental skills or in emotional areas (Employment Security Department, 2010). Table 2-6 contains the types of questions Wilmoth, Prigmore, and Bray (2002) suggest to get you very close to the human roots of an incident.

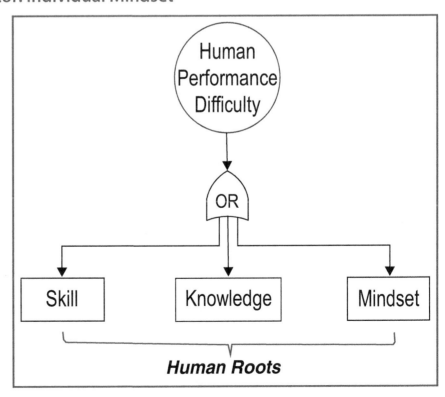

Figure 2-9. Individual Ability and Mindset Problem Areas

Table 2-6. Individual Ability and Mindset Questions

Questions	Purpose/Clarification
A. What is the human performance difficulty?	‣ What is actually happening vs. what "should be" happening? Establishes the gap.
B. Is there clear direction and support to perform as desired?	‣ Expectations clear and understood? ‣ Risks? Conflicting directions? ‣ Resources available & adequate?
C. Could job performer do it if really required to do it? Already know how?	‣ Job performer qualified? ‣ Done it before? Successfully? ‣ Job done often enough to maintain proficiency?
D. Anything preventing desired performance? Hindering right behavior?	‣ Internal factors: Personal problems? Medical? ‣ External factors: Ergonomic challenges? ‣ Task demands? Complexity?
E. Are there appropriate consequences for worker performance (behavior)?	‣ Is desired performance perceived as punishment? ‣ Is undesired performance perceived as being rewarded? ‣ Are there consistent positive consequences for effective performance?

2.3.3   Question Generator: Personal and Organizational Accountability

When it appears an individual is culpable for an incident, you need to check into the possibility of culpability on the part of the organization also. See Figure 2-10. The organization is supposed to set up the individual for success. When a serious incident occurs, there is usually something about the system that has set up the worker to fail. Besides looking at the individual, also look into tangible factors such as the work environment and into the intangible factors associated with the prevailing organizational culture (Wile, 2014).

Figure 2-11 is a flowchart aimed at determining the degree of accountability that should be assigned to an individual versus the accountability of the organization. Start with the human performance difficulty you are investigating and work your way through the types of questions Hobbs (2008) suggests in Table 2-7 to pinpoint where the individual needs adjustment and where the organization needs fixing.

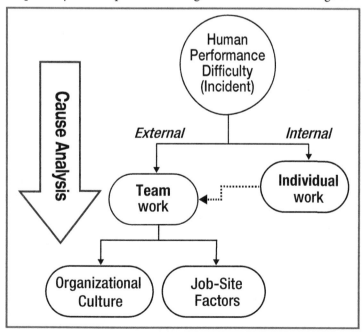

Figure 2-10. Individual/Team Accountability

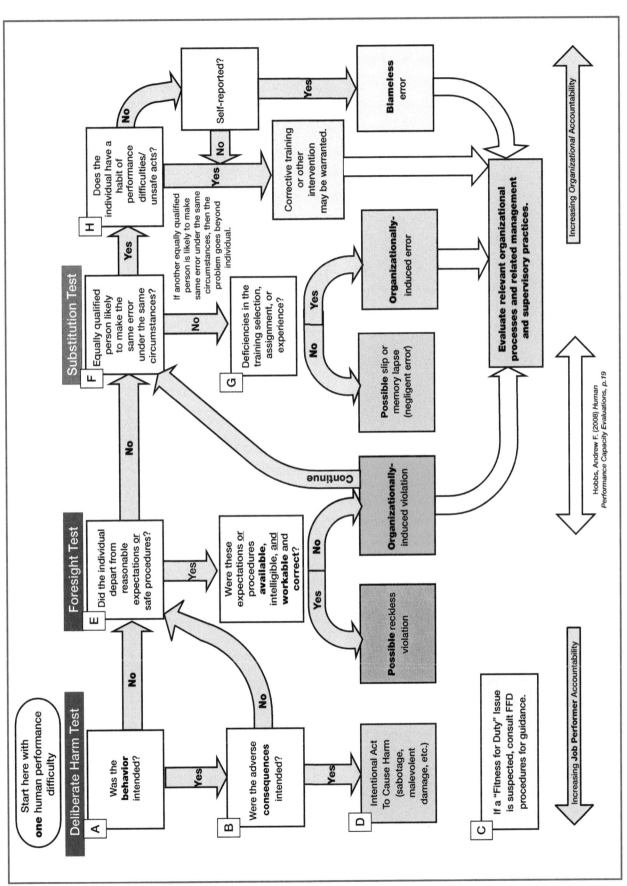

Figure 2-11. Accountability Decision Tree

Table 2-7. Accountability Questions

Questions	Purpose/Clarification
A. Was the job performer's behavior intended?	▸ IF the actions were not as intended (I meant to push button "A," but somehow pushed button "B"), then we are probably dealing with a mental slip or lapse. These generally are skill-based errors.
B. Did the job performer intend the adverse consequences?	▸ IF the actions were as intended, but the consequences were not, then the error was most likely a mistake (not willful). These are rule and knowledge-based errors. ▸ IF the answer is "YES," you are probably not dealing with an error at all (intentional act) and should consult your management.
Note: IF both the actions and the consequences were as intended, then this was not an error.	
C. Was there a fitness for duty issue (i.e., use of an unauthorized substance, or fatigue)?	▸ IF the worker's behavior indicates a suspected problem related to drug or alcohol use or due to fatigue, take action in accordance with business fitness for duty (FFD) procedures.
D. Were reasonable expectations knowingly violated?	▸ IF it is established that the individual was aware of the expectations, but consciously elected not to conform to those expectations, then the answer would be "YES."
Note: Reasonable expectations consist of guidance communicated through procedures, policies, training, work practices, or verbally. Once again, it is necessary to establish the "intent" of the job performer being evaluated.	
E. Were reasonable expectations readily available, workable, intelligible, and correct?	▸ IF it is established that the reasonable expectations were readily available, workable, intelligible and correct, then the answer would be "YES." ▸ IF it is established or suspected that non-compliance has become more or less automatic (as happens in the case of routine short-cuts), you should question the accuracy of the expectations.
Note: The availability, workability, and accuracy of reasonable expectations are important concepts. This must be evaluated from the perspective of the immediate user. Gaining an understanding of the job performer's perception on this matter is important.	
	▸ IF in establishing the intent (or motive) of the violation it can be argued that "the job performer was attempting to achieve the proper desired outcome but the situation at hand rendered the expectations unsuitable," then the answer will most likely be "NO" to this question. ▸ IF the answer to this question is "YES," then there was a possible reckless violation.

Note: Violations generally involve a conscious decision to bend or break the rules. However, while the actions are deliberate, the potential bad consequences are not, in contrast to sabotage, etc.	

Note: You must also consider another error or violation at this point. The expectation to stop and seek additional guidance in situations like these (unworkable procedures) is generally understood by all job performers. Failure to adhere to this and other expectations of this nature should be evaluated as separate acts.	

F. Is an equally qualified person likely to make the same error under the same circumstances? (Substitution Test)	▸ IF the answer is "probably," then apportioning culpability has no material role to play other than possibly to obscure potential systemic deficiencies and blame one of the victims. ▸ One method of conducting the substitution test is to ask the individual's peers, "Given the circumstances that prevailed at the time, is it likely you would have done the same thing (committed the same or similar error)?" IF the answer is "probably," then assigning culpability to the job performer is inappropriate. The answer to the substitution test is "YES." ▸ IF the answer to the substitution test is "YES," the error is most likely blameless. Proceed to the question asking whether or not the individual has a history of unsafe acts.

Note: This is probably the most critical and difficult evaluation to conduct. Substitute the individual concerned with someone else coming from the same domain of activity, possessing comparable qualifications and experience. Ask the following question, "In the light of how events unfolded and were perceived by those involved in real time, is it likely that this new individual would have performed the same?"	

G. Considering this job performer's training and experience, should this task have been assigned to this person in the first place?	▸ IF it is established that there were no deficiencies in the job performer's training, selection, or experience, then a possible negligent error must be considered. ▸ IF there are questions about the person's training, qualification, or selection for the task, then there is a good likelihood that the unsafe act was largely a system-induced error.

H. Does the job performer have a history of performance difficulties or unsafe acts?	▸ IF the evaluation determines that the error (or violation) was system induced, ensure the proper follow-up actions are taken. The condition identified as creating or complicating the error should be identified and resolved.

Note: Consider only documented incidents involving this worker in the previous six months. IF the person in question has a history of unsafe acts or errors, it does not necessarily bear upon the culpability of the error committed on this particular occasion. However, it probably indicates the necessity for corrective training or other intervention to reinforce desired performance and take full advantage of lessons learned.	

2.3.4   Question Generator: Management Control Elements

The management control questions probe the following aspects of an incident's causal factors in order to get insights into the organizational system's weaknesses. It starts with the human performance difficulty that resulted in an incident at your site, but is aimed at finding flaws in organizational defenses that either triggered or allowed the incident (Nuclear Regulatory Commission, 1993).

☐	Response	The nature of an individual's visible actions and behaviors	**Act**
☐	Decision-making	The mental and information processing requirements	**Think**
☐	Stimulus	The cues that initiated the actions involved in the incident	**Sense**
☐	Management	Programmatic, leadership, organizational, and staffing issues	
☐	Teamwork	Performance difficulties where more than one person was involved	

Work your way backwards using the stimulus-response model as illustrated in Figure 2-12. Start with the human action that directly triggered the incident. That act would be the response to some stimulus. Use questions A through C in Table 2-8 to find out more about the context of the individual's response — what he or she was focused on and was supposed to do, and what the job set-up was like. When a worker has difficulty responding correctly, it's time to look into the human-machine interface (a.k.a. human factors engineering). Look into any written instructions the worker was using, training he or she had been given, and whether supervisor was in the field and engaged. This will help explain the worker's response which may have been inappropriate.

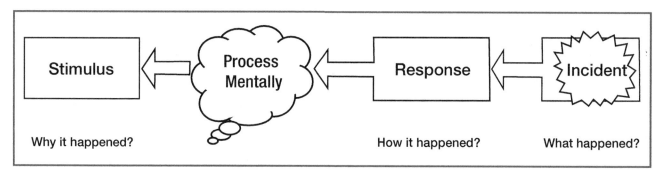

Figure 2-12. Stimulus Response Cause Analysis Flow

The goal of questions D through H in Table 2-8 is to assess how the worker was processing the signals from the work environment at the time of the incident. Find out how the worker was accessing knowledge acquired in the past to apply to the current situation. If you find issues with mental processing, look into the human factors set-up of the environment, past instruction, procedure use and quality, and supervisor field presence. You're trying to find the answer to the question, "What was the job performer thinking?"

Questions I through J in Table 2-8 are looking for the visual, audible, and other cues the worker was receiving (or not receiving). You are looking for the worker's capability to detect and recognize information available in the immediate vicinity of the work. It's hard to pay attention to detail when there are too many details. Before you conclude someone was not paying attention to detail, find out how many and what details he or she was paying attention to. If you find problems with sensing signals and cues, look into the human factors in the work area, the written instructions governing the work, past training, and supervision. You'll find the deeper causes in these areas.

Table 2-8. Act-Think-Sense

Question	Purpose/Clarification
A. Was work performed in an adverse environment (hot, humid, dark, cramped, or hazardous)?	*Individual Response.* **Yes** answer points to the following types of concerns/causal factors: <ul><li>Human Factors Engineering</li></ul>
B. Were displays, alarms, controls, and equipment identified and operated properly?	*Individual Response.* **No** answer points to the following types of concerns/causal factors: <ul><li>Human Factors Engineering</li><li>Written Instructions (Procedures)</li><li>Learning Environment (Training)</li></ul>
C. Was procedure used correctly?	*Individual Response.* **No** answer points to the following types of concerns/causal factors: <ul><li>Written Instructions (Procedures)</li><li>Supervision/Oversight</li></ul>
D. Did work involve repetitive motion, uncomfortable positions, vibration, or heavy lifting?	*Individual Response.* **Yes** answer points to the following types of concerns/causal factors: <ul><li>Human Factors Engineering</li><li>Learning Environment (Training)</li><li>Supervision/Oversight</li></ul>
E. Was knowledge of task performance or equipment response missing?	*Individual Response.* **Yes** answer points to the following types of concerns/causal factors: <ul><li>Learning Environment (Training)</li><li>Supervision/Oversight</li></ul>
F. Was the missing knowledge required for analysis, interpretation, identification, or planning to perform task?	*Individual Decision-Making.* **Yes** answer points to the following types of concerns/causal factors: <ul><li>Learning Environment (Training)</li></ul>
G. Were displays, alarms, controls, and equipment provided for analysis, interpretation, identification, or planning needed to perform task?	*Individual Decision-Making.* **No** answer points to the following types of concerns/causal factors: <ul><li>Human Factors Engineering</li></ul>
H. Did available information guide person to procedure?	*Individual Decision-Making.* **No** answer points to the following types of concerns/causal factors: <ul><li>Human Factors Engineering</li><li>Written Instructions</li></ul>
I. Was reason to begin actions present and seen?	*Individual Stimulus.* **No** answer points to the following types of concerns/causal factors: <ul><li>Human Factors Engineering</li></ul>
J. Was there any indication of excessive fatigue, impairment, or inattentiveness?	*Individual Stimulus.* **Yes** answer points to the following types of concerns/causal factors: <ul><li>Human Factors Engineering</li><li>Learning Environment (Training)</li><li>Supervision/Oversight</li></ul>

Questions K through Q in Table 2-9 are asking for information about the controls the organization had in place at the time of the incident and about teamwork and interface concerns. See Figure 2-13. You are working at identifying any barrier or defenses that were missing, not used, or ineffective. For critical tasks in high reliability organizations, businesses set up defense-in-depth for protection and for production. Primarily you are looking for the flaws in any defenses that should have prevented the incident. These flaws or weaknesses will be the *latent roots* of the incident or will lead you to the latent roots. Make sure you also identify any defenses that held or kept the consequences of the incident from being much worse.

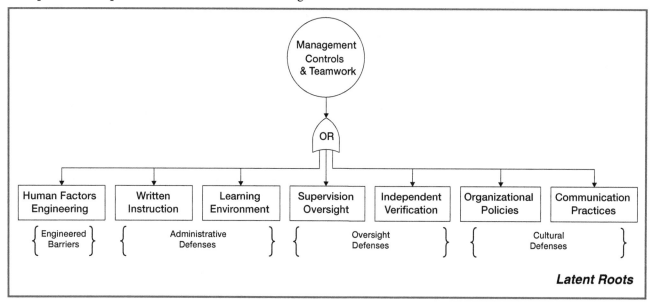

Figure 2-13. Management Controls and Teamwork Concerns

Engineered barriers are designed to protect your business from people's errors thus preventing incidents and ensuring continued production of whatever your business produces. Besides the structures, systems, or other hardware designed to reduce risk, engineered barriers also involve warning devices and safety devices. The remainder of the defenses — administrative, oversight, and cultural — help, but are generally considered much weaker than physical defenses (Department of Defense, 2012). People are the weakest link in a chain of defenses.

The programmatic weaknesses are generally found in the areas of administrative and oversight controls. If a task relies largely on administrative and organizational controls and results in a significant incident or recurring annoying problems, your business may want to consider a hardware fix.

In the area of teamwork, you will be looking for interface and integration concerns. You will be looking for how well one program has been integrated with other programs. You will be determining the degree of commitment groups have for implementing specific programs. You will be assessing how well one group interfaces with another group. Here, you are especially looking for communications problems.

Table 2-9. Organizational Management and Teamwork

Question	Purpose/Clarification
K. Was task performed in a hurry or a short-cut used?	*Management.* **Yes** answer points to the following types of concerns/causal factors: ‣ Supervision/Oversight ‣ Organizational Policies
L. Did employee have personal stresses (overtime, monotonous work, heavy workload, illness, or personal problems)?	*Management.* **Yes** answer points to the following types of concerns/causal factors: ‣ Human Factors Engineering ‣ Supervision/Oversight
M. Was this a recurring error or was potential for failure known before failure occurred?	*Management.* **Yes** answer points to the following types of concerns/causal factors: ‣ Organizational Policies
N. Were administrative controls or policies to prevent, identify, or mitigate the error not used or missing?	*Management.* **Yes** answer points to the following types of concerns/causal factors: ‣ Written Instructions ‣ Supervision/Oversight ‣ Organizational Policies
O. Was coordination required between team members or did shifts change?	*Team.* **Yes** answer points to the following types of concerns/causal factors: ‣ Communications Practices
P. Was there agreement about the "who/what/when" of task performance?	*Team.* **No** answer points to the following types of concerns/causal factors: ‣ Written Instructions ‣ Learning Environment (Training) ‣ Supervision/Oversight ‣ Communications Practices
Q. Was communication across organizational boundaries or other facilities required?	*Team.* **Yes** answer points to the following types of concerns/causal factors: ‣ Communications Practices ‣ Organizational Factors

2.4   Pareto Analysis

What is it?

Pareto analysis is a method of organizing data to determine the "vital few" factors responsible for a particular problem. A Pareto chart is a bar chart of failures ordered by frequency of failure, cost of failure, or contribution to system unavailability. The bars are arranged, in descending order, from left to right. The horizontal axis represents categories of interest. Percent of total is plotted on a separate line to show the cumulative effect.

Why is it useful?

A Pareto chart helps to prioritize multiple problems visually by using a process that allows you to focus on areas where the largest opportunities exist. Pareto analysis helps focus on the areas that must be improved the most. The Pareto chart highlights which of the concerns comprise the "vital few," and which are the "trivial many." The basis for Pareto analysis is the "80-20" rule — 80% of the problems result from 20% of the causes (Department of Energy, 1995).

When is it used?

The Pareto diagram can be used in Step 2 (Investigate the Factors) to display the major problems to address. It also can be used to show the major causes of the problem. After a solution is developed during Step 6 (Plan Corrective Actions), the results of the solution can be displayed by comparing a "before" Pareto diagram with an "after" Pareto diagram.

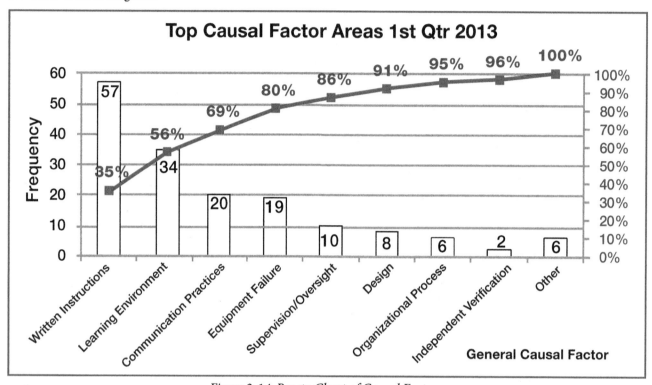

Figure 2-14. Pareto Chart of Causal Factors

How is it done?

1. IDENTIFY what problem or concern is to be analyzed.
2. SELECT the time period for the data to be analyzed.
3. DETERMINE how to measure the problem. (For example, frequency of failure is used to measure reliability; duration of failure is used to measure availability.)
4. COLLECT the data.
5. GROUP the data by meaningful categories. (Equipment failures are typically stratified by system, component, model, or vendor although other groupings may be used.)
6. RECORD the data.
7. ARRANGE the categories in descending order from left to right (frequency, unavailability, etc.).
8. LABEL the vertical axis. Frequencies go on the vertical line.
9. LABEL the horizontal axis. Horizontal bars are labeled with categories.
10. DRAW/PLOT bars for each category; each bar's height equals the category's frequency/duration. (The categories represented by the tall bars on the left are relatively more important than those on the right.)
11. ADD up the counts.
12. DRAW the cumulative percentage line (total = 100%) above the bars, adding the impact of each category from left to right.
13. ADD title, legend, and date.
14. ANALYZE the diagram by checking into the 2 to 4 categories that add up to approximately 80%. Ask yourself what the data reveal and which failures or causes are the "vital few."

2.4.1   Pareto Chart Template

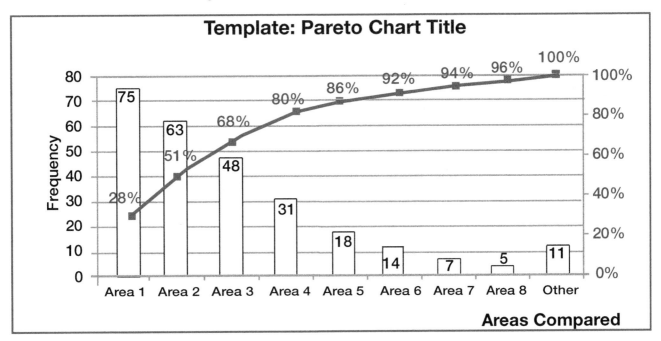

Figure 2-15. Pareto Chart Template

2.4.2   Pareto Analysis Examples

Example 1:

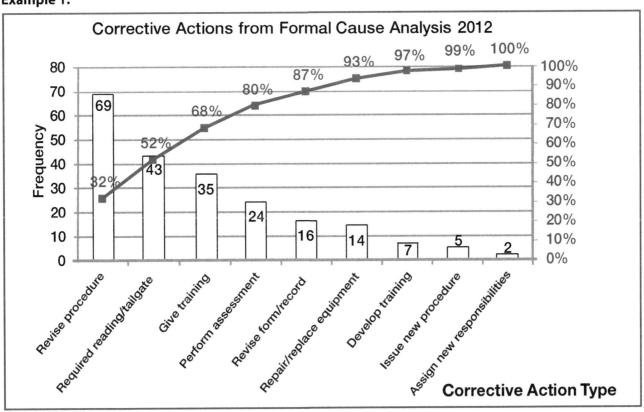

Figure 2-16. Pareto Chart of Corrective Action Types

Example 2: The following example shows how Pareto analysis might be used during an investigation.

A company manufactures clothing in six different locations. Figure 2-17 shows the Taos location with 56% of the 487 rejects nation-wide during the week of August 3-7, 2015.

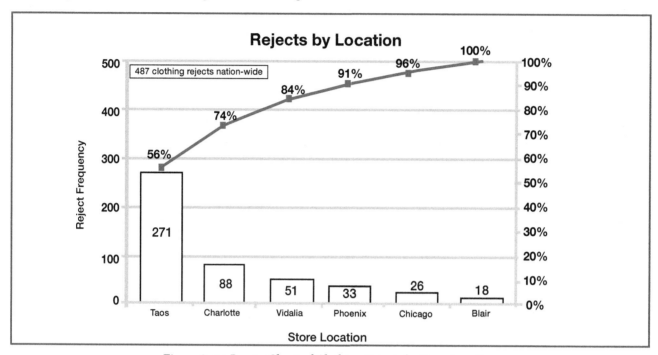

Figure 2-17. Pareto Chart of Clothing Rejects by Store Location

The company sends investigators to the Taos location to look into the reasons for the high number of clothing rejects (271). Figure 2-18 shows 42% of the rejects were blouses.

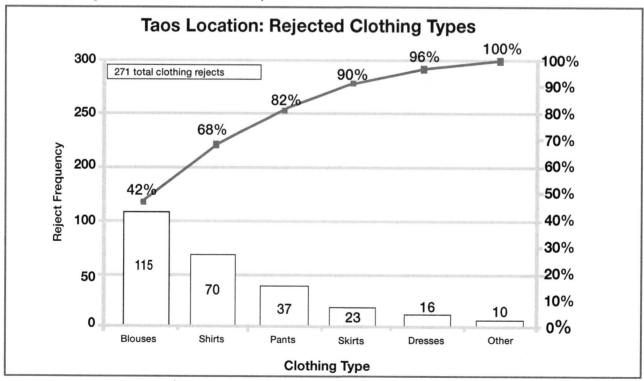

Figure 2-18. Pareto Chart of Type of Clothing Rejected

The investigators use the check sheet below (Table 2-10) to quantify the types of blouse rejects by type during the week of August 3-7, 2015.

Table 2-10. Type of Clothing Rejects

Subject: *Types of Women's Blouse Reject* Dates Data Collected: *August 3-7, 2015*			Recorder: *I. N. Vestigate* Special Events: *None*			
REJECT TYPE	**MON**	**TUES**	**WED**	**THURS**	**FRI**	**TOTAL**
No Label	11		1	1	1	5
Deformed Collar	卌 1	卌	卌 11	卌	111	26
Buttons missing	卌 111	卌 卌 1	卌 11	卌 111	卌 卌 111	47
Discoloration	11	11	11	11	11	10
Snags	卌 11	1111	卌	1111	111	23
Tears	1		11		1	4
TOTAL BY DAY	26	22	24	20	23	115

The data from the check sheet is plotted on a Pareto chart in Figure 2-19. Based on these numbers, it might lead an investigator to pursue the reasons why buttons were missing on so many blouses. But other factors need to be considered.

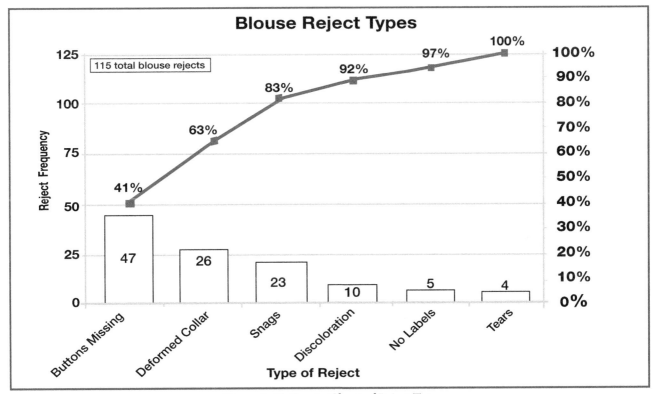

Figure 2-19. Pareto Chart of Reject Types

The investigators gather information about the cost of rework for each type of blouse defect. The results are plotted on Figure 2-20. Blouses with snags, tears, or discoloration are scrapped; so there are no rework costs. Defective collars show up as the biggest issue on Figure 2-20, but the investigator needs to look at other types of cost.

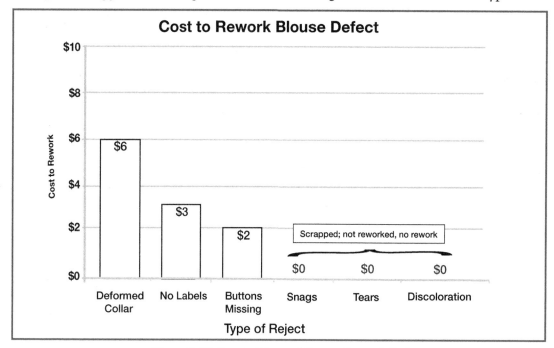

Figure 2-20. Pareto Chart of Cost to Rework Defect

The cost of scrapping blouses is determined, then plotted along with the cost of reworking blouses. The results are displayed on Figure 2-21. This shows blouses with snags, tears, and discoloration carry the most cost per reject.

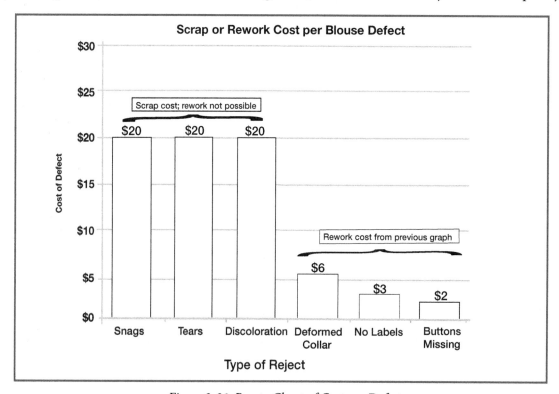

Figure 2-21. Pareto Chart of Cost per Defect

Figure 2-22 shows what happens when cost for each type of defect is multiplied by the number of each type of defect. Using this information, the investigators should look deeper into the reasons for the high reject rate caused by snags in blouses. This is a beginning point for an investigation, not the end point.

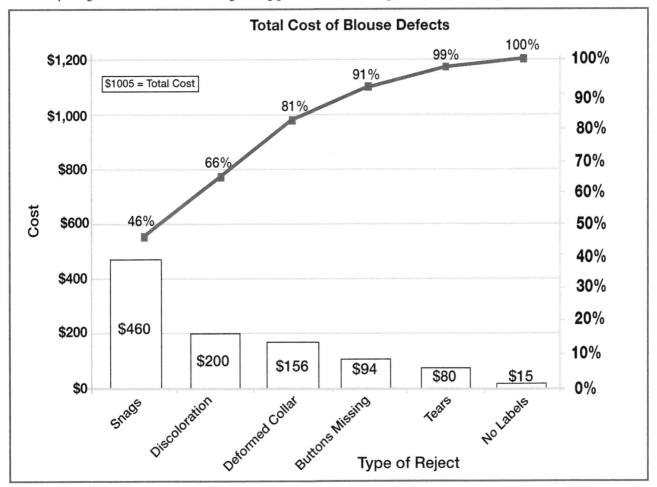

Figure 2-22. Pareto Chart of Type of Clothing Reject

One of the key points in a Pareto analysis is to make sure an attempt is made to look at the data gathered from several different angles. Data displayed from only one direction often misses bigger issues that need to be resolved. If the Pareto analysis in this example had been stopped after development of Chart 1, the investigators would have been looking at missing buttons on blouses — with a total cost of $94 for the week compared to $460 for the snags in blouses.

Looking Forward

You will continue to gather information as you go throughout Steps 3 to 6. The information you have collected about actions that happened or conditions that actually exist are considered *facts*. Other information you have collected, such as actions that should have happened but didn't or conditions that should exist but don't, are considered *counterfactuals* (Dekker, 2002). Both types of information are important. But first, your investigation needs to pursue the causes of things that actually happened, i.e., facts. Then chase the reasons why expected actions did not happen or conditions did not exist. Since it is difficult to find a direct cause and effect for a non-event, counterfactuals have only an indirect influence on the outcome of a situation or problem.

In Step 3, the information you have compiled will help you to begin to reconstruct the story of the incident. You will use the facts you have gathered to establish the string of triggering actions along with the factors that influenced the performance of equipment or workers.

Questions for Understanding

1. Why is it a mistake for an investigator to assume that he or she already knows what caused the problem?
2. What are some of the basic questions that should be answered for any type of cause investigation?
3. If you are investigating an equipment failure, what will you determine with your first set of questions?
4. What are the three sets of questions you need to pursue to see how an incident unfolded from an individual's perspective?

Questions for Discussion

1. What are some of the concerns you might encounter as you attempt to preserve evidence before and during the course of an investigation?
2. As an investigator, what are some steps you would do in preparation for an interview?
3. What should be your focus during an interview?

References

Bloch, H. P. (2005, April). Successful failure analysis strategies. *Reliability Advantage: Training Bulletin.* Retrieved from http://www.heinzbloch.com/docs/ReliabilityAdvantage/Reliability_Advantage_Volume_3.pdf.

Bloch, H. P. (2011, May). Structured failure analysis strategies solve pump problems. *Machinery Lubrication.* Retrieved from http://www.machinerylubrication.com/Read/28467/pump-failure-analysis

Dekker, S. (2002). *The field guide to human error investigations.* Burlington, VT: Ashgate Publishing Company.

Department of Defense (DOD). (2012, May). *Standard practice: System safety.* (MIL-STD-882E). Wright-Patterson Air Force Base, OH: Headquarters Air Force Materiel Command/SES.

Department of Energy (DOE). (1995, October). *How to measure performance: A handbook of techniques and tools.* (DOE DP-31 and EH-33). Washington, DC: US Department of Energy.

Employment Security Department, Washington State. (2010). Bloom's taxonomy: KSA's. Retrieved from http://www.wa.gov/esd/training/toolbox/tg_bloom.htm

Hobbs, A. F. (2008). *Human performance culpability evaluations: A comparison of various versions of the culpability decision tree from various Department of Energy sites.* Retrieved from http://www.drillscience.com/dps/Andy%20Hobbs%20-%20Research%20Paper%20%20Human%20Performance%20Culpability%20E.pdf

Muschara, T. (2007, August). INPO's approach to human performance in the United States commercial nuclear power industry. *IEEE Xplore Digital Library.* Retrieved from http://ieeexplore.ieee.org/xpl/login.jsp?tp=&arnumber=4413179&url=http%3A%2F%2Fieeexplore.ieee.org%2Fxpls%2Fabs_all.jsp%3Farnumber%3D4413179

Nuclear Regulatory Commission (NRC). (1993). *Development of the NRC's human performance investigation process (HPIP): Investigator's manual.* (NRC NUREG/CR-5455, S1-92-101). Washington, DC: US Government Printing Office.

Wile, D. E. (2014). Why doers do — Part 1: Internal elements of human performance. *Performance Improvement, 53*(2), 42.

Wilmoth, F. S., Prigmore, C., & Bray, M. (2002). HPT models: An overview of the major models in the field. *Performance Improvement, 41*(8), 18.

For Further Reading

Daniels, A. C. & Daniels, J. E. (2004). *Performance management: Changing behavior that drives organizational effectiveness.* Atlanta, GA: Performance Management Publications.

Dekker, S. (2006). *The field guide to understanding human error.* Brookfield, VT: Ashgate Publishing Company.

Mager, R. F. (1999). *What every manager should know about training: An insider's guide to getting your money's worth from training.* Atlanta, GA: The Center for Effective Performance, Inc.

Rummler, G. A. & Brache, A. P. (1995). *Improving performance: How to manage the white space on the organization chart.* San Francisco, CA: Jossey-Bass Publishers.

Step 3

Reconstruct the Story

Those who don't know history are doomed to repeat it.

— Edmund Burke, Statesman

Using the factors you uncovered in Step 2 (Investigate the Factors) about the incident, you will start using those pieces of information to clearly illustrate the sequence of steps that led to the problem. You will need tools to concisely document the initiating actions, inappropriate actions, error precursors, flawed defenses, and organizational weaknesses to ensure decision-makers have a complete story of the incident.

Four techniques are explained in Step 3. Implementing these techniques in an investigation will help you *reconstruct the story* behind an incident.

1. Use *fault tree analysis* to diagram the possible ways a piece of equipment could have failed.
2. Perform *task analysis* to understand how people normally do a job.
3. Pinpoint the most important and risky steps in the work using *critical activity charting*.
4. Display the progression of the incident on a timeline using *actions and factors charting*.

A well-developed fault tree will help reveal the *physical roots* of an incident. Task analysis and critical activity charting will expose the *human roots* of a problem. Finally, actions and factors charting will assist in identifying the *latent roots* — the underlying programmatic and organizational weaknesses — that allowed the business to experience an accident or incident. The four tools presented in this section will help you illustrate, in context, the progression of the problem and the factors that drove, influenced, or allowed the incident.

You will rebuild the history of the problem with the detailed answers to these questions:

 ▸ HOW did each action happen?
 ▸ WHAT were people involved focused on?
 ▸ WHEN and WHERE did each pertinent action occur?

Basics of Cause Analysis for Step 3

If you are investigating a significant incident that involves machinery, it is generally a mistake to believe you can get to the underlying human issue *before* you have established what the equipment problem is. For example, a driver involved in a vehicle accident may have a percentage of alcohol on his or her breath, but the actual cause of the vehicle accident is a broken steering mechanism. Both the problem with the alcohol and the steering mechanism need to be addressed, but if you focus solely on the person's use of alcohol you will miss the problem with the machine. Generally speaking, make sure you have pinpointed the hardware problem before you

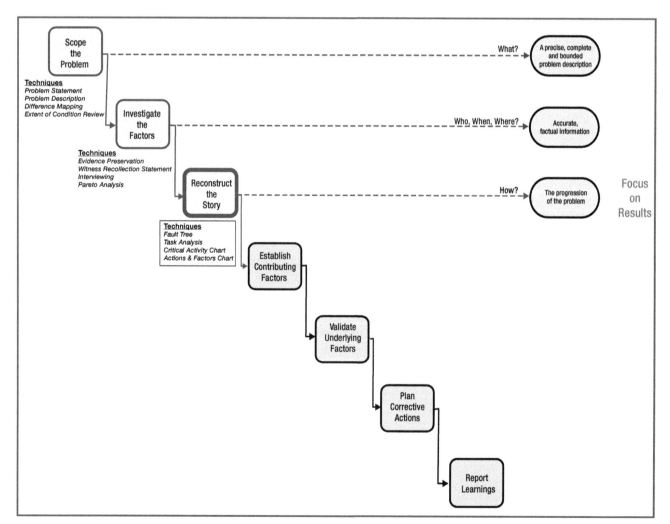

Figure 3-1. Step 3 Reconstruct the Story

make any conclusions about the people portion of the problem. An incident can appear to have been caused by an operator's error when there is a more important design flaw or installation error that needs to be found and corrected. Using a fault tree for equipment problems will ensure you consider all the potential equipment and human performance concerns that may have caused an incident.

When a worker appears to have difficulty performing a job such as operating a piece of equipment, a task analysis is needed to identify any gaps between the desired or expected performance and the actual performance. If there is a variation between the work as planned and the work as done, determine why the difference exists.

As you establish what should have happened versus what actually happened, graphically display actions and key decision points in time sequence. In order to establish cause and effect, the cause must precede the effect (in time). You also need to make sure that you and others can see the connection between a cause and its effect. Did the cause trigger the effect? Did the cause allow a condition to exist? Did the cause aggravate the outcome of the situation? See Figure 3-2.

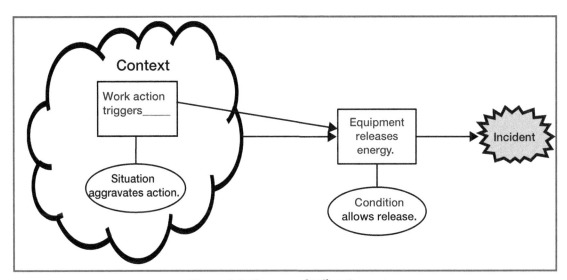

Figure 3-2. Cause and Effect Context

It is also necessary to determine and study the more important steps of a task. These are steps where potential threats and existing hazards could interact to cause an accident. These are actions that have to be performed for production reasons; so businesses generally have workers take extra precautions at these critical steps. Use a critical activity chart to determine how an important task is performed and what safeguards are used or available at that step. Also determine any worker attitude or belief that might cause the production importance of the task to prevail over conscious consideration of the hazards associated with the job.

Reconstruct how work was progressing and how information was processed by the workers involved. This needs to be done for each pertinent action leading up to the incident to make sure you understand the context in which workers' decisions were made and actions were taken. Decisions are not made in a vacuum. Display this framework on an actions and factors chart so you and key decision-makers understand how the situation unfolded.

Use Table 3-1 as a checklist to guide you through Step 3 of the investigation. The following techniques and tools (listed by section number) will help you complete the checklist:

3.1 Fault Tree Analysis

3.2 Task Analysis

3.3 Critical Activity Chart

3.4 Actions and Factors Charting

Table 3-1. Step 3 Jump Start Checklist

☑ Behaviors [Sub-Tasks]	Tools/Techniques	Required		
☐ Determine if a procedure/process flowchart exists. If so, use it.		RC	AC	AD
☐ Construct a preliminary timeline or flowchart identifying chronology, activities, conditions/factors, consequences/effects (as applicable).		RC	AC	AD
☐ *FOR equipment-related incidents, diagram all credible failure scenarios that may have caused the problem.*	*Fault Tree Analysis*	RC	AC	
☐ *FOR human performance difficulties, evaluate the assigned actions and behaviors for error precursors, error-likely situations, and flawed defenses.*	*Task Analysis*	RC	AC	
☐ *FOR some human performance difficulties, identify any critical human actions that would have prevented or mitigated the incident.*	*Critical Activity Chart*	RC	AC	
☐ FOR discrete incidents, develop a detailed actions and factors chart to clearly show WHAT happened WHEN. **FOR** other incidents, display using a logical [success] model.	*Actions and Factors Chart*	RC	AC	
☐ *Begin construction of the actions and factors chart as soon as preliminary information has been gathered. Helps focus investigators on where information is missing.*		RC	AC	
☐ *Initially, the actions and factors chart can be done on chart paper with self-sticking notes that can be rearranged as the incident is fleshed-out.*		RC	AC	
☐ *Show actions/behaviors that occurred prior to, during, and after the incident so that the big picture is understood.*		RC	AC	
☐ *When complete, convert the actions and factors chart to a graphics file so that the document can be attached to the associated condition report.*		RC	AC	
☐ *As more information/data is received, continue modifying the actions and factors chart until the circumstances that led up to the incident are understood.*		RC	AC	
☐ *From the beginning, display the actions and factors chart where everyone on site can see it and contribute to it.*		RC	AC	
☐ Determine "HOW" the incident happened (i.e., the failure modes, the behaviors, the visible actions).		RC	AC	
☐ IF other issues (OI) are identified, show on the actions and factors chart or discuss in the report. (Optional)		RC	AC	
☐ IF appropriate, update the Corrective Action Review Board.		RC	AC	
☐ Critical action completed. Involve responsible management.		RC		

RC = Root Cause Analysis; **AC** = Apparent Cause Analysis; **AD** = Adverse

☑ **Results** Required [R]/Desired [D]			
☐ The progression of HOW the incident happened presented in a logical manner.	RC$_R$	AC$_R$	
☐ Documented equipment failures, related actions, and error precursors.	RC$_R$	AC$_R$	AD$_R$
☐ Documented flawed defenses (physical, human, or programmatic vulnerability factors).	RC$_R$	AC$_R$	AD$_D$
☐ Documented latent organizational weaknesses (systemic/cultural vulnerability factors).	RC$_R$	AC$_D$	

3.1   Fault Tree Analysis

What is it?

A *fault tree* is a top-down graphical representation used to diagram all credible failure scenarios that may have caused an incident, generally involving equipment. Failure mechanisms which may have contributed to the undesired incident are depicted using a tree branching structure. Through further research and deductive reasoning, the investigator determines the actual path to the system failure by verifying or refuting possible causes (Nuclear Regulatory Commission, 1981).

Why is it useful?

The fault tree analysis method is useful for systematically identifying and graphically displaying the many ways something can go wrong. Fault tree analysis helps to quickly identify all possible failure modes and causes needed for an incident to occur, which of these factors may have failed, and what can be added or modified to reduce the probability of repetition.

When is it used?

Fault trees are excellent troubleshooting tools for equipment-initiated incidents. Fault trees are generally used to determine the reasons for a failure that has already occurred. Begin building the fault tree when the investigation starts. The tree diagrams can also be used in planning processes to determine possible vulnerabilities and to ensure the future reliability of a procedure or piece of equipment.

How is it done?

1. DEVELOP a problem statement that defines what undesired incident is being analyzed and enclose it in a circle. This is the reason for the investigation. See Figure 3-3.

Figure 3-3. The Incident in a Circle

Problem Statement: An equipment operator's flashlight would not work.

2. IDENTIFY the first tier inputs to the incident. Consider the basic components of the piece of equipment. If the defective component has been identified, consider possible form, fit, or function concerns. See Figure 3-4.

> ‣ Ask "How could this situation happen?"

> ‣ Brainstorm ALL possible inputs or known failure modes and mechanisms.

> ‣ List each possible input in a box below the incident circle.

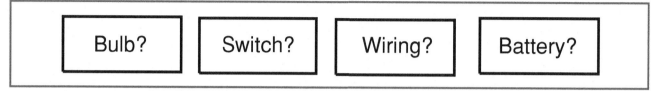

Figure 3-4. First Tier Inputs

3. DEFINE the relationship between the first tier inputs to the incident. Connect each input to the incident using logic for their occurrence. IF any one of the inputs listed would cause the failure, it would go through an **OR** Gate (*independent — any of the inputs may exist*). IF two or more inputs must occur together to cause the failure, they would go through an **AND** Gate (*dependent — all inputs must exist*). See Figure 3-5.

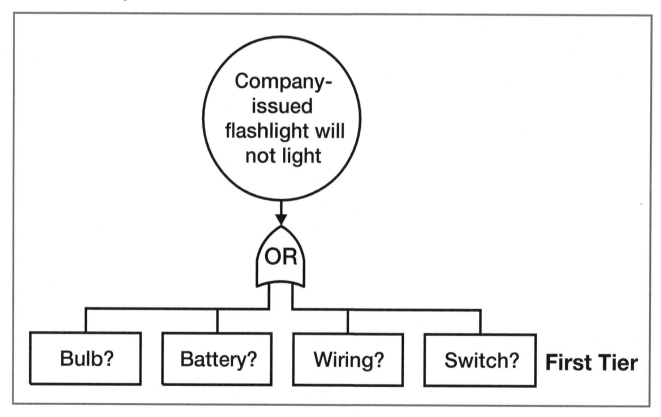

Figure 3-5. First Tier Inputs' Relationship to the Incident

4. From left to right, EVALUATE each first tier input for second-level inputs (second tier). See Figure 3-6.

> ‣ Ask, "How could this situation happen?"

> ‣ Brainstorm **ALL** possible inputs or known degradation mechanisms and influences.

> ‣ List each possible input in a box below the first tier input.

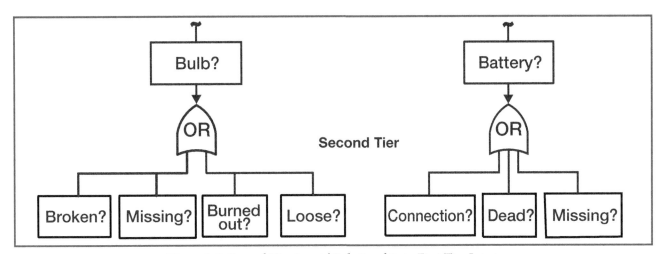

Figure 3-6. Second Tier Inputs' Relationship to First Tier Inputs

5. DEFINE the relationship between the second tier inputs to the first tier. Connect lines from first tier input boxes to the second tier using logic gates **AND** (both conditions must exist), and **OR** (either condition may exist).

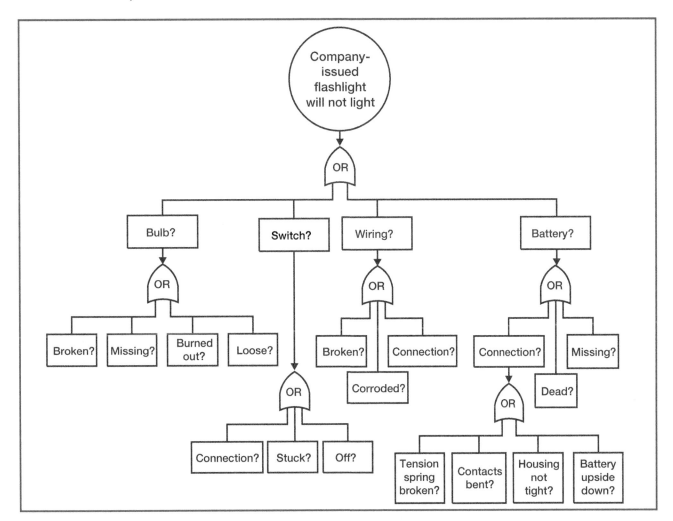

Figure 3-7. Possible Failure Scenarios for the Incident

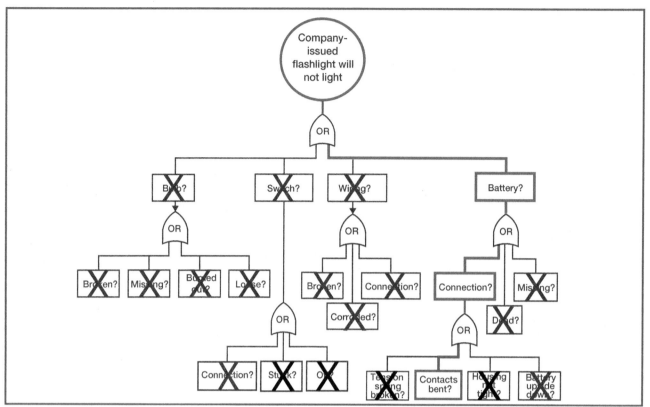

Figure 3-8. Plot Investigation Results

6. CONTINUE to drill down to a tier level corresponding to the significance of the issue. See Figure 3-7.

7. IF needed, GATHER additional information to complete missing or invalidated information in the fault tree. The goal is to support or refute the validity of inputs. WHEN eliminating inputs, as shown in Figure 3-8, use the following as guidance:

   ▸ Eliminate inputs based on interviews, documentation, walk-downs, trend data, deductive reasoning, etc.

   ▸ Investigate and eliminate possible inputs until only one credible failure path is evident.

   ▸ Document justification for each input eliminated.

8. DOCUMENT your resulting cause(s) in the report. Include supporting data to validate the failure path and resulting contributing factor(s).

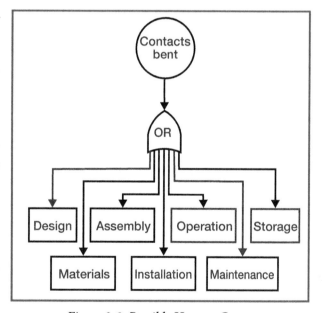

Figure 3-9. Possible Human Causes

Note: Once you find the form, fit, or function problem, you will start looking for causes. In the example, the underlying hardware problem is that the battery's contacts are bent. So how did the contacts get bent? Too much force? Are the contacts old? Corroded?

If the contacts were bent by excessive force, you will need to start looking for the potential human causes of the bent contacts. Figure 3-9 shows some of the ways a person can interact with a machine.

3.1.1   Fault Tree Example

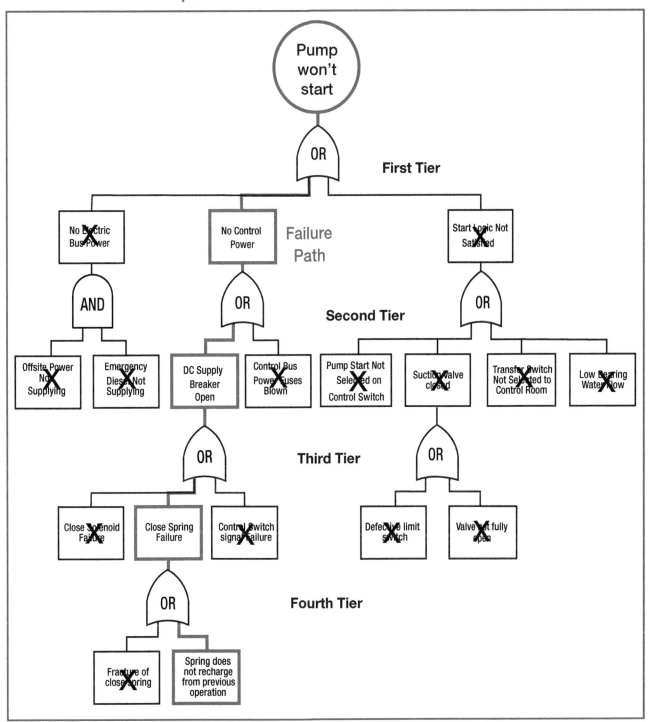

Figure 3-10. Example Fault Tree

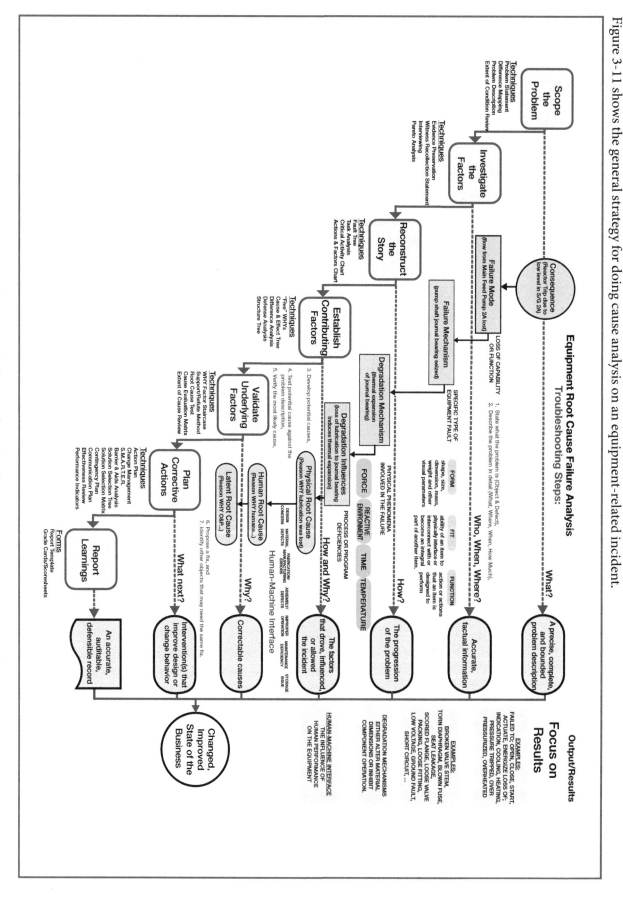

Figure 3-11 shows the general strategy for doing cause analysis on an equipment-related incident.

Figure 3-11. Equipment Failure Analysis (Nuclear Regulatory Commission, 1993)

3.2 Task Analysis

What is it?

*Task analysi*s is a technique in which participants conduct a step-by-step reenactment of their actions for an investigator without carrying out the actual function. The technique is used to understand a work activity related to an incident. There are two phases to a task analysis (International Atomic Energy Agency, 2008):

1. **Paper and pencil (a.k.a. "table top") phase.** The investigator obtains enough written guidance associated with task completion so that skill and knowledge deficiencies can be determined without actually observing performance of the task.

2. **Walk-through phase.** The investigator actually observes or performs the task noting any difficulties encountered during task performance. The walk-through task analysis technique involves a step-by-step reenactment of the task.

   Limitations may exist to access the area after an incident. If appropriate, it may be possible to use a simulator or a "mock-up" for performing the walk-through rather than the actual work location.

This investigation technique is similar to simplified *job task analysis* (JTA) used by those in the training profession.

Why is it useful?

Performing a task analysis will provide the investigator with:

▸ A clear understanding of how the task is normally performed.

▸ Questions to be answered during the course of the investigation, usually through interviewing.

The benefits of the paper and pencil phase are that it is:

▸ Useful for an investigator not familiar with the task.

▸ Provides investigators with a good insight of the task and sub-tasks. (May not identify how the task was actually done.)

▸ Identifies questions to use later for interviewing.

The features of the walk-through phase are:

▸ Re-enactment of the task with the job performers involved with the incident. (If these workers are not available, the task is performed with other job performers who normally perform the work.)

▸ Notation of differences between actual re-enactment and procedure steps.

▸ Helpful identification of contributing factors that relate to physical work environment and human-machine interface.

When is it used?

Task analysis is a tool that is used on evaluations where problems during execution of tasks contributed to the incident. Task analysis should be considered for all incidents involving human performance difficulties. Task analysis is usually performed in the early stages of the investigation process (generally during Steps 2 through 4) and the information provided is used throughout the investigation.

Prerequisite: Participants must be people who actually do or have done the task.

How is it done?

Figure 3-12 shows the flow of the basic steps of a simple task analysis (Department of Energy 1992).

1. OBTAIN preliminary information so that it is known what activities were taking place when the problem or performance difficulty occurred. Identify the sequence of actions.

2. SELECT task(s) of interest. Decide specifically which tasks will be investigated.

3. OBTAIN the necessary background information.
   - Obtain relevant procedure(s), work documents, logs, and technical manuals.
   - Obtain training materials (lesson plans and manuals).
   - Obtain system drawings, block diagrams, piping and instrumentation diagrams, etc.
   - Interview individuals who have performed the task (but not those who will be observed) to obtain understanding of how the work should be performed.

4. PREPARE a task performance guide outlining how the task will be carried out. Document how the task should be performed.
   - An existing procedure with key items underlined is the easiest way of doing this.
   - Indicate steps of interest in the task and key controls and displays so that:
     - ❏ You will know what to look for.
     - ❏ You will be able record observations and actions more easily.

5. GET FAMILIAR with the guide and decide what information is to be recorded and how it will be recorded.

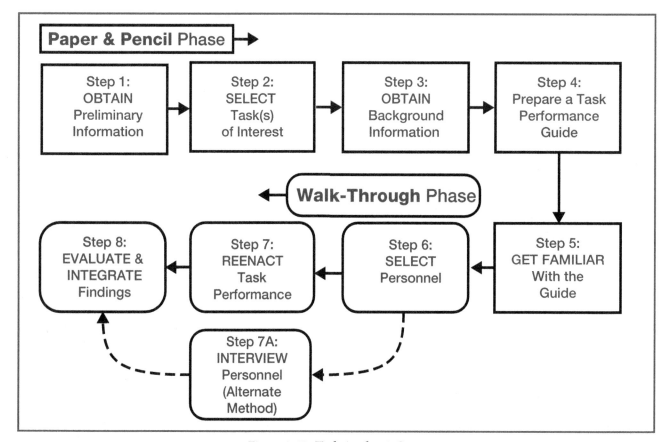

Figure 3-12. Task Analaysis Steps

> ▸ Check off each step and controls or displays used as they occur.
> ▸ Note discrepancies and problems in the margin or in a space provided for comments, adjacent to the step.

6. SELECT personnel to determine how the task was actually performed.

> ▸ If the incident was related to human performance, select personnel who performed the task or normally perform the task or both.
> ▸ If the task is performed by a crew, crew members should play the same role they fulfill when normally carrying out the task.

7. REENACT task performance/interview personnel in order to reconstruct the incident step-by-step. Observe a walk-through.

> ▸ Try to re-create the situation to obtain a sense of how the actual incident occurred.
> ▸ The actual task may be observed or a mock-up or simulation may be used depending on plant conditions.
> ▸ Observe personnel walking through the task.
> ▸ The walk-through may be done in slow motion or even stopped to facilitate asking questions.

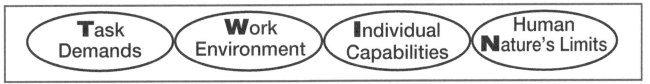

Figure 3-13. Error Precursor Categories

> ▸ Using the four categories shown in Figure 3-13, look for error precursors (Department of Energy, 2012).
> ▸ Using the four categories shown in Figure 3-13, look for error-likely situations that may exist (Department of Energy, 2012). Determine whether there was:
> ❏ A mismatch between the worker's capabilities and the demands of the task.
> ❏ A mismatch set up by work conditions that challenge a worker's personal limits.

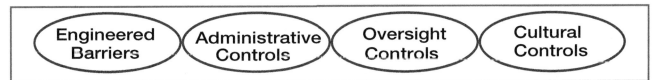

Figure 3-14. Organizational Defense Categories

> ▸ Using the four categories shown in Figure 3-14, look for factors associated with organizational defenses (Department of Energy, 2009).

8. EVALUATE and INTEGRATE findings. Summarize all information collected. See Table 3-2.

> ▸ Record workers' actions and use of displays and controls.
> ▸ Consolidate any problem areas noted.
> ▸ Identify all probable contributors to the performance difficulties.

Table 3-2. Task Analysis Worksheet

(1) **Paper and Pencil Input Steps in Procedure or Practice** (Enter step number and short description.)	(2) **Walk-Through by Analyst or Trained Individual** (State how actual behavior matches procedure.)	(3) **Questions/Conclusions** (Ask/state how task was/should be performed.)

3.2.1   Task Analysis Example

(1) **Paper & Pencil Input Steps in Procedure or Practice** (Enter step number an short description.)	(2) **Walk-Through by Analyst or Trained Individual** (State how actual behavior matches procedure.	(3) **Questions/Conclusions** (Ask/state how task was/should be performed.)
1. Locate proper "drain trap." 2. De-pressurize line pressure. 3. Verify that the line has been de-pressurized. 4. Open line. 5. Insert drain trap. 6. Close line. 7. Re-pressurize line.	Drain trap is not labeled. Nearest pressure gauge is up 2 flights of stairs about 50' away. All other drain traps have pressure gauges near opening.	Is there a requirement to label? Why is this location without a pressure gauge? Has it been modified? Steps are all very general. How does the equipment operator know how to do them?

3.3   Critical Activity Charting (Critical Incident Technique)

What is it?

A *critical activity chart* is used to identify critical human actions in a work process that if performed correctly would have prevented an incident from occurring or would have significantly reduced the incident's consequences. This is accomplished by defining and breaking down a task in order to identify problem areas associated with the activity and its control requirements (Nuclear Regulatory Commission, 1993).

Why is it useful?

The critical activity chart helps an investigator identify worker tasks critical to the successful completion of levels of steps that preceded an incident. The process is very useful in identifying problem areas within a work activity. It can also be used to help several different people get an equal understanding of the problem. The critical activity chart provides information by answering the following questions:

-) Who was to perform the action (behavior) and with what?
-) When was the action performed and what cues (antecedents) signaled its start?
-) Where was the action performed and under what conditions?

When is it used?

The critical activity chart can be used to analyze how a work process works. It helps identify problem areas in the work process. A critical activity chart is usually developed in the early stages of the investigation process (generally during Steps 2 through 4) and the information provided is used throughout the investigation. Also, ask "Are there ways that each activity could be made more efficient or effective?" In Step 6 (Plan Corrective Actions) the chart is used in the effectiveness review.

A critical activity chart does not have to be used for every investigation, but should be used whenever at least one of the following is true:

-) Identification of the causes of the incident is difficult or controversial.
-) Extremely complete documentation of the incident is required.
-) Assistance from human performance experts is needed.

How is it used?

Table 3-3. Critical Activity Chart

Action/ Step #	Performed By	Required Human Action(s)	Equipment Component(s)	Tools	Observations: Questions/Comment	☑ Critical Human Action
		Paper & Pencil Input Step			Walk-Through Remark	
		Paper & Pencil Input Step			Walk-Through Remark	

1. IDENTIFY all the human actions. To develop a list of the relevant human actions:

   ‣ Obtain the applicable operating, maintenance, test, abnormal, alarm response, or emergency procedures and list each step to be evaluated.

   ‣ Collect all relevant reference documents (such as user's manuals, procedures, previously completed task analyses, and training material) and review them for the human actions that would be associated with the incident.

   ‣ Do a "table top" talk through the incident with those involved and experts on performing the work. (See 3.2 Task Analysis: Paper and pencil phase.)

   ‣ Walk through the incident with qualified personnel. Recreate the incident in the field by using actual trained personnel and the applicable procedures. Consider use of a simulator or "mock-up." The steps will be walked through or, if possible, actually performed. (See 3.2 Task Analysis: Walk-through phase.)

   > **Note:** Not all steps of a work activity are equally important.

2. IDENTIFY the "risk-important" steps of the task (Nuclear Regulatory Commission, 2004). Risk-important steps are actions/behaviors that expose products, services, or assets to the potential for harm (Muschara, 2010). Consider the following four risk factors:

   1. The significance of the potential harm.
   2. The irreversibility of the action.
   3. The irreversibility of the potential harm.
   4. The immediacy of the potential harm.

3. IDENTIFY the critical human actions (CHAs) from the list of risk-important steps (Nuclear Regulatory Commission, 1993). CHAs include:

   ‣ Actions aimed at changing the state of facility structures, systems, or components.

   ‣ Steps that are irrecoverable or actions that cannot be reversed.

   ‣ Steps where the outcome of an error is intolerable for personnel or facility safety.

   It is a CHA if the step:

   ‣ Might cause an incident if it is not done.

   ‣ Might cause an incident if an error is made.

   ‣ Might cause an incident if done some other way.

   ‣ Makes incident less severe if done the right way.

   The key question for identifying a CHA is:

   If this action had been performed correctly, would it have prevented the incident from occurring or would it have significantly reduced the incident's consequences?

   A CHA could be a "critical step" related to the incident.

4. IDENTIFY any critical steps. Critical steps are actions in written instructions that, if performed improperly, ***will trigger immediate, irreversible harm*** (Muschara, 2010). For each critical step identified, the following should have been addressed up front in the planning process:

   ‣ Conditions that would cause work to stop and work activities to be placed in a safe condition if the safety of the worker, environment, or equipment is threatened.

   ‣ The expected actions/behaviors to be taken if these conditions are reached.

5. RECORD the answers to each of the following questions about each CHA and critical step:

- Who was to perform the action/step? Technician? Operator? Supervisor?
- With what? Tools? Displays? Procedures? Drawings?
- When was the action/step performed? Timing? Time of day?
- Where was the action/step performed? Layout of the work place?
- Under what conditions? Lighting? Noise? Temperature? Weather? Multi-tasking?

6. For each CHA and critical step, RECORD *error precursors*.

Figure 3-15. Error Precursor Categories

7. For each CHA and critical step, RECORD *error likely situations*.

8. For each CHA and critical step, RECORD *error reduction tools*.

9. For each CHA and critical step, RECORD *defenses* that were weak, missing, or not used.

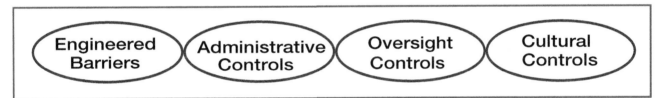

Figure 3-16. Organizational Defense Categories

3.3.1   Critical Activity Chart Example

Action/ Step #	Performed By	Required Human Action(s)	Equipment Component(s)	Tools	Observations: Questions/Comment	☑ Critical Human Action
3.1.1	Rad/Chem Technician	Notify Control Room of intent to sample.		Phone		
3.1.2	Rad/Chem Technician	Open demineralizer outlet grab sample valve.	DA-V0112		Is this the correct valve (per system design)?	
3.1.3	Rad/Chem Technician	Open sample pane isolation valve.	DA-V0421		Is this the correct valve (per system design)?	
3.1.4	Rad/Chem Technician	Observe pressure indicator.	DA-PI-5129			
3.1.5	Rad/Chem Technician	Adjust/maintain sample pressure <20 psig.	DA-V0112 DA-PCV-5129A			
3.1.6	Rad/Chem Technician	Observe flow rate on meter.	DA-FI-5129			

3.1.7	Rad/Chem Technician	Purge at least 2.5 gallons of water through sample lines.		Stop-watch or clock?	Critical step in order to ensure sample is representative. Were sample lines flushed the proper amount based on flow?	☑
3.1.8	Rad/Chem Technician	Throttle open grab sample valve.	DA-V0112		Why does step 3.1.8 say to open valve when it is already open per step 3.1.2?	
3.1.9	Rad/Chem Technician	Draw sample from grab sample valve.		Sample bottle	Sample contamination could occur here. Did Technician ensure sample bottle was clean and empty? How many times was the bottle rinsed?	☑
3.2.1	Rad/Chem Technician	Close sample valve.	DA-V0112			

3.4   Actions and Factors Charting

What is it?

Actions and factors charting graphically displays an incident on a timeline highlighting:

▶ Human behaviors and equipment operations that happened.

▶ Associated conditions, situations, or circumstances.

The chart is used primarily for compiling and organizing thoughts and evidence to portray the sequence and progression of the incident in context which, in turn, leads to the potential reasons for those behaviors and operations.

When complete, the chart is a timeline showing the sequence of behaviors and operations that led up to, and occurred after, the incident. The chart includes factors associated with the incident and pinpoints differences (changes), contributing factors, and flawed defenses (Nuclear Regulatory Commission, 2001).

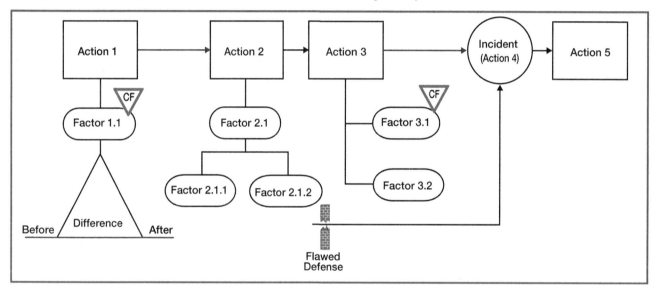

Figure 3-17. Actions and Factors Chart (AFC) Diagram

Why is it useful?

Actions and factors charting is the single investigative tool that does all the following (Department of Energy, 2012):

▶ Tells the story. Readers will understand the sequence of actions leading to the incident.

▶ Integrates information. Shows connections among individual job performer acts and decisions, team/leader shortfalls, and management system control weaknesses.

▶ Makes contributor factors evident. Helps prove suspected relationships among triggering factors, error-inducing situations, flawed defenses, and underlying latent organizational weaknesses.

▶ Helps spot missing information or inconsistencies.

▶ Helps demonstrate visually why the incident occurred.

▶ Focuses discussions on what really happened and helps avoid getting sidetracked on problems investigators found, but that did not cause the incident.

▶ Organizes thoughts and presents a good picture of the incident to decision-makers.

When is it used?

Actions and factors charting is used throughout the problem solving process starting with Step 1 (Scope the Problem) through Step 7 (Report Learnings). However, it is the primary focus of Step 3 (Reconstruct the Story). When *difference (change) analysis* or *barrier analysis* is used, incorporate the results into the chart using the appropriate symbols.

How is it done?

> **Prerequisite:** Before starting the actions and factors chart, understand the symbols that are used.

Table 3-4. Actions and Factors Charting Terms and Symbols (Department of Energy, 2012)

TERM	DEFINITION	SYMBOL
Incident	The adverse condition, or consequence, that is the focus of investigation. The incident can be described by a short sentence with one noun and one active verb.	○
Action (Event or Occurrence)	A real-time happening or operation that leads to a result. A discrete, relevant deed or occurrence that preceded or followed the incident being investigated. Could be a human behavior, or equipment performance, that leads to an outcome. Use a dotted box for an assumption **(Presumptive Action)**.	▭ (solid box) ⬚ (dotted box)
Factor	Any circumstance, situation, or condition that produces, shapes, or allows the consequence (effect/result). Information, including problems, related to an action. Use a dotted oval for an assumption **(Presumptive Factor)**.	⬭ (solid oval) ⬭ (dotted oval)
Difference (Change)	A change that is introduced sometime in the sequence of actions and determined to be relevant to the incident.	⟁ Before / After

Flawed Defense **(Broken Barrier)**	The physical, administrative, oversight, or cultural control that was intended to inhibit an inappropriate act or equipment failure. Weak or missing defenses allow incidents to occur.	
Contributing Factor **(Causal Factor)**	Any action, situation, or condition that occurred or existed prior to an error without which the error is less likely to have occurred. A contributing factor may have initiated the incident, allowed its outcome, or exacerbated its consequences. Contributing factors are those actions, conditions, or events which directly or indirectly influence the outcome of a situation or problem. Sometimes called "causal factor."	

To develop an actions and factors chart:

1. EVALUATE initial information and data — the facts about what occurred and how, when and where the incident occurred, who was involved, and the consequences.

2. DEFINE the incident by writing a problem statement providing factual information identifying what has gone wrong (*defect/deviation*) with what (*object*). Put it in a circle. See Figure 3-18.

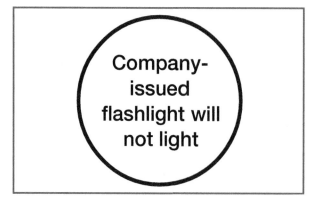

Figure 3-18. The Incident in a Circle

3. CONSTRUCT a preliminary timeline of actions or occurrences leading up to the incident. Put each action in a separate box. See Figure 3-19.

   As a general rule, actions should be described using one noun (subject) and one verb (predicate). Add date/times above boxes or in boxes (but maintain a consistent format). Connect actions by solid arrows (→) in relative time sequence (left to right). Consider the use of the task analysis technique to get started. State facts. Get rid of judgmental words. Limit to one action per rectangle.

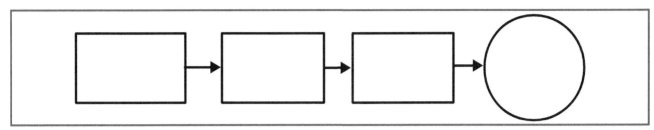

Figure 3-19. Time Sequence

4. CONDUCT the investigation using applicable techniques (barrier analysis, difference analysis (a.k.a. change analysis), critical activity charting, etc.) to identify "factors" associated with each action. Factors are information, including problems, related to an action. Put each factor in an oval and attach with lines to its associated action or factor. See Figure 3-20.

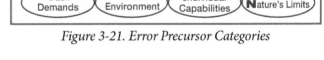

Figure 3-20. Action Context

Using the four categories shown in Figure 3-21, look for error precursors (Department of Energy, 2012).

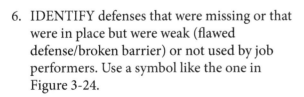

Figure 3-21. Error Precursor Categories

Using the four categories shown in Figure 3-22, look for factors associated with organizational defenses (Department of Energy, 2009).

Figure 3-22. Organizational Defense Categories

5. IDENTIFY every relevant difference (change). Use a symbol like the one in Figure 3-23.

.

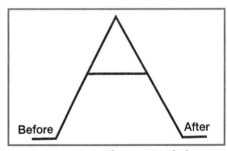

Figure 3-23. Difference Symbol

6. IDENTIFY defenses that were missing or that were in place but were weak (flawed defense/broken barrier) or not used by job performers. Use a symbol like the one in Figure 3-24.

7. IDENTIFY defenses that held (i.e., functioned as expected). Defense functions are to create awareness, detect and warn, protect, recover, contain, or enable escape. Use a symbol like the one in Figure 3-25.

Figure 3-24. Flawed Defense Symbol

Figure 3-25. Defense Held Symbol

8. IDENTIFY the contributing factors with a triangle or shaded oval as illustrated in Figure 3-26.

9. ENSURE facts are validated and conclusions are supported by facts.

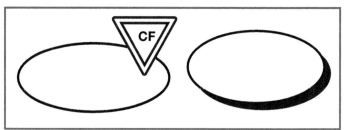

Figure 3-26. Contributing Factor Symbols

Note: At this point, it is possible to start building a *WHY factor staircase* to diagram contributing causes and root causes. This is covered in Step 5 (Validate Underlying Factors).

3.4.1   Actions and Factors Chart Example

Figure 3-28 is an example of an actions and factors chart for the following problem statement: Employee breaks wrist in forklift incident.

3.4.2   Notes

1. You may ask, "How do I know how far back in time to go?" Keep asking the question until you go backwards in time enough to understand what happened — how the problem progressed.

2. You may need to work from both directions. This happens when you have conflicting stories or the time period covers several shifts or days.

3. Look at each box (action) and ask, "What facts or data do we have about this action?" Put these factors in ovals.

4. Once a large collection of data is on hand, facts have a way of vanishing and logic flaws have a habit of creeping in. From the beginning, display the actions and factors chart where everyone onsite can see it and contribute to it. Tucking an actions and factors chart away on a laptop, or waiting to draft one for the final report, deprives evaluators of a valuable "group memory" and discussion tool. The actions and factors chart puts the cards on the table for everyone to see.

5. The actions and factors chart captures the whole incident in an integrated format and presents the situation in a single glance. The actions and factors chart helps the investigator understand the incident's progression by helping to identify missing information and inconsistencies in the information. It also enables the investigator to explain the incident to others, such as key decision-makers.

6. Include information about policies, actions that were omitted, what was wrong about the action, equipment information, vendor procedures, etc.

7. IF any of the following criteria are met, THEN a factor should be designated as a *contributing factor* (a.k.a. causal factor, contributing cause):

   ‣ Identifies an action, condition, or event which directly or indirectly influenced the outcome of the situation or problem.

   ‣ Identifies a clear driver or reason for the stated problem and is supported by the facts of the investigation.

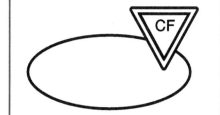

Figure 3-27. Contributing Factor

   ‣ Identifies conditions or situations that could have prevented the incident.

   ‣ Identifies actions or circumstances that, if removed or prevented, the incident would not have occurred or its consequences would be significantly mitigated.

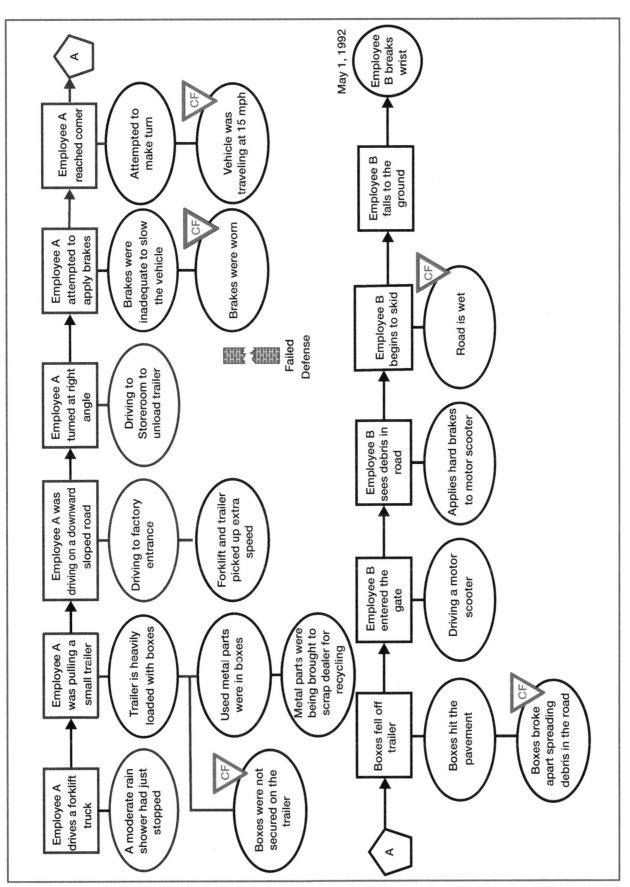

Figure 3-28. Actions and Factors Chart (Center, 1992)

Looking Forward

By this time, you should be able to present a good picture to interested parties of how the incident unfolded. You will be able to do this because you have used a structured method for collecting, organizing, and integrating the evidence you collected in Step 2 (Investigate the Factors). The clear display of information will serve you well as you write the incident report.

For equipment-initiated incidents, your fault tree should show a diagram of all the possible failure mechanisms you researched and how you verified or refuted possible causes. For machinery, it is often possible to determine the specific physical mechanism that triggered the incident. You will label that cause the *physical root* of the incident.

Your actions and factors chart should illustrate the sequence of activities that led to the incident and the conditions that influenced each pertinent action. The chart may have shown you gaps in the information you already collected and given you the opportunity to gather more data about certain activities or situations. Others looking at your chart should be able to see the context of each important or critical act. Your management and other key decision-makers will have an effective visual aid explaining the history of the incident.

You have probably also established some actions or conditions as potential contributing factors — direct or indirect influences that led to the incident. In Step 4 (Establish Contributing Factors), you will learn tools and techniques that will help you refine and validate conclusions about cause and effect relationships.

Questions for Understanding

1. What should your first step be in developing a fault tree for equipment-initiated incidents?
2. Why is task analysis useful?
3. What makes a step of a task a critical human action (CHA)?
4. What is actions and factors charting?
5. What is the purpose for developing an actions and factors chart?
6. What are some ways of ensuring you have determined all the possible ways a machine part or component failed?

Questions for Discussion

1. How does the task analysis technique relate to interviewing?
2. Why is actions and factors charting a critical tool during your investigation and what are the benefits for using this tool?
3. How would you determine if a factor should be a contributing factor (a.k.a. causal factor)?

References

Center for Chemical Process Safety of the American Institute of Chemical Engineers. (1992). *Guidelines for preventing human error in process safety*. New York, NY: American Institute of Chemical Engineers.

Department of Energy (DOE). (1992, February). *DOE guideline: Root cause analysis guidance document*. (DOE-NE-STD-1004-92). Washington, DC: US Department of Energy.

Department of Energy (DOE). (2009, June). *DOE standard: Human performance improvement handbook: Volume 1: Concepts and principles*. (DOE-HDBK-1028-2009). Washington, DC: US Department of Energy.

Department of Energy (DOE). (2012, July). *DOE handbook: Accident and operational safety analysis: Volume I: Accident analysis techniques*. (DOE-HDBK-1208-2012). Washington, DC: US Department of Energy.

International Atomic Energy Agency (IAEA). (2008, July) *Best practices in the organization, management and conduct of an effective investigation of events at nuclear power plants*. (IAEA-TECDOC-1600). Vienna, Austria: Operational Safety Section, International Atomic Energy Agency.

Muschara, T. (2010). *A risk-based approach to managing the human risk*. Retrieved from http://www.slideshare.net/muschara/managing-human-risk

Nuclear Regulatory Commission (NRC). (1981, January). *Fault tree handbook*. (NUREG-0492). Washington, DC: US Government Printing Office.

Nuclear Regulatory Commission (NRC). (1993, October). *Development of the NRC's human performance investigation process (HPIP)*. (NRC NUREG/CR-5455, S1-92-101). Washington, DC: US Government Printing Office.

Nuclear Regulatory Commission (NRC). (2001, September). *The human performance evaluation process: A resource for reviewing the identification and resolution of human performance problems*. (NUREG/CR-6751). Washington, DC: Office of Nuclear Regulatory Research.

Nuclear Regulatory Commission (NRC). (2004, February). *Human factors engineering program review model*. (NUREG-0711, Rev. 2). Washington, DC: Office of Nuclear Regulatory Research.

For Further Reading

Causal factors analysis: An approach for organizational learning. (2008). Amarillo, TX: Babcock and Wilcox (B&W) Technical Services Pantex LLC.

Center for Chemical Process Safety of the American Institute of Chemical Engineers. (1994). *Guidelines for investigating chemical process incidents*. New York, NY: American Institute of Chemical Engineers.

Step 4

Establish Contributing Factors

There is something in all of us that loves to put together a puzzle, that loves to see the image of the whole emerge. The beauty of a person, or a flower, or a poem lies in seeing all of it.

— Peter Senge, Author

In Step 4, you will evaluate the pertinent factors that should have contributed to success so you can find out how an incident happened instead. Cause and effect analysis is most effective when used within the framework of success models and the actions and factors chart. Establishing contributors is all about sifting through the information that you have gathered while scoping the problem, investigating the factors, and reconstructing the story in Steps 1 to 3.

To be a valid causal factor, an action or condition must be supported by the evidence and must have had some effect on the incident's circumstances and consequences. You have already asked what drove, influenced, or allowed this incident to happen; however, the tools and techniques you will be using in Step 4 will help you establish which factors are linked directly or indirectly to the incident you are investigating.

Basics of Cause Analysis for Step 4

Benjamin Franklin's version of an old nursery rhyme, which he published in 1758, (illustrated in Figure 4-1) shows that you should not ignore information that seems minor or insignificant, especially early in the investigation. You never know about potential cause and effect.

For want of a nail the shoe was lost,
for want of a shoe the horse was lost;
and for want of a horse the rider was lost;
being overtaken and slain by the enemy,
all for want of care about a horseshoe nail.

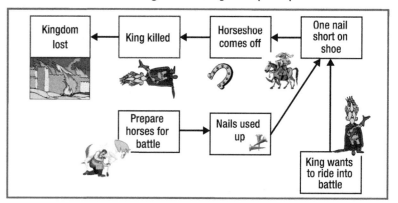

Figure 4-1. Why Did This Happen?

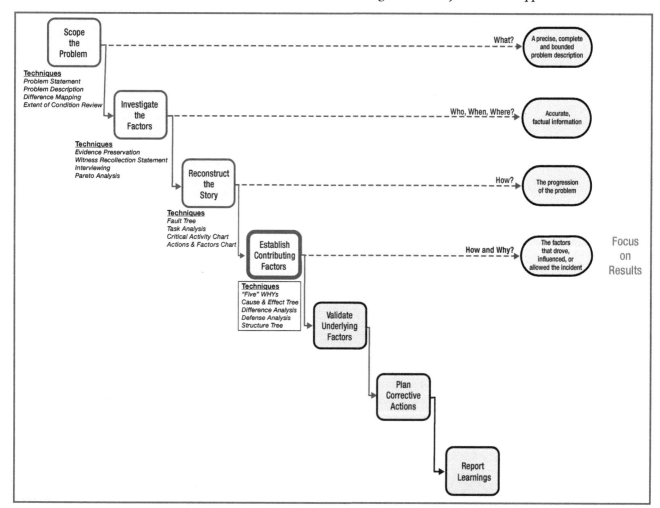

Figure 4-2. Step 4 Establishing Contributing Factors

As defined by Avatar International (1985), there are several ways you can establish a cause (C) and effect (E) relationship. See Figures 4-3 through 4-6. Notice the effect (E) can become the cause (C) of the next effect in a sequence of events.

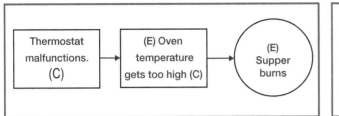

Figure 4-3. Chained Cause and Effect

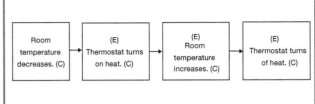

Figure 4-4. Control and Effect

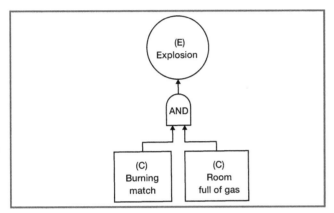

Figure 4-5. Conditional Cause and Effect

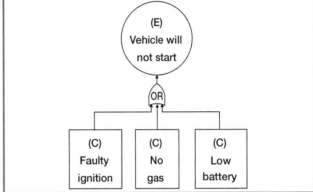

Figure 4-6. Compound Cause and Effect

This is a good time to get some working definitions for terms you will be using:

▸ A *contributing factor* is an action, condition, or event which directly or indirectly influenced or permitted an incident to occur. Equivalent terms for a contributing factor are *contributing cause* and *causal factor*. Some contributing factors are actions or conditions that set the stage for an incident to occur but, alone, may not have been sufficient to cause the incident. Other contributing factors may be longstanding situations or a series of prior incidents and problems that, while inconsequential standing alone, increased the probability of failure.

▸ A *root cause* is an underlying contributing factor or reason that explains the existence of workplace conditions or the permitting of worker actions that resulted in a harmful business incident. A root cause will explain the actions that triggered the incident, the weak controls that allowed the incident, or the conditions that intensified the consequences of the incident. "A root cause of a human performance problem is the set of conditions that, if eliminated or modified, would minimize the likelihood that the problem would reoccur as well as prevent similar problems from occurring" (Nuclear Regulatory Commission, 2001, p. 5-2). Once you find a root cause, there may be other underlying factors but they are generally outside the control of the organization or not important enough to correct.

The following observations should guide your thinking as you search for and establish the contributors to the incident you are investigating:

Caution must be taken in applying analytic methods. First, no single method will provide all the analyses required to completely determine the multiple causal factors of an accident. Several techniques that can complement and cross-validate one another should be used to yield optimal results. Second, analytic techniques cannot be used mechanically and without thought. The best analytic tools can become cumbersome and ineffective if they are not applied to an accident's specific circumstances and adapted accordingly. (Department of Energy, 2012, p. 2-40)

Frequently the investigator will identify more than one root cause/contributor to an incident. Often this occurs when several causal factors are identified that contributed to a single accident/incident. It can also occur when more than one root cause for a single causal factor is found. (Nuclear Regulatory Commission, 1993, p. 11)

On your way to establishing contributors, you should also look into both the human and organizational factors. According to Muschara (2010), these factors can be categorized as engineered, administrative, oversight, or cultural controls or defenses. The human aspect focuses on worker practices, whereas the organizational aspect focuses on the process the worker is expected to use.

Use Table 4-1 as a checklist to guide you through Step 4 of the investigation. Step 4 contains a variety of logical and structured tools (listed below by section number) that can be used to ensure the factors that drove, influenced, or allowed the incident are identified:

4.1   Contributing Factor Test

4.2   "Five" WHYs

4.3   Cause and Effect Trees

4.4   Difference Analysis (a.k.a. Change Analysis)

4.5   Defense Analysis (a.k.a. Barrier Analysis)

4.6   Structure Tree Diagram

You will be introduced to several specific types of structure trees:

4.6.1 Fishbone (Ishikawa) Diagrams

4.6.2 Defense-in-Depth Analysis

4.6.3 MORT Analysis

4.6.4 Production/Protection Strategy Analysis

4.6.5 Safety Culture Analysis

Table 4-1. Step 4 Jump Start Checklist

☑ Behaviors [Sub-Tasks]	Tools/Techniques	Required		
☐ Map **cause and effect** relationships. Include refuting facts.	*Cause and Effect Tree/ "Five" WHYs*	RC	AC	AD
☐ *Evaluate findings to determine "why" the incident happened.* *Seek to understand the contributing causes of risk significant performance issues. Identify conditions that could have prevented the incident.*		RC	AC	
☐ *Identify a clear cause that addresses the stated problem and is supported by the facts of the investigation.*		RC	AC	AD
☐ *Ensure cause (C) prior to effect (E) in time.*		RC	AC	AD
☐ Conduct a difference analysis to identify more causal factors (as applicable).	*Difference Analysis (a.k.a. Change Analysis)*	RC	AC	
☐ Conduct an analysis of **production/protection strategy**.	*Production/Protection Analysis*	RC		
☐ *Evaluate the error reduction strategy used during work preparation.*		RC		
☐ *Evaluate the error reduction strategy used during work performance (execution).*	*Critical Human Activity Charting*	RC		
☐ *Evaluate the error reduction strategy used during work feedback.*		RC		
☐ *Evaluate the defense-in-depth strategy for engineered barriers.*		RC		
☐ *Evaluate the defense-in-depth strategy for administrative controls.*		RC		
☐ *Evaluate the defense-in-depth strategy for oversight controls.*		RC		
☐ *Evaluate the defense-in-depth strategy for cultural controls.*	*Safety Culture Analysis*	RC		
☐ Conduct a factor chart analysis.	*Actions and Factors Chart*	RC	AC	
☐ *Identify triggering factors on the actions and factors chart or model (initiating action).*	*Fault Tree/Task Analysis output*	RC	AC	
☐ *Identify aggravating factors on the actions and factors chart or model.*	*Fault Tree/Task Analysis output*	RC	AC	
☐ *Identify exposure factors on the actions and factors chart or model.*	*Defense Analysis*	RC	AC	
☐ *Identify moderating factors on the actions and factors chart/model (defenses held).*	*Defense-in-Depth Analysis*	RC		
☐ Identify contributing factors on the actions and factors chart (or other logical [success] model used).	*Actions and Factors Chart*	RC	AC	
	Contributing Factor Test			
☐ Continue the extent of condition review.	*Extent of Condition Review*	RC	AC	AD
☐ Continue the search for operating experience.		RC	AC	
☐ To gather information about equipment trends and failures, use industry sources.		RC	AC	
☐ Critical action completed. Involve responsible management.		RC		

RC = Root Cause Analysis; **AC** = Apparent Cause Analysis; **AD** = Adverse

☑ **Results** Required [R]/Desired [D]			
☐ Factors that triggered (released) the incident are identified.	RC$_R$	AC$_R$	AD$_R$
☐ Factors that made the situation worse are identified.	RC$_R$	AC$_R$	AD$_D$
☐ Exposure factors (holes in defenses) are identified.	RC$_R$	AC$_R$	
☐ Factors that prevented the incident from being worse than it was are identified.	RC$_R$	AC$_D$	

4.1   Contributing Factor Test

What is it?

The *contributing factor test* is an evaluation to see what actions, events, or situations contributed to the incident significantly enough to go on to root cause evaluation.

Why is it useful?

It is useful for clarifying exactly which issues need a further expenditure of resources so that underlying causes can be investigated.

When is it used?

This test will be done in Step 4 (Establish Contributing Factors) to see which issues will be taken through root cause analysis.

How is it done?

1. CONDUCT an actions and factors chart analysis to accomplish the following tasks:
    - Identify the triggering factors on the actions and factors chart or model.
    - Identify the shaping factors on the actions and factors chart or model.
    - Identify the exposure factors on the actions and factors chart or model.
    - Identify the moderating factors on the actions and factors chart or model.

2. Then PRESENT information to help understand the contributing causes of risk-significant performance issues.

3. IF any of the following criteria are met, DESIGNATE the factor as a *contributing factor*:
    - Identifies an action, event, condition, situation, or circumstance that directly triggered the incident.
    - Identifies an action, event, condition, situation, or circumstance that indirectly influenced or allowed the incident or shaped its outcome.
    - Identifies a clear cause that addresses the stated problem and is supported by the facts of the investigation (a.k.a. "a sin of commission").
    - Identifies actions or conditions that could have prevented the incident (a.k.a. "a sin of omission").

4. USE the decision-making flowchart to determine the most probable path of deeper evaluation called *root cause analysis*. See Figure 4-7. That is, you will do one of the following:
    A. FIND root causes (generally for direct influences such as triggering factors).
    B. CONSTRUCT root causes (for indirect influences like exposure factors and exacerbating factors).

> **Note:** It takes a lot more work to determine "root cause(s)" for indirect causes because these are usually actions that should have happened but did not or conditions that should have existed but did not. You will generally have to build a "case" with a "preponderance of evidence" to infer the deeper underlying causes of an incident.

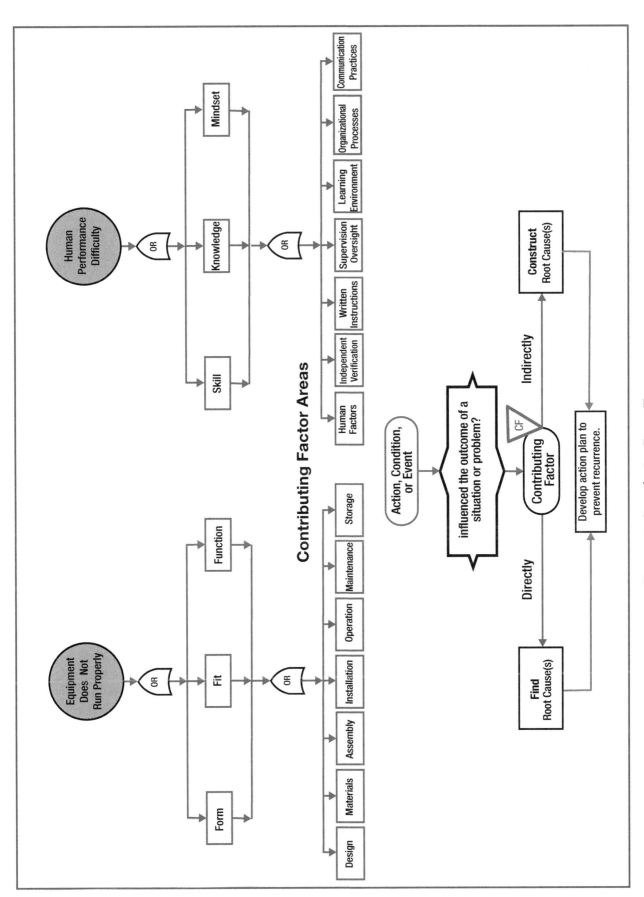

Figure 4-7. Contributing Factor Test

4.2   "Five" WHYs

What is it?

"Five" WHYs is an elementary technique used to diagram the cause and effect sequence of an incident or accident. This is a technique for discovering causal factors by repeatedly asking "why." This technique can also help spur understanding of how different causes might be related. Another advantage of using this technique is that it allows you to focus on the process instead of personalities. It is similar to a cause and effect tree (described in section 4.3) with only one branch.

Why is it done?

By asking "why" up to five times, an investigator can:

> ▸ Investigate the reasons for an incident or accident.
> ▸ Identify solutions to prevent an incident from happening again.
> ▸ Make links between the causes of good or inappropriate actions.

When is it used?

The quest for explanations and the reasons that drove or allowed the incident or accident begins in Step 1 (Scope the Problem) and continues into Step 5 (Validate Underlying Factors).

How is it done?

This technique consists of describing the problem in very specific terms and then asking "why" it happens successive times until the question no longer yields any useful information.

1. DESCRIBE the problem in very specific terms. Be specific in the choice of words to help keep everyone focused.
2. ASK "why" the problem happens. Ask "why" five times, then for each answer, ask "why" again. By the fifth time, the answer should reflect the most likely cause of a situation.
3. If the answer does not identify a deeper cause, ASK "why" again.
4. CONTINUE asking until the deepest causes are identified (this may take more or less than FIVE WHYs).
5. STOP when the answer is outside management's control OR where going deeper adds no value.

After as few as two to three WHYs, but sometimes seven WHYs (an average of five WHYs) the most probable cause is identified. For example, five WHYs can be presented as a tree diagram, which highlights the chain of causes. It starts with the effect and the major group of causes, by step or category.

Although called "Asking WHY Five Times," five is a rule of thumb. There may be more or fewer questions depending on the particular situation. It is important to beware of channeling your analysis down one avenue and completely ignoring other possible causes of the same problem.

4.2.1   "Five" WHYs Example

Problem Statement: Equipment operator doing rounds in the turbine building broke right forearm which was classified as a lost-time away injury. See Figure 4-8.

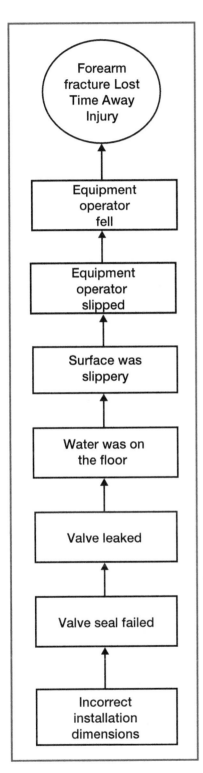

WHY 1   Why [how] did the equipment operator break his right forearm doing rounds in the turbine building?

Answer: The equipment operator fell.

WHY 2   Why did the equipment operator fall?

Answer: The equipment operator slipped.

WHY 3   Why did the equipment operator slip?

Answer: The equipment operator stepped on a slippery spot on the turbine building floor.

WHY 4   Why was the turbine building floor slippery?

Answer: Water was on the turbine building floor making it slippery.

WHY 5   Why was there water on the turbine building floor?

Answer: Valve XYZ leaked water.

WHY 6   Why did valve XYZ leak water?

Answer: A seal in valve XYZ failed.

WHY 7   Why did the seal in valve XYZ fail?

Answer: Mechanical maintenance installed the seal following the instructions in a work package that had incorrect installation dimensions.

Figure 4-8. Asking WHY

4.2.2   Exxon-Valdez Oil Spill Example

Problem Statement: Supertanker *Exxon-Valdez* spilled 10.8 million gallons of crude oil into the waters of Prince William Sound.

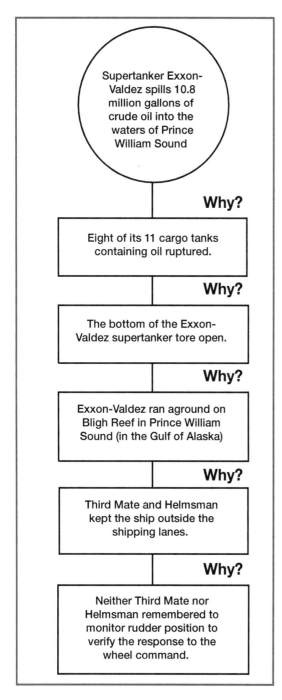

Figure 4-9. Exxon-Valdez

4.2.3   Tokai-Mura Criticality Incident Example

Problem Statement: Two of three workers preparing fuel for an experimental reactor died after receiving high doses of radiation.

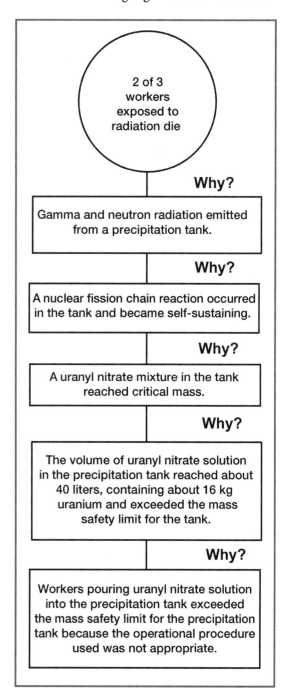

Figure 4-10. Japan Tokai-Mura

4.2.4 Reactor Trip Example

Problem Statement: Port Clay Nuclear Station Unit 2 reactor trip.

"Why did the reactor trip?"

    …because level in steam generator 2B dropped below the actuation set point…

"Why did the level in steam generator 2B drop below the actuation set point?"

    …because feedwater regulating valve 2B went closed…

"Why did feedwater regulating valve 2B close?"

    …because its circuitry received a signal to close…

"Why did the circuitry receive a signal to close?"

    …because a controls technician placed a jumper across its terminals on the circuit board…

"Why did a controls technician place a jumper across its terminals on the circuit board?"

    …because the work instructions told them to…

"Why did the work instructions say to land the jumper?"

    …because the work instructions were incorrect…

"Why were the work instructions incorrect?"

    [Answer 1] …because the work planner listed the wrong terminals …AND

    [Answer 2] …the work crew supervisor did not implement management expectations to verify the work instructions were accurate.

4.3   Cause and Effect Trees

What is it?

A *cause and effect tree* diagram highlights the chain of causes. See Figure 4-11. It starts with the effect and the major groups of causes and then asks for each branch, "Why is this happening? What is causing this?" The tree

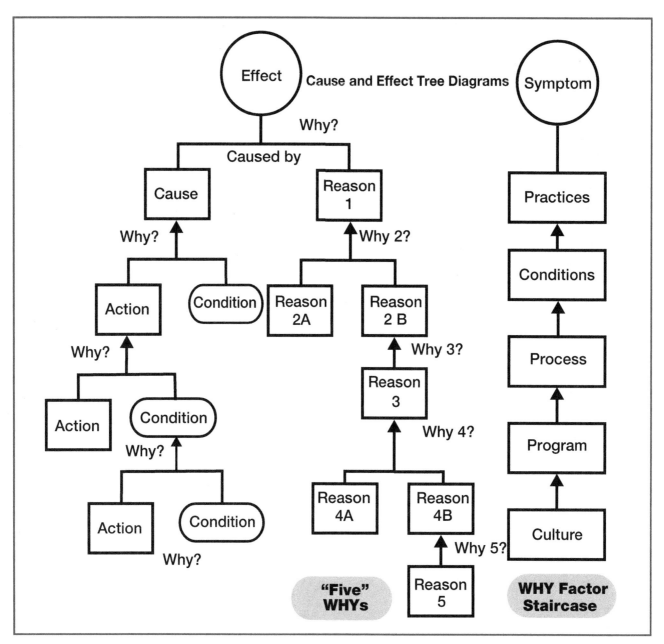

Figure 4-11. Cause and Effect Tree Structures

diagram is a graphic display of a simpler method known as the "Five" WHYs (described in section 4.2). It displays the layers of causes, looking for the *deeper* cause. This tool can be used alone or with other incident systems analysis techniques.

Remember, cause and effect diagrams begin as hypotheses (i.e., educated guesses) about causes, not facts. Failure to test these hypotheses — treating them as if they were facts — often leads to implementing the wrong solutions and wasting time. To determine the actual cause(s), collect data to test these hypotheses.

Why is it done?
A cause and effect tree diagram provides a structure for analyzing data and information and, subsequently, identifying gaps and deficiencies in the knowledge of the investigator.

When is it used?

The quest for explanations and the reasons that drove or allowed the incident or accident begins in Step 1 (Scope the Problem) and continues into Step 5 (Validate Underlying Factors).

How is it done?

Although there are several ways to construct a cause and effect diagram, the steps of construction are essentially the same. AGREE on the problem or the desired state and write it in the effect box. Try to be specific. Problems that are too large or too vague can bog down the investigation. Describe the effect in very specific terms defining the object and the defect. See Figure 4-12.

Figure 4-12. Reason
for the Investigation

1. COLLECT data to support the evaluation. Analyze any readily available data to support your evaluation.

2. DEFINE from two to eight major "branches" of causes or steps. Or brainstorm first about likely causes and then sort them into major branches. Add or drop categories as needed when generating causes. Each branch (or step) should be written into the box. See Figure 4-13.

3. ASK WHY the problem happened or WHY the object has the defect. See Figure 4-14.

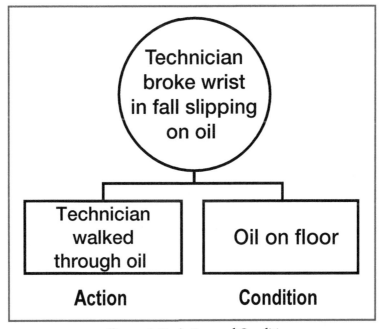

Figure 4-13. Action and Condition

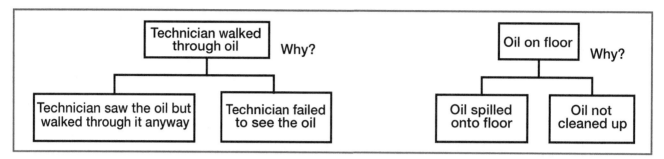

Figure 4-14. Asking Why

4. IDENTIFY specific causes and fill them in on the correct branches or sub-branches. Use simple brainstorming to generate a list of ideas before classifying them on the diagram, or use the development of the branches of the diagram first to help stimulate ideas. Either way will achieve the same end; use the method that feels most comfortable. If an idea fits on more than one branch, place it on both. Be sure that the causes as phrased have a direct, logical relationship to the stated problem or effect. Each major branch (category or step) should include three or four possible causes. If a branch has fewer, lead the group in finding some way to explain this lack, or ask others who have some knowledge in that area to help. See Figure 4-15.

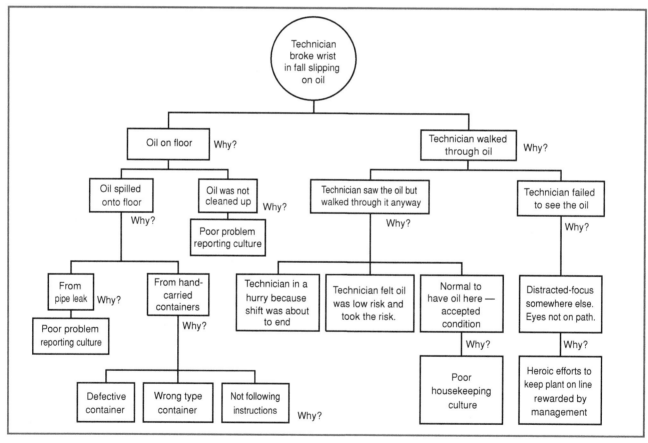

Figure 4-15. Cause and Effect Tree

5. From your answer to the previous question, KEEP ASKING "why" and "why else" for each cause until a potential cause has been identified. A cause is one that: (a) can explain the "effect," either directly or through a series of events, and (b) if removed, would eliminate or reduce the problem. Try to ensure that the answers to the "why" questions are plausible explanations and that, if possible, they are correctable.

6. CONTINUE ASKING "why" until you have identified the most likely cause(s) of the original defect. Asking "why" simply involves repeatedly asking "why" until the answer is "because that's the way it is." At this point, it is likely that you have identified a probable cause of the problem. If tackled and removed, the observed symptoms of the problem should also disappear. Keep asking "why" and "why else" for each case until a likely cause has been identified.

7. TEST each likely cause against the problem description. Any cause identified as the most likely cause must fit all the facts in the investigation. Many possible causes will be discarded during this phase because they cannot explain all the data.

Check the logic of the chain of causes; read the diagram from the most probable cause to the effect to see if the flow is logical. Each possible cause should be tested against the problem description. Any cause identified as the most probable cause must fit all the facts in the investigation. Many possible causes will be discarded during this phase because they cannot explain all the data. Make needed changes.

4.3.1   Cause and Effect Tree Examples

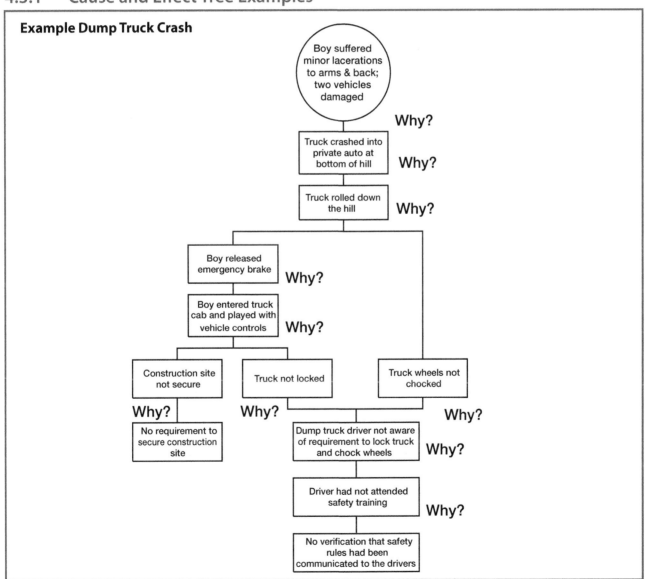

Figure 4-16. Dump Truck Crash

Example Eye Injury

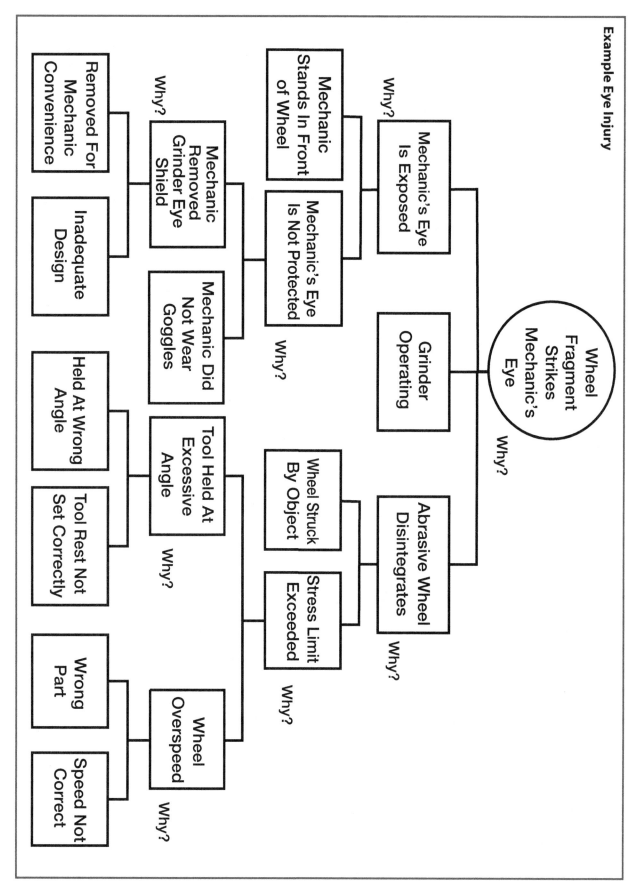

Figure 4-17. Eye Injury

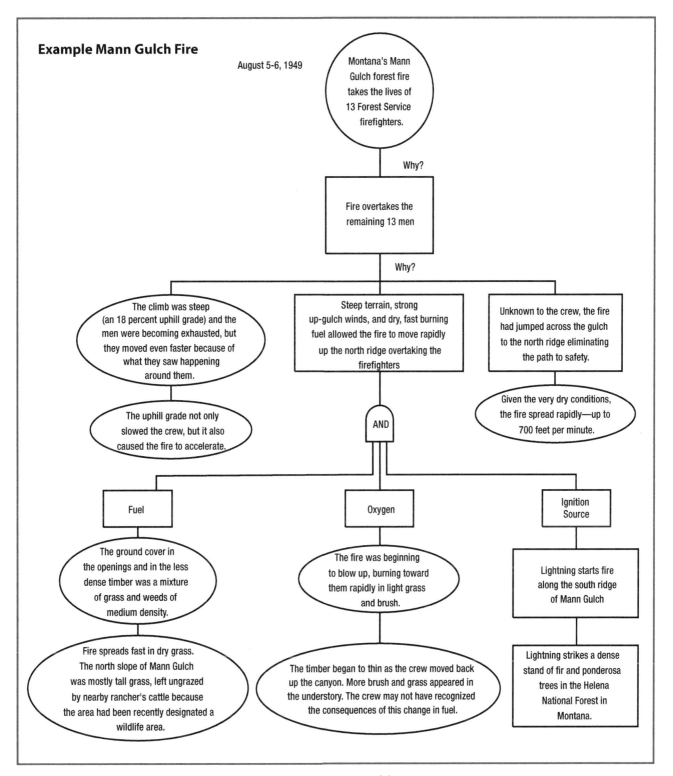

Figure 4-18. Mann Gulch Fire

4.4 Difference Analysis (a.k.a. Change Analysis)

What is it?

Difference analysis focuses on those elements that were different or changed during the incident as compared to a previous, trouble-free activity. It is sometimes called *change analysis* (Department of Energy, 2012).

Why is it done?

Difference analysis is a good starting point for an investigation. It is not only quick and easy, but it is also a great way to focus a room full of anxious team members. Difference analysis generates good questions for interviewing.

When is it used?

Use difference analysis when the problem is obscure. So difference analysis could be used as early as Step 1 (Scope the Problem) and at any time during Steps 2 through 5.

How is it done?

1. Beginning with a problem statement, DESCRIBE the nature of the problem in terms of known facts in *object/defect* format. See Figure 4-19 and Table 4-2 columns to guide your analysis.

2. CONSIDER the current problem statement and list factors that influenced performance, equipment, or the process. Record all factors impacting the incident with the undesirable consequences. (Column A)

3. DESCRIBE the way the task was performed, and how equipment or process functioned during the incident. (Column B)

4. IDENTIFY AND DESCRIBE one or more examples of situations where the problem could have existed but did not. Describe the "old" way the task was performed, and how equipment or process functioned when performance was successful. Consider a comparable, reference incident that did not have undesirable consequences. (Column C)

5. COMPARE the incident with undesirable consequences (Column B) to the reference incident (Column C). Compare the two sets of data to determine what differences or distinctions may exist between the two situations.

6. WRITE questions for interviews to help you identify changes. Document any distinctions, differences, or changes (Column D). Establish all known differences whether they appear relevant or not. Regarding the differences that are identified, determine what if any changes may have occurred regarding these differences.

7. ANSWER the question: Is this a contributing factor? (Yes or No.) (Column E)

8. [Later] ANALYZE all the differences for their effects in producing the undesirable result. Attempt to confirm the cause(s) identified through testing or other methods, such as:

   ‣ List of possible causes.

   ‣ Confirmed true cause (based on testing).

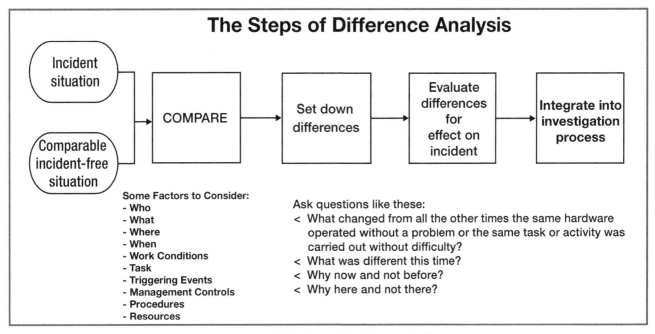

Figure 4-19. The Steps of Difference Analysis

Use the format in Tables 4-2 and 4-3 as a means of organizing and analyzing information using this approach. Questions used to complete the second column (B) should correspond horizontally to the same question asked in the third column (C). Likewise, changes and differences should horizontally correspond to the related information in the second and third columns.

Table 4-2. Difference Analysis Form

Problem Statement: Object/defect or deviation				
A	**B**	**C**	**D**	**E**
Factors that Influence Performance	**Failed Performance**	**Past Successful Performance**	**Differences or Changes**	**Contributing Factor? (Yes/No)**
Conditions/situations that drive or control performance, the equipment, or the process	Problem situation (List of information that results from questions regarding the nature of the problem)	Problem-free situation (List of information that results from the same questions asked in the second column, but for the nonproblem situation)	Distinctions (What is different about the information in the second column compared to the information in the third column? What changed?)	Effects of the change or difference (Triggered, released, allowed, permitted, or aggravated the situation or circumstances)
Factor 1				
Factor 2				
Factor 3				
List of Possible Causes:				
Confirmed True Cause (based on testing):				

Table 4-3. Difference Analysis Form Template

A	B	C	D	E
Factors that Influence Performance	**Failed Performance**	**Past Successful Performance**	**Differences or Changes**	**Contributing Factor? (Yes/No)**
List of Possible Causes:				
Confirmed True Cause (based on testing):				

Instructions for Use of Difference Analysis (a.k.a. Change Analysis) Form

1. CONSIDER the current problem situation and list factors that influenced performance, equipment, or the process. Record all facts concerning the incident with the undesirable consequences.

2. WRITE questions for interviews to help you identify changes.

3. DESCRIBE the "old" way the task was performed, and how equipment or process functioned when performance was successful. Consider a comparable, reference incident that did not have undesirable consequences.

4. DESCRIBE the way the task was performed, and how equipment or process functioned during the incident. Compare the incident with undesirable consequences to the reference incident (Step 3).

5. DOCUMENT any differences or changes. Establish all known differences whether they appear relevant or not.

6. ANSWER the question: Is this a contributing factor? (Yes or No). Analyze all the differences and changes for their effects in producing the undesirable result. Be sure to include the obscure and indirect effects.

4.4.1   Broken Back Example

Table 4-4. Broken Back Difference Analysis Example

Problem Statement: Employee broke back in fall from ladder				
Factors that Influence Performance	**Failed Performance**	**Past Successful Performance**	**Differences or Changes**	**Contributing Factor? (Yes/No)**
WHEN	Job performer came in early to avoid the heat.	Job performer started day the same time as co-workers.	No co-workers were available to help with the job.	Yes. Worker came to work early, so was working alone, carrying tools.
SUPERVISION	Employee did not meet with supervisor the morning of the accident.	Employee met with supervisor to discuss the day's work activities.	Work activities were not discussed.	Yes. Because worker came to work early, job hazards were not discussed.

4.4.2   Falling Objects Example

Table 4-5. Falling Objects Difference Analysis Example

Problem Statement: Refueling Outage Adverse Trend of Falling Objects				
Factors that Influence Performance	**Failed Performance**	**Past Successful Performance**	**Differences or Changes**	**Contributing Factor? (Yes/No)**
WHAT	Tools Scaffold pieces	Small Instruments Small parts	Value Care in Handling	Crews more careless with tools & scaffold pieces (Could this be a cause? Yes)
WHERE	Containment	Turbine Building Aux. Building	Amount of material handling, space	Higher amount of activities, tighter quarters, more people working in containment (Could this be a cause? Yes)
WHEN	Nights (11/14) End of Night Shift Sunday (5) Monday (3)	Days End of Day Shift Tuesday (0) Thursday (1) Friday (1) Saturday (1)	Supervision Circadian Rhythms	Less available supervision on nights (Could this be a cause? Yes) Times of incidents correspond with Circadian patterns for likely error (Could this be a cause? Yes)
WHO	ACME personnel	AJAX personnel	Safety Focus	Reward systems different for safety (different culture) (Could this be a cause? Yes)

4.4.3   Breaker Trip Example

Table 4-6. Breaker Trip Difference Analysis Example

Problem Statement: 11A RCP Breaker is tripping free while attempting to start the pump				
Factors that Influence Performance	**Failed Performance**	**Past Successful Performance**	**Differences or Changes**	**Contributing Factor? (Yes/No)**
WHAT	11A RCP breaker Tripping free	Other RCP breakers, other 13KV breakers Failing to close, failing to trip, fault signals	Different crew installed up-grade on this breaker	Crew had not been trained on new tripping device and relied on procedure for guidance (Could this be a cause? Yes)
WHERE	Installed on the 13KV bus In operating mechanism of breaker	Installed in breaker cubicle in test position, out of cubicle in switchgear room NA	Breaker connected to bus, breaker located deeper in cubicle New operating mechanism	New tripping mechanism location changed (Could this be a cause? Potentially) New design installed two days ago is much more complex (Could this be a cause? Yes)
WHEN	Today at 8:05 a.m. Every attempt to operate breaker First attempt to operate breaker on bus after upgrade	Any time prior Periodic, or sporadic Operating breaker in test position after upgrade	None observed None observed Breaker connected to the bus (See above)	Occurred only since new upgrade installed (Could this be a cause? Yes) Breaker worked in test but not when installed (Could this be a cause? Yes)
EXTENT	11A RCP breaker Tripping mechanism NA Unknown trend	One or more 13KV breakers Other parts of the breaker NA Unknown trend	Upgraded breaker New operating mechanism	Need more information

4.5   Defense Analysis (a.k.a. Barrier Analysis)

What is it?

Defense analysis a systematic process used to identify engineered barriers and administrative, oversight, and cultural controls and other defenses that should have prevented or mitigated an incident. See example in Figure 4-20. It is sometimes called *barrier analysis*.

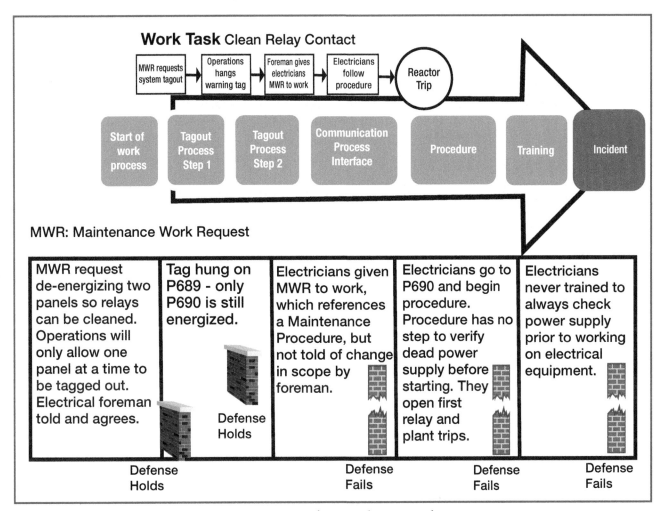

Figure 4-20. Defense Analysis Example

Why is it done?

Defenses are used to serve two purposes: (1) to prevent the release of hazardous energy, and (2) to mitigate harm to people and equipment in the event hazardous energy is actually released. Defense analysis is done to determine if all the defenses pertaining to an incident were present and effective. The defense analysis technique applies the concept that various hazards exist in relationship to a specific target and that pre-designed defenses have failed to prevent the hazard from affecting the target. This technique requires an iterative process to be performed on each defense that has failed in order to identify the underlying cause(s). This method has the advantage of quickly documenting the failure of known defenses but relies heavily on the creativity and knowledge level of the investigator.

When is it used?

It is most effectively used as a technique for supporting portions of the actions and factors charting method during Step 3 (Reconstruct the Story). It is also used during Step 4 (Establish Contributing Factors) and Step 6 (Plan Corrective Actions).

How is it done?

1. Beginning with the problem statement, IDENTIFY the target of concern.

2. IDENTIFY one or more hazards related to the problem, and which directly affected the target of concern.

3. DEVELOP a list of all the defenses (considering the following forms, physical, natural, human, administrative, programmatic, etc.) that should have prevented the hazard from affecting the target of concern.

4. DETERMINE defenses that held or were not used, were missing, or were ineffective. Examples of the questions that may be asked follow this section.

Table 4-7. Defense Analysis* Form

Problem Statement: Object/Defect or Deviation				
Target (Person, Equipment, Process)	**Hazard** (Threat/ Concern)	**Defense** (Physical, or Administrative)	**Assessment**	
			☐ Held?	
			☐ Not used?	
			☐ Missing?	
			☐ Ineffective?	

*also known as Hazard-Barrier-Target analysis

5. Use Table 4-7 or Table 4-8 for organizing the results of each hazard-barrier-target analysis step.

6. For each failed defense, REPEAT the above process by making the failed defense a new target with its own hazards and defenses.

7. For defenses that were not used, were missing, or were ineffective, DETERMINE why.

8. Continue this process and periodically ASSESS each failed barriers until its root causes are identified.

9. INCORPORATE the answers/information collected, from each question, into the investigation for the root cause(s).

10. When all potential causes have been identified, carefully REVIEW each causal factor and enter the potential cause(s) for each inappropriate action under the corresponding item number.

11. If more than one potential cause appears, each cause should be ranked.

12. Each cause may be considered a potential root cause.

13. For each potential root cause, CONSIDER the following three criteria:

    ‣ The problem would not have occurred had the cause(s) not been present.

    ‣ The problem WILL NOT recur due to the same causal factors if the cause(s) are corrected or eliminated.

    ‣ Correction or elimination of the cause(s) WILL prevent recurrence of similar conditions.

14. If a potential root cause satisfies all three criteria, CONSIDER it a valid root cause.

15. With all root causes identified and validated, REFER to the corrective action procedure, as necessary, for development, documentation, implementation, and reporting of the root causes and associated corrective action.

Instructions for Use of Defense Analysis Form Template (Table 4-8)

1. IDENTIFY each target of the hazards/threats (i.e., reactor, safeguards equipment, personnel, valve, etc.).

2. IDENTIFY each hazard/threat (adverse effect/consequence).Typically start with the activity in progress at the time that the human performance difficulty occurred (i.e., reactor scram, safeguards equipment actuation, personnel injury, valve wrongly positioned, etc.).

3. IDENTIFY defenses that should have controlled hazard — failed or allowed the incident to progress.

    ‣ Prevented contact between hazard and target.

    ‣ Mitigated consequences of hazard/target contact.

4. ASSIGN a safety precedence sequence number to each defense.

5. ASSESS how defense failed.

    ‣ Not provided/missing (not in place).

    ‣ Not used/circumvented (but were in place).

    ‣ Ineffective.

6. DETERMINE why defense failed (during Step 5, Validate Underlying Factors).

7. VALIDATE the results of the analysis with the information learned. The integrated method for using defense analysis involves superimposing defenses into the actions and factors chart analysis which was discussed earlier.

8. INTEGRATE this information in actions and factors chart.

9. Finally DETERMINE what corrective action is needed to restore the defense to effectiveness.

> **Note:** While defense analysis identifies missing or defective defenses, it has one weakness. If the investigator does not recognize ALL the failed defenses, the evaluation may be incomplete. Because using defense analysis alone is very time-consuming, it is recommended that defense analysis be used in conjunction with other techniques.

Table 4-8. Defense Analysis Form Template

Target	Hazard/ Threat	Defense		Failed?		HOW Defense Failed			WHY Defense Failed	Corrective Action to Restore Defense to Effectiveness
			SPS #*	No	Yes	Missing	Not Used	Ineffective		
			☐							
			☐							
			☐							
			☐							
			☐							

*SPS # refers to the S**afety Precedence Sequence Number** which is a tool that can be used to manage risk.

1. Extreme risk: Design for minimum hazard. Include fail-safe features and redundancy.
2. High risk: Control hazards to an acceptable risk level with safety devices.
3. Important: Provide devices that warn targets of hazards.
4. Moderate: Develop procedures to reduce and control hazards.
5. Uneconomic: Select, train, supervise, and motivate personnel to work safely in presence of hazard.
6. Negligible: Identify residual hazards and accept the risks at the proper management level.

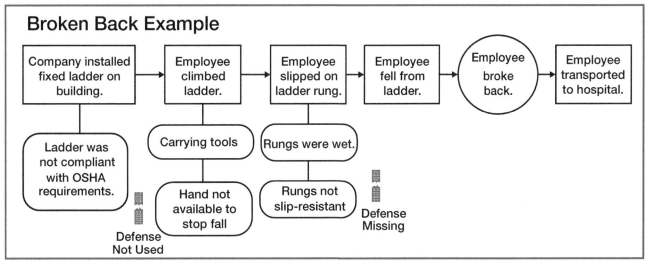

Figure 4-21. Actions and Factors with Flawed Defenses

Using the information from the example displayed on the actions and factor chart in Figure 4-21, the defense analysis form (Table 4-9) was completed.

Table 4-9. Broken Back Defense Analysis

Target	Hazard/ Threat	Defense		Failed?		HOW Defense Failed			WHY Defense Failed	Corrective Action to Restore Defense to Effectiveness
			SPS #*	No	Yes	Missing	Not Used	Ineffective		
Employee	Slip on rungs	Slip-resistant rungs (provide traction)	2		Yes	X			Did not exist; so did not provide traction	
Employee	Falling from heights	Proper climbing technique	5		Yes		X		Carrying tools; so second hand not available to stop fall	

*SPS # refers to the **Safety Precedence Sequence Number** (Department of Defense, 2000), which is a tool that can be used to manage risk.

1. Extreme risk: Design for minimum hazard. Include fail-safe features and redundancy.
2. High risk: Control hazards to an acceptable risk level with safety devices.
3. Important: Provide devices that warn targets of hazards.
4. Moderate: Develop procedures to reduce and control hazards.
5. Uneconomic: Select, train, supervise, and motivate personnel to work safely in presence of hazard.
6. Negligible: Identify residual hazards, and accept the risks at the proper management level.

4.5.1   Breaker Fire Example

Incident: On October 31, 2012, a fire occurred at Port Clay Plant in the breaker cubicle of the 480 volt class 1E load center 2W1E.

Table 4-10. Breaker Fire Defense Analysis

Target Protected	Hazard/Threat	Defenses	SPS #	Failed? No	Failed? Yes	HOW Missing	HOW Not Used	HOW Ineffective	Why Defense Failed
West Switchgear Breaker Cubicle 2W1F	High resistance connection	Human-Machine Interface	3		Y			Y	The bus side of the switchgear is extremely difficult to access. Design did not consider difficulty of access to perform periodic inspections.
West Switchgear Breaker Cubicle 2W1F	High resistance connection	Design	1		Y			Y	The design change specifications did not consider the partial plating of the WS EJ-5 switchgear stabs, resulting in the replacement breaker cradles engaging the bus stabs at the edge of and beyond the silver-plated contact area. The inadequate design assessment has been determined to be causal.
West Switchgear Breaker Cubicle 2W1F	High resistance connection	Post-Maintenance Test	4		Y		Y		Failure to confirm as left resistance from the line to load side of the switchgear following the modification has been determined to be a contributing cause to the incident.
West Switchgear Breaker Cubicle 2W1F	High resistance connection	Individual Tool: Procedure Use and Adherence	4		Y			Y	A low resistance seating area was not established by cleaning. EA-PM-FY-1100, Inspection and Maintenance of Model EJT-5 Low Voltage Switchgear, does not contain sufficient instructions to remove load center bus side inspection covers. Electrical maintenance has interpreted this to mean the requirement does not exist, just perform what can easily be accessed.
West Switchgear Breaker Cubicle 2W1F	High resistance connection	Training	5		Y			Y	Engineering staff relied on breaker vendor because plant staff had limited knowledge of what was physically in the plant at the point in time the Mod 12347 modification was taking place.

4.6   Structure Tree Diagrams

If you can't describe what you are doing as a process, you don't know what you're doing.

— W. Edwards Deming, Engineer and Management Consultant

What is it?

A tree diagram/structure diagram breaks down a broad area into increasing levels of granularity. The tree graphically represents the separation of broad, general information into increasingly detailed information. The *structure tree diagram* is used to graphically depict the forces and factors needed to produce successful results in the performance of a task or operation. So a structure tree is a success model and is any flowchart, diagram, drawing, or picture showing the expected flow or methodology related to how a job performer, leader, or organization is expected to do well at a given task. Figure 4-22 depicts two very simple success models.

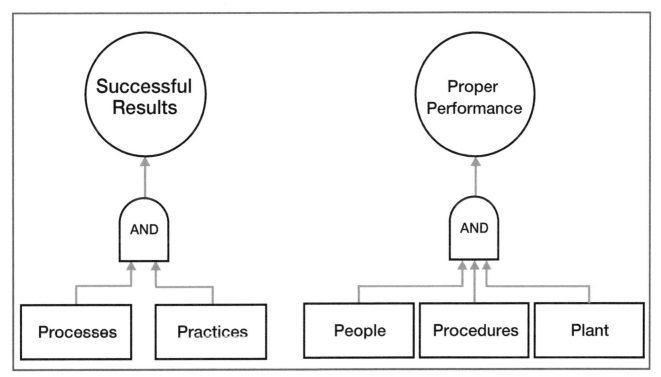

Figure 4-22. Structure Tree Success Path

Conversely, when an incident or failure occurs, the structure tree diagram can be used in the reverse direction to detect the place(s) along the path that broke down and resulted in the adverse consequences. See Figure 4-23. During investigations, the structure tree helps depict both the success path (usually AND logic) and the failure path (usually OR logic) for a given result. The goal is to look back through the work activity and find the ways the job performer or the equipment may have been set up to fail.

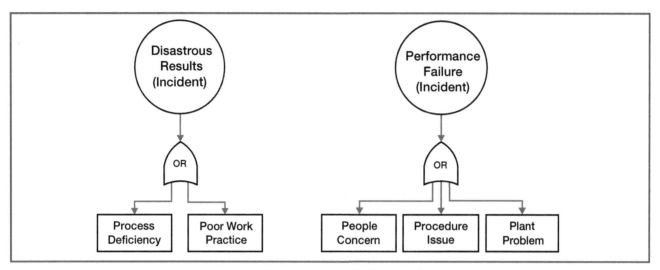

Figure 4-23. Structure Tree Failure Analysis

Why is it used?

A structure tree diagram helps the investigator understand how the organization planned to succeed before the incident happened. Since a structure tree is divided into ordered groups or categories (i.e., it is a taxonomy), the diagram provides a way of analyzing cause-and-effect relationships for a given subject.

When is it used?

The quest for explanations and the reasons that drove or allowed the incident or accident begins in Step 1 (Scope the Problem) and continues into Step 5 (Validate Underlying Factors). After the problem related to the incident has been carefully described, choose or construct a structure tree diagram pertinent to the process, system, or organization. Then systematically analyze the cause-and-effect relationship within that structure to identify the possible root cause(s) of the incident or accident. A structure tree will also be good to use during Step 6 (Plan Corrective Actions).

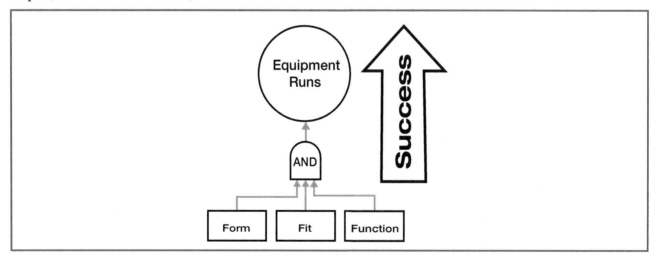

Figure 4-24. Equipment Success Tree

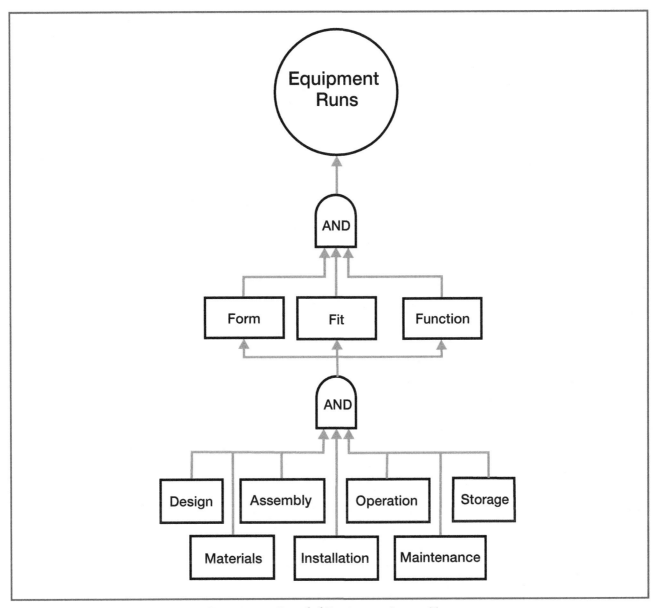

Figure 4-25. Detailed Equipment Success Tree

How is it done?

1. DOCUMENT the task the way it should be performed to be successful. See Figures 4-24 and 4-25.

2. GROW the tree into branches that the group members consider likely to contain the underlying factors. See Figure 4-26.

The following tools are specialized types of structure trees/diagrams:

- ▸ Fishbone Diagram (Section 4.6.1)
- ▸ Defense-in-Depth Analysis (Section 4.6.2)
- ▸ MORT Analysis (Section 4.6.3)
- ▸ Production/Protection Strategy Analysis (Section 4.6.4)
- ▸ Safety Culture Analysis (Section 4.6.5)

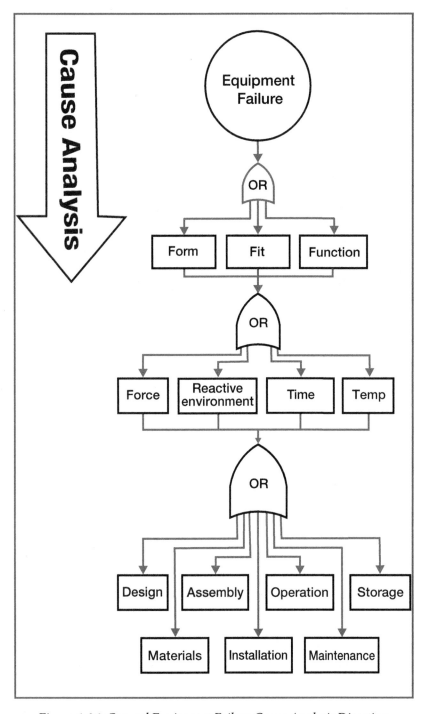

Each of these concepts will be covered as a subset of the structure tree section because, in reality, each tool is a somewhat "pre-packaged" structure tree or diagram. There are advantages and disadvantages to having a tree or taxonomy laid out in advance. The biggest caution is avoiding the belief that the tree has ALL the possible causal factor categories or, for that matter, ALL the possible causal factors. The investigator may have to develop "branches" of the "tree" by research or by getting help from a subject matter expert. The biggest advantage is that the trees can act as checklists to remind investigators and teams to check into some areas that they may not have thought of during a pure "brain" storming session.

Figure 4-26. General Equipment Failure Cause Analysis Direction

Lawn Chair Breaks Example

Build a success tree first (Figure 4-27); then reverse the process to determine the causal area (Figure 4-28).

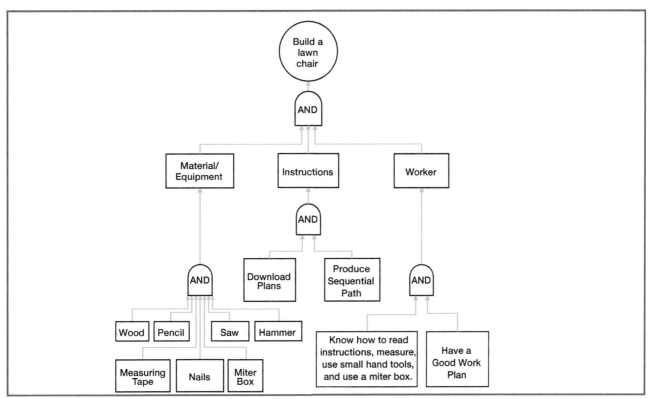

Figure 4-27. Lawn Chair Building: Success Tree

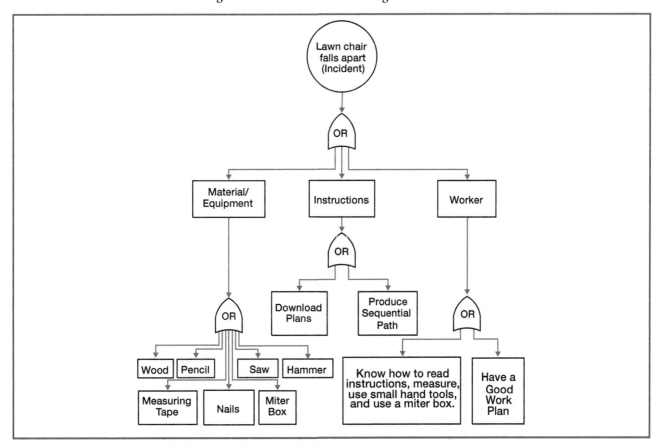

Figure 4-28. Lawn Chair Breaks: Failure Analysis

4.6.1   Fishbone (Ishikawa) Diagram

What is it?

The *fishbone diagram* is a simple defense analysis tool that helps generate a graphical overview of possible causes of an incident into generalized categories. Figure 4-29 shows that a fishbone diagram is a specialized form of a structure tree.

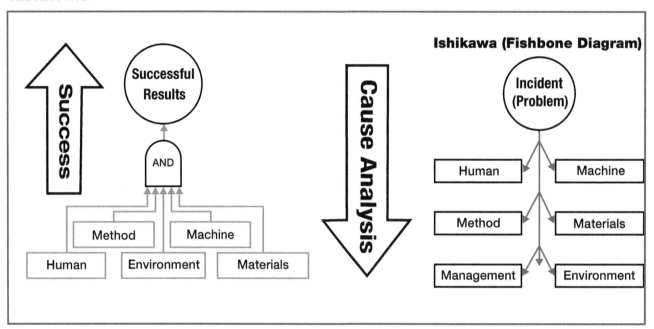

Figure 4-29. Structure Tree Compared to Fishbone Diagram

Why is it useful?

A fishbone diagram is used for recording the possible causes of failures or performance difficulties. It can be helpful to trigger ideas and to display the relationships of many causes with a single effect (or incident).

When is it used?

After the problem statement has been written, construct a fishbone diagram to systematically analyze the cause-and-effect relationship and identify the possible root cause(s) of the problem.

How is it done?

1. WRITE the problem statement in a circle. Be sure everyone agrees on the problem before beginning.

2. DEFINE the major categories of possible causes or use generic branches (Human, Method, Materials, Machine, and Environment).

3. BRAINSTORM possible causes or reasons for the incident and list them under the appropriate category.

4. KEEP ASKING "Why does this condition exist?" or "What causes this?" and branch off of brainstormed ideas.

5. CREATE a separate diagram for causes with many sub-causes or branches (i.e., consider splitting up overcrowded branches or "bones").

6. CONSIDER grafting relatively empty branches ("bones") onto other branches.

7. CLARIFY that each sub-cause relates to the effect (the incident) by going in reverse from cause to effect (the problem statement in the circle).

8. NARROW the list of possible causal factors by using data already collected to eliminate causes that clearly do not apply.

4.6.1.1 Forearm Fracture Example

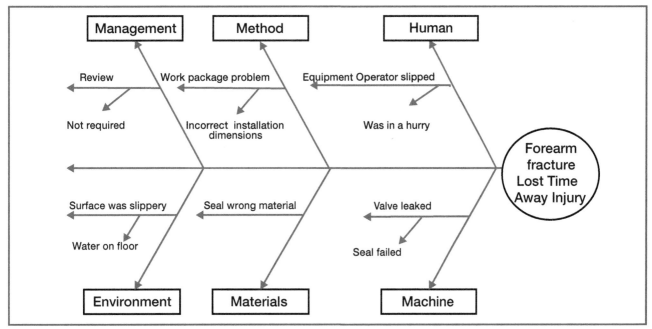

Figure 4-30. Fishbone Diagram Example: Forearm Fracture

4.6.1.2 Poor Safety Culture Example

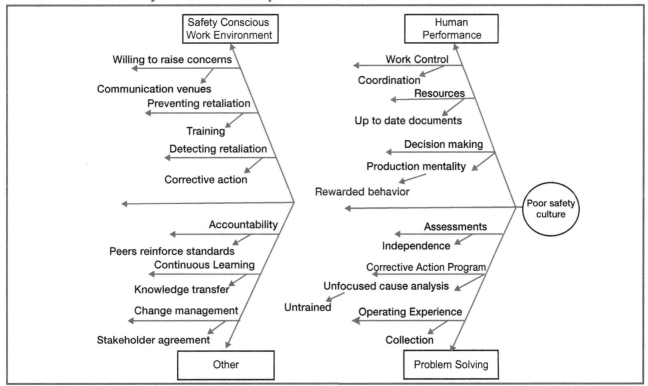

Figure 4-31. Fishbone Diagram Example: Poor Safety Culture

4.6.2   Defense-in-Depth Analysis

What is it?

Defense-in-depth is the overlapping capacity of various barriers and controls to protect personnel and equipment from human error while accomplishing the mission of the business (Figure 4-32). *Defense-in-depth analysis* looks at the defenses that the organization thought were in place or should have been in place to prevent a business incident. According to Tosti (2007), results and behaviors must be aligned to drive organizational performance. Said another way, what a business produces must have cultural values and practices driving how work is accomplished.

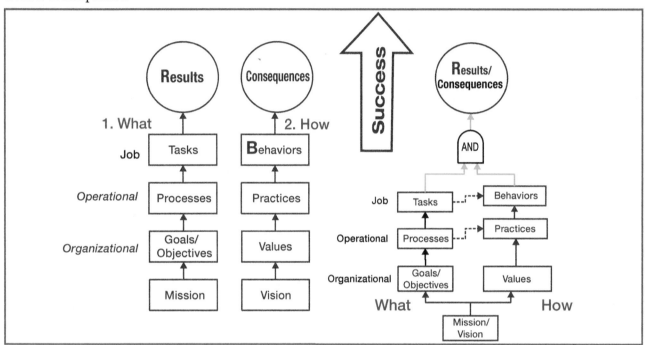

Figure 4-32. Success Drivers

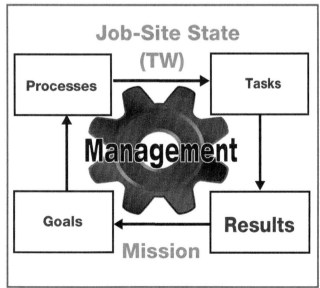

Figure 4-33. Strategic Alignment

Figure 4-34. Cultural Alignment

The "WHAT" side is used to achieve strategic alignment for accomplishing the mission of the business (Figure 4-33); the "HOW" side shows the cultural alignment and reflects the vision, beliefs, and values of the organization (Figure 4-34).

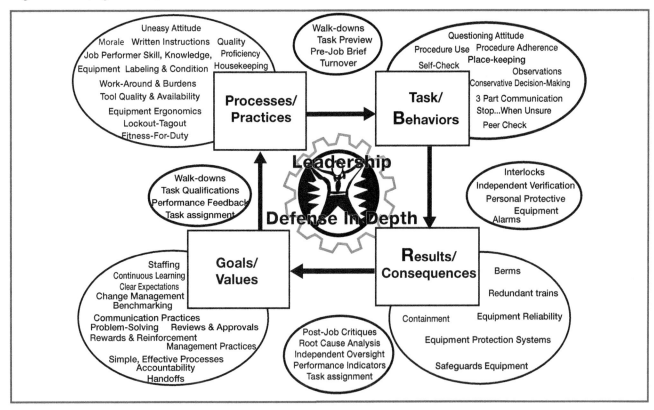

Figure 4-35. Strategic Defense-in-Depth

The model in Figure 4-35 shows the integration of the general steps [boxes] of strategic alignment and cultural alignment. The tools and techniques in the balloons [ovals] show defenses, barriers, and controls that help prevent incidents while accomplishing production goals. According to the Department of Energy (2012), it is important to take a systems view of operating performance.

Why is it useful?
If a failure occurs with one defense, another would compensate for that failure, thereby preventing harm. The four lines of control — engineered, administrative, oversight, and cultural controls (or defenses) — should work together to anticipate, prevent, or catch active errors before suffering a significant incident. If they did not, you need to find out why. It is especially useful in common factor analysis.

When is it used?
Defense-in-depth analysis is done in Step 4 (Establish Contributing Factors) to determine flawed defenses that need to be taken through root cause analysis. It is also used during Step 6 (Plan Corrective Actions).

How is it done?
Controls include various devices, methods, or practices that make an activity or process go safely, effectively, efficiently, predictably, and according to high standards to protect key assets from human error — usually taking an engineered, administrative, cultural, or oversight form.

Figure 4-36. Barrier

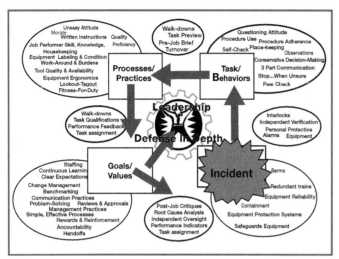

Figure 4-37.
Defense-In-Depth Cause Analysis Flowpath

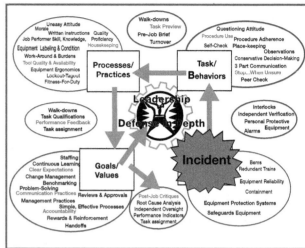

Figure 4-38.
Example Incident Defense-in-Depth Analysis

Note: Example shows (in red) flawed, missing, or unused defense.

Use the model in Figure 4-37 (with example defenses) to backtrack through the performance process to identify weak defenses or broken barriers (Figures 4-37 and 4-38). Integrate the results of the defense analysis into the actions and factors chart using the broken brick wall symbol (Figure 4-36).

4.6.3   MORT Analysis

What is it?

Management oversight and risk tree (MORT) analysis is a form of fault tree analysis. MORT was developed by William Johnson under the auspices of the US Atomic Energy Commission. MORT is a type of defense analysis in a tree structure used to systematically deduce the causes and contributing factors of significant incidents. The MORT chart is the key diagram for the whole MORT system safety program. This chart sets down, in an orderly way, many potential causal factors for accidents. Analysis is carried out by means of a fault tree. See Figure 4-39. A typical MORT investigation will use other root cause analysis tools such as difference analysis (a.k.a. change analysis), defense analysis, and actions and factors charting (Department of Energy, 1992).

Why is it useful?

The MORT chart helps identify the underlying management and oversight root causes of incidents. The MORT chart visually shows the elements present and serves to call the investigator's attention to any missing elements. The chart can also be used to predict the adequacy of control elements already in place to prevent future incidents.

When is it used?

The MORT analysis effort begins immediately after the incident occurs. A MORT tree is a "cause tree" generally completed in Step 4 (Establish Contributing Factors) to determine flawed defenses that need to be taken through root cause analysis. The MORT tree is also used during Step 6 (Plan Corrective Actions).

How is it done?

1. OBTAIN a copy of the MORT diagram.

2. STATE the final consequences of the adverse incident at the top of the tree (TOP incident).

3. CONSTRUCT the fault tree using the technique of deductive reasoning (e.g., reasoning from the general to the specific) to progressively isolate the contributing factors to the incident being considered.

> **Note:** When the MORT tree is used as a kind of a "master checklist" to analyze a specific incident or evaluate an existing system, the investigator will usually see immediately that certain sections of the tree are or are not applicable to the particular situation being analyzed. Even in the branches that are used, some details at the lower levels may not apply.
>
> Conversely, the user may find it helpful to further develop some branches of the more complex concepts of the diagram. This may help isolate and evaluate an important aspect of the situation being analyzed.
>
> Each element in an analytic tree need not be any more complex than the subject being analyzed. The complete diagram should be recognized as a tool to assist in performing a task rather than a burden or additional work load.

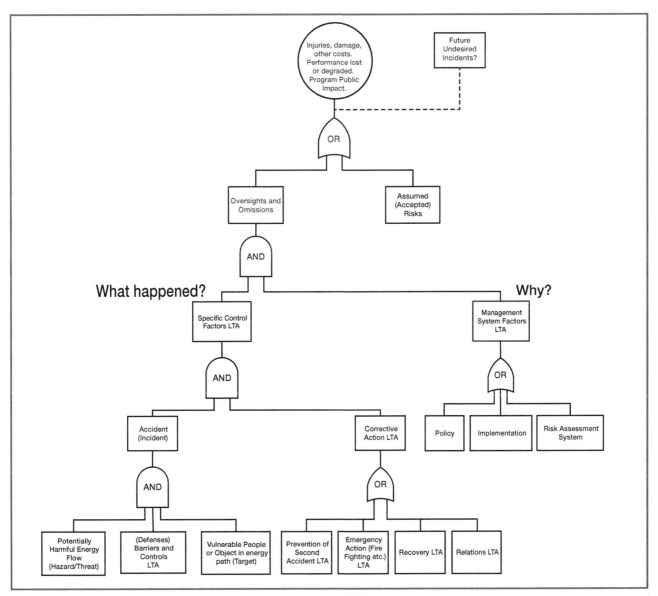

Figure 4-39. MORT Areas

▸ IDENTIFY the elements on the "what" side of the tree that describe what happened in the occurrence (what barrier or control problems existed). [See Figure 4-39.]

▸ For each barrier or control problem, IDENTIFY the management elements on the "why" side of the tree that permitted the barrier control problem. [See Figure 4-40.]

▸ COLOR *red* any factor found to be less than adequate (LTA) on the chart.

▸ COLOR *green* any factor found to be adequate on the chart.

▸ COLOR *blue* any factor that has insufficient evidence to reach a conclusion.

4.   CONTINUE constructing the tree until a system component is identified for which a failure is considered primary or basic (i.e., no further breakdown of contributing factors to the failure is necessary).

5.   DESCRIBE each of the identified inadequate elements (problems).

6.   SUMMARIZE your findings.

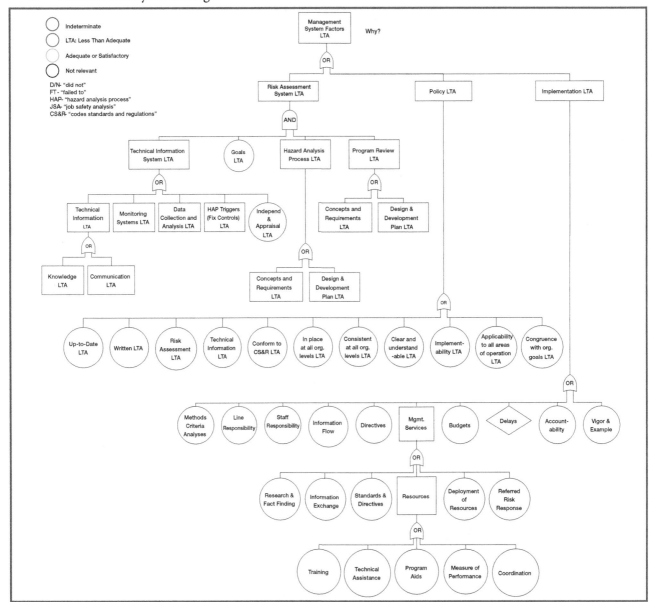

Figure 4-40. MORT Chart

MORT uses similar symbols and logic to that used in fault tree analysis (FTA). However, MORT represents a fault tree that has already been constructed. Therefore, the investigator is not required to build the tree. The investigator works through the existing model and discards those branches which are not relevant to the incident being investigated. See Figure 4-40. MORT looks at not only *what happened* during an incident, but also traces causal factors back to management systems to identify *why incidents happened*. Generic problems are represented by text in rectangular boxes, while circles are used to identify basic causes (Livingston, Jackson & Priestly, 2001). The Nuclear Regulatory Commission (2011, p. 5) defines root cause(s) as "the basic reason(s) (i.e., hardware, process, human performance), for a problem, which if corrected, will prevent recurrence of that problem."

4.6.3.1 MORT Maintenance Example

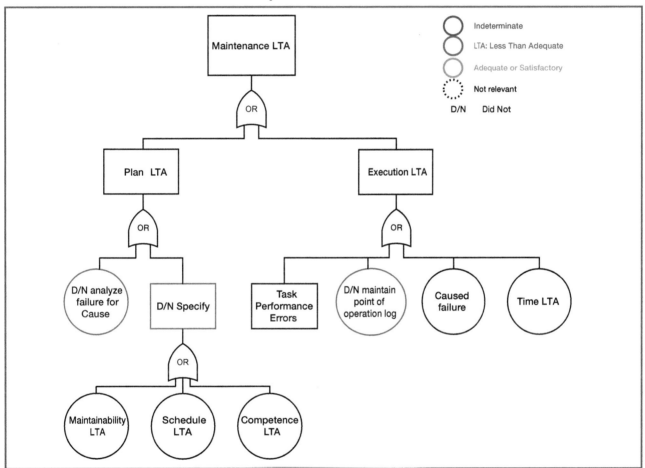

Figure 4-41. MORT Maintenance Example

4.6.4   Production/Protection Strategy Analysis

What is it?

Muschara (2007) indicates a *production/protection strategy analysis* is needed to evaluate an organization's rigorous use of error-prevention tools (R_e) and its ability to aggressively control the four lines of control — engineered, administrative, oversight, and cultural controls (M_d). See Figure 4-42. These tools and controls should have worked together to anticipate, prevent, or catch latent weaknesses and active errors before the business experienced a significant incident. The tools and controls should have kept the business in safe, legal, and effective production while protecting the equipment and the safety of the workers, the public, and the environment.

Why is it useful?

The taxonomy of the structure trees and corresponding checklists used in production/protection strategy analysis are based on logical success models. This allows investigators to systematically evaluate the strategy and tactics the organization considered to be in place to accomplish the business mission before the incident happened. Because the analysis uses a series of structure trees divided into ordered groups or categories (i.e., it is a taxonomy), the diagrams provide a way of analyzing cause-and-effect relationships for a given incident. The structure trees help identify the underlying programmatic and organizational root causes of incidents. The structure trees visually show the elements present and serve to call the investigator's attention to any missing elements.

When is it used?

This technique is used for significant incidents and can be used for common factor analysis. The production/protection strategy analysis begins in Step 1 (Scope the Problem) and continues through Step 6 (Plan Corrective Actions). Muschara (2010) recommends that work practices must be examined during each of three general phases of a job: preparation, performance, and feedback. Figure 4-43 is a general structure tree showing the inputs needed for a worker to execute a job error-free. Figure 4-47 (shown later in this section) is a general structure tree showing the defenses an organization needs to have in place to either prevent a human's error or to handle the consequences of an error without having an incident.

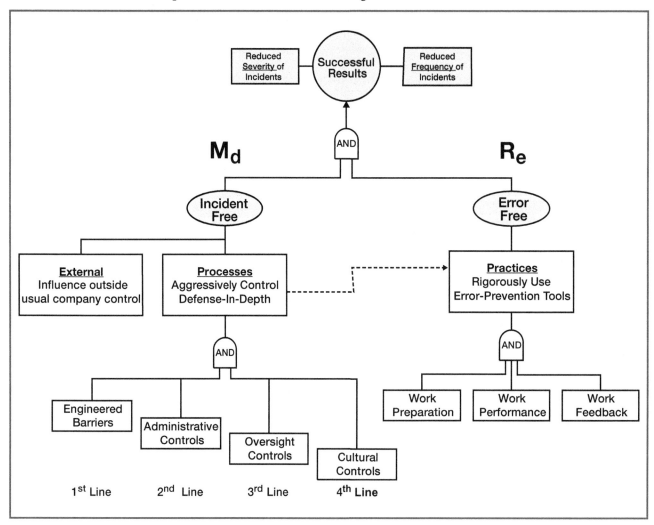

Figure 4-42. Production/Protection Strategy

How is it done?

1. EVALUATE each item of the trees and checklists described here against the information and evidence available.

2. USE the trees and checklists to determine if more information and evidence needs to be gathered.

Work Preparation

In preparing for a task, a worker needs to walk down the job and eliminate distractions. A well-prepared job performer knows the potential hazards and threats, critical steps, important parameters, and error-likely situations and their potential consequences before starting the work activity. This knowledge helps the job performer more readily notice situations that are not normal (Figure 4-44).

Work Performance (Work Execution)

Workers need to execute tasks with a sense of uneasiness — an attitude of wariness regarding the capacity to err when performing specific human actions. Evaluate not only the physical and motor capabilities of the job performer, but also decision-making and communication habits. Ask the worker about the frequency and quality of supervisor in-field observations of the work activity (Figure 4-45).

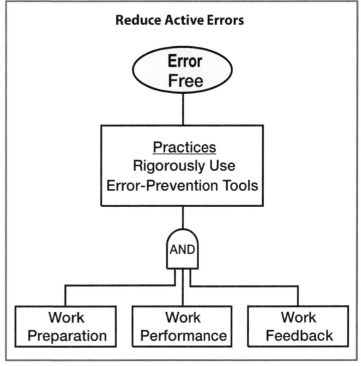

Figure 4-43. Worker Reduction of Active Errors

Work Feedback

Errors that trigger significant incidents are organizational failures. Therefore, feedback on work preparation and performance is very important information for management. Procedure and equipment problems and minor human performance difficulties require management's attention. Such factors tend to be latent in nature and accumulate within the system if uncorrected. If job performers do not communicate the information, key decision-makers miss an opportunity to improve (Figure 4-46).

You will be reversing the success path diagrammed in Figures 4-43 through 4-46 in order to find the underlying causes of the incident. Table 4-11 will help you to systematically go through each phase of the job and determine a worker's contribution to the incident.

In evaluating work practices, evaluate the tools and methods a job performer routinely uses to ensure the safe and successful execution of a task. Consider the worker's practices for

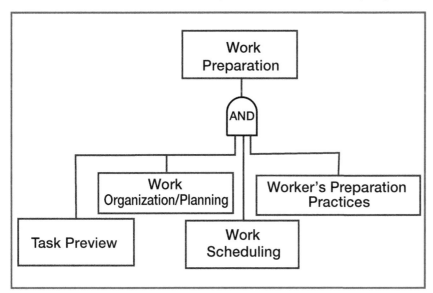

Figure 4-44. Work Preparation Drivers

work preparation, error detection, equipment/material use, and document use. Evaluate whether individuals are receptive to feedback and continuously strive to improve their knowledge, skills, and performance. Workers should coach and provide feedback to others, especially during post-job reviews.

Manage Defenses

The organization can improve incident-free operation by installing a variety of overlapping defenses (barriers, controls, and safeguards) and by aggressively monitoring their effectiveness. Management needs to be aggressive because equipment, procedures, the organization and its culture, and even its oversight processes all contain hidden flaws or latent conditions which can accumulate without anyone's knowledge. Human errors occur commonly during work performance and could combine with latent conditions in unforeseen ways resulting in harm to a person, property, or the environment — an incident. By aggressively managing defenses, the resilience of the business against residual errors is improved. Figure 4-48 depicts how defense-in-depth might be sequenced. Front-line workers are fallible and errors still occur despite the best efforts of the organization to avoid

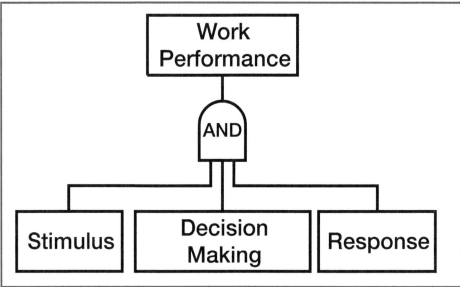

Figure 4-45. Work Execution Drivers

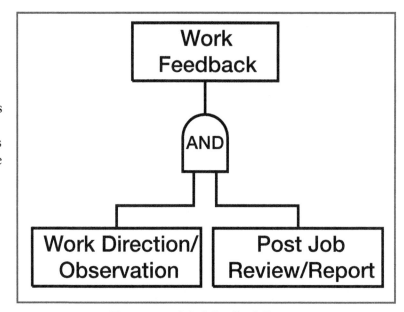

Figure 4-46. Work Feedback Drivers

them. Managing defenses seeks to quickly detect a latent adverse condition and resolve the situation as soon as practicable. Use Table 4-12 to guide you through the evaluation of organizational defenses.

Table 4-11. Reduce Active Errors: Reduce Frequency of Incidents (Error Free)

Components Within Strategy	Any Concerns About Strategy?		Corrective Action Needed
Work Preparation	☐ **Yes**	☐ **No**	
1. Task Preview	☐ Yes	☐ No	
2. Work Organization/Planning	☐ Yes	☐ No	
3. Work Scheduling	☐ Yes	☐ No	
4. Worker's Preparation Practices	☐ Yes	☐ No	

Work Performance (Work Execution)	☐ **Yes**	☐ **No**	
1. Error Detection Practices (Use of error prevention tools)	☐ Yes	☐ No	
2. Document Use Practices	☐ Yes	☐ No	
3. Equipment/Material Use Practices	☐ Yes	☐ No	

Work Feedback	☐ **Yes**	☐ **No**	
1. Work Direction/Observations	☐ Yes	☐ No	
2. Post-Job Review and Reporting	☐ Yes	☐ No	

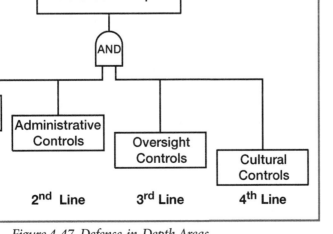

Training   Job Aid   Peer Check

Figure 4-48. Defense-in-Depth

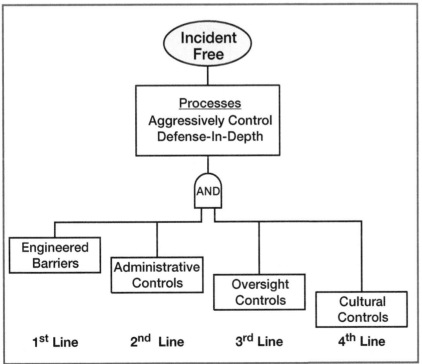

Figure 4-47. Defense-in-Depth Areas

Table 4-12. Managing Defenses: Reduce Severity of Incidents (Incident Free)

Components Within Strategy	Any Concerns About Strategy?		Corrective Action Needed
Engineered Barriers	☐ **Yes**	☐ **No**	
1. Human Factors/Human-Machine Interface	☐ Yes	☐ No	
2. Design	☐ Yes	☐ No	
3. Configuration Control	☐ Yes	☐ No	
4. Equipment Performance Programs	☐ Yes	☐ No	

Components Within Strategy	Any Concerns About Strategy?		Corrective Action Needed
Administrative Controls	☐ **Yes**	☐ **No**	
1. Procedures/Written Instructions	☐ Yes	☐ No	
2. Training/Qualification	☐ Yes	☐ No	
3. Resource Management	☐ Yes	☐ No	
4. Change Management	☐ Yes	☐ No	
5. Correction Action Program	☐ Yes	☐ No	

Components Within Strategy	Any Concerns About Strategy?		Corrective Action Needed
Oversight Controls	☐ **Yes**	☐ **No**	
1. Work Supervision/Coaching	☐ Yes	☐ No	
2. Accountability	☐ Yes	☐ No	
3. Independent Assessment	☐ Yes	☐ No	
4. Management Control Elements	☐ Yes	☐ No	
5. Performance Monitoring (Indicators/Trending)	☐ Yes	☐ No	

Components Within Strategy	Any Concerns About Strategy?		Corrective Action Needed
Cultural Controls	☐ **Yes**	☐ **No**	
1. Communication/Interfaces	☐ Yes	☐ No	
2. Individual Excellent Behaviors	☐ Yes	☐ No	
3. Leader Excellent Behaviors	☐ Yes	☐ No	
4. Organizational Process and Values	☐ Yes	☐ No	
5. Safety Culture	☐ Yes	☐ No	

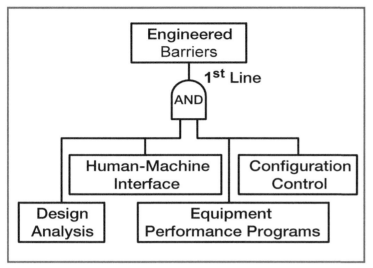

Figure 4-49. Engineered Causal Factors

Engineered Barriers

Engineered barriers provide the business with the physical ability to protect itself from the errors of humans. Engineering controls are used to remove a hazard or place a barrier between the worker or the equipment and the hazard. Well-designed engineering controls can be highly effective in protecting workers and equipment and will typically be independent of worker interactions to provide this high level of protection. The initial cost of engineering controls can be higher than the cost of administrative controls or personal protective equipment, but over the longer term, operating costs are frequently lower, and in some instances, can provide a cost savings in other areas of the process (Figure 4-49).

Administrative Defenses

Administrative defenses and personal protective equipment are frequently used with existing processes where hazards are not particularly well controlled. Administrative controls and personal protective equipment programs may be relatively inexpensive to establish but, over the long term, can be very costly to sustain. These methods for protecting workers have also proven to be less effective than other measures, requiring significant effort by the affected workers (Figure 4-50).

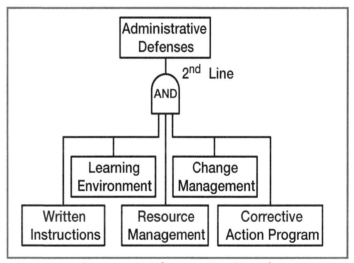

Figure 4-50. Administrative Controls

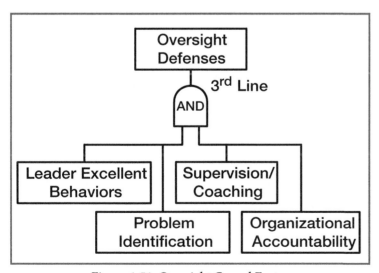

Figure 4-51. Oversight Causal Factors

Oversight Defenses

Management defines the line of authority and responsibility for work activities. Supervisory and management oversight of work activities, including contractors, helps verify margins, the integrity of defenses and processes, as well as the quality of work execution. Accountability is maintained for important safety decisions in that the system of rewards and sanctions is aligned with safety policies and reinforces behaviors and outcomes which reflect safety as an overriding priority. Both management and the workforce reinforce safety principles. Problems are promptly identified and fully evaluated. Corrective actions are taken in a timely manner (Figure 4-51).

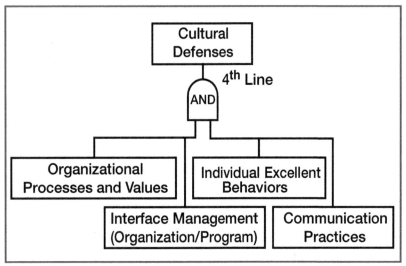

Figure 4-52. Cultural Causal Factors

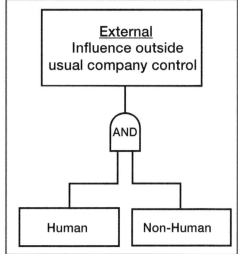

Figure 4-53. External Factors

Cultural Defenses

Leaders understand that, when an individual's actions lead to an incident, the conditions associated with the person's behaviors were shaped by organizational processes or the prevailing culture — the system. Aggressive leaders set up cultural controls that explicitly emphasize the assumptions, values, beliefs, and attitudes that encourage high standards of performance and open communication. Production tends to take priority over protection unless there is a strong safety culture nurtured by strong leadership (Figure 4-52).

External Factors

The organization needs to consider using defenses or safeguards to compensate for influences outside the usual control of the business. Some of these influences may be human (e.g., theft) and some non-human (e.g., weather) (Figure 4-53).

The fault tree diagrams specific human and non-human factors that can influence incidents (Figure 4-54).

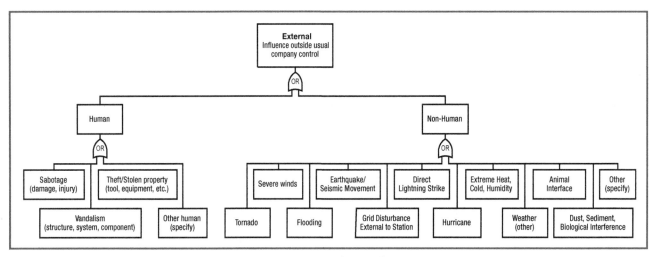

Figure 4-54. External Causal Factors

4.6.5   Safety Culture Analysis

What is it?

Safety culture analysis compares each of the cross-cutting aspects of safety culture to the circumstances surrounding the incident to determine if the safety culture contributed to the performance deficiency (Figure 4-55). This analysis is required for certain types of incidents or conditions at commercial nuclear power plants to determine whether the organization has any safety culture weaknesses. Cross-cutting aspects of safety culture are described in the Nuclear Regulatory Commission's Regulatory Issue Summary (RIS) 2006-13 and addressed by its baseline inspection program. A cross-cutting issue is a Nuclear Regulatory Commission (2013) inspection finding associated with a cross-cutting aspect that is a significant contributor to the performance deficiency (Figure 4-56).

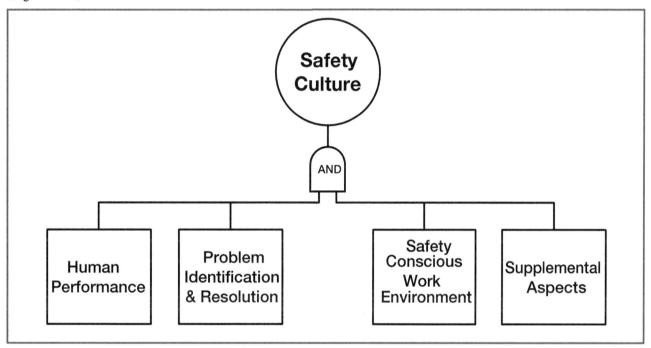

Figure 4-55. Nuclear Regulatory Commission Safety Culture Areas

Why is it useful?

The purpose of this evaluation is to identify issues with cross-cutting tendencies that warrant enhanced corrective action to address adverse impacts to safety culture.

How is it done?

1. FAMILIARIZE yourself with the safety culture definitions and questions. (See Table 4-14 for details.)

    ‣ REVIEW the questions/issues related to safety culture.

    ‣ FACTOR these questions/issues into the investigation as it progresses.

    ‣ CONSIDER these questions and issues when generating the actions and factors chart, when reviewing defenses, and when evaluating changes/differences.

2. ENSURE your employee concerns department is engaged in the assessment of corporate safety culture to assure the root cause analysis team is aware of any employee concern trends in a particular area.

3. COMPLETE the investigation (i.e., the root cause, apparent cause, or common cause analysis) including identification and analysis of causal factors.

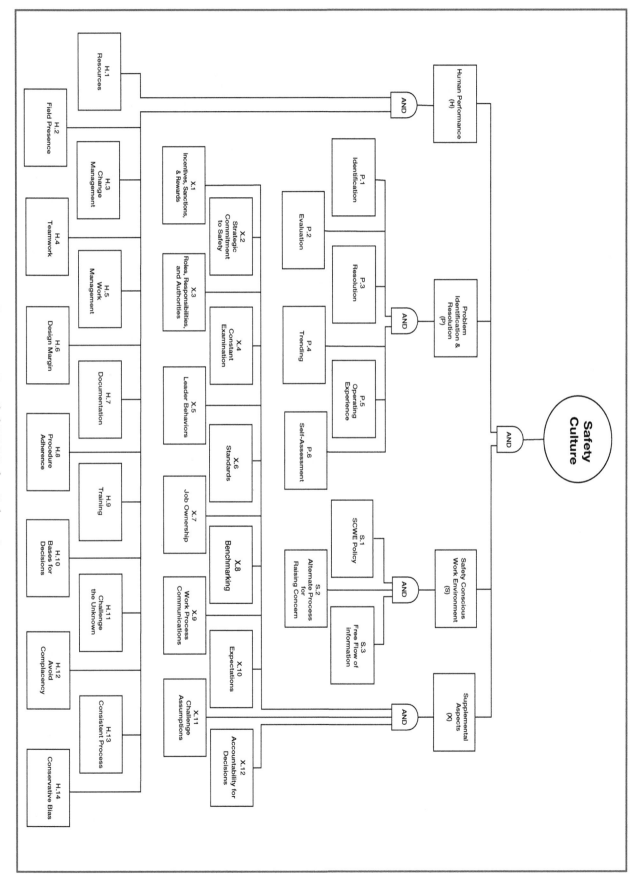

Figure 4-56. Detailed NRC Safety Culture Aspects

- ‣ IF the work activity was previously performed successfully, DETERMINE what was different this time. (*Substitution test/difference analysis results*)
- ‣ IDENTIFY tools, barriers, and management controls that were weak, missing, or not used. (*Defense analysis results*)
- ‣ MAP the cause-and-effect relationships of the findings to determine WHY the incident happened.
- ‣ PRESENT information to help understand the contributing causes of risk significant performance issues. IF any of the following information applies, THEN DESIGNATE the factor as a causal factor:
  - ❑ IDENTIFY conditions that could have prevented the incident.
  - ❑ IDENTIFY a clear cause that addresses the stated problem and is supported by the facts of the investigation.
  - ❑ IDENTIFY conditions that, if removed or prevented, the incident would not have occurred or its consequences would be significantly mitigated.

4. VERIFY and VALIDATE the causal factors.
   - ‣ LIST all those actions, conditions, or events which directly or indirectly influenced the outcome of a situation or problem.
   - ‣ IDENTIFY each causal factor/inappropriate action (CF) in the space provided on the checklist.
   - ‣ DETERMINE if any aspect of safety culture contributed to the incident.

5. EVALUATE each causal factor (CF) against each of the safety culture aspects listed in Table 4-13.
   - ‣ ANALYZE each causal factor in its entirety before moving to the next causal factor.
   - ‣ During the investigation, DETERMINE:
   - a) IF any of the factors the investigation identified (i.e., documented) were **weaknesses** (i.e., any factor that initiated the incident, contributed to its outcome, or exacerbated its consequences).
     - ❑ What set the stage for the consequence? (Vulnerabilities)
     - ❑ What triggered the incident? (Released)
     - ❑ What made the incident as bad as it was? (Exacerbated/Aggravated)
     - ❑ What kept it from being worse than it was? (Mitigated)
   - b) IF a factor was a weakness, determine whether that factor was a **significant contributor** (i.e., a "root cause" (RC) or a "contributing cause" (CC)) by considering:
     - ❑ Risk.
       - ◆ Impact on the safe operation of the plant (nuclear safety significance).
       - ◆ Impact on the reliable operation of the enterprise (revenue and cost).
       - ◆ Impact on the environment.
       - ◆ Personnel radiation safety threat.
       - ◆ Personnel industrial safety hazard.
     - ❑ Recurrence.
       - ◆ Repeat incidents (known frequency).
       - ◆ Adverse trends (known frequency).
       - ◆ Acceptability of the potential for recurrence (likelihood of occurrence).
     - ❑ Precursors and defenses.
       - ◆ Precursor to a much more serious incident.
       - ◆ Potential to be more severe if different conditions that could be reasonably expected, had been present.

- ◆ Defenses penetrated (number and dependability).
- ◆ Defenses remaining (number and dependability).
- ❏ Exposure.
  - ◆ Regulatory margin exposure.
  - ◆ Degree of regulatory impact.
  - ◆ Amount of public impact.
  - ◆ Safety culture aspect contribution to any risk significant performance issue.

c) For each aspect delineated as a significant contributor (i.e., a root cause (RC) or contributing cause (CC), MAP the aspect to cause by providing the cause number (e.g., RC-# or CC-#).

d) IF the aspect's weakness was a significant contributor, evaluate the relationship between aspects to determine if a weakness in one aspect drove another aspect's weakness (e.g., didn't have a procedure because we failed to adequately evaluate external operating experience).

e) If the weakness was a significant contributor, what corrective actions are needed to address that significant contributor?

Table 4-13. Safety Culture Aspect Assessment

Code	Area/Aspect	Any Concerns Within Area or Aspect?		Significant Contributor? Weakness? Factor?
H	**Human Performance**	☐ **Yes**	☐ **No**	
H.1	Resources	☐ Yes	☐ No	
H.2	Field Presence	☐ Yes	☐ No	
H.3	Change Management	☐ Yes	☐ No	
H.4	Teamwork	☐ Yes	☐ No	
H.5	Work Management	☐ Yes	☐ No	
H.6	Design Margins	☐ Yes	☐ No	
H.7	Documentation	☐ Yes	☐ No	
H.8	Procedure Adherence	☐ Yes	☐ No	
H.9	Training	☐ Yes	☐ No	
H.10	Bases for Decisions	☐ Yes	☐ No	
H.11	Challenge the Unknown	☐ Yes	☐ No	
H.12	Avoid Complacency	☐ Yes	☐ No	
H.13	Consistent Process	☐ Yes	☐ No	
H.14	Conservative Bias	☐ Yes	☐ No	

Code	Area/Aspect	Any Concerns Within Area or Aspect?		Significant Contributor? Weakness? Factor?
P	**Problem Identification and Resolution**	☐ **Yes**	☐ **No**	
P.1	Identification	☐ Yes	☐ No	
P.2	Evaluation	☐ Yes	☐ No	
P.3	Resolution	☐ Yes	☐ No	
P.4	Trending	☐ Yes	☐ No	
P.5	Operating Experience	☐ Yes	☐ No	
P.6	Self-Assessment	☐ Yes	☐ No	

Code	Area/Aspect	Any Concerns Within Area or Aspect?		Significant Contributor? Weakness? Factor?
S	**Safety Conscious Work Environment (SCWE)**	☐ **Yes**	☐ **No**	
S.1	SCWE Policy	☐ Yes	☐ No	
S.2	Alternate Process for Raising Concerns	☐ Yes	☐ No	
S.3	Free Flow of Information	☐ Yes	☐ No	

Code	Area/Aspect	Any Concerns Within Area or Aspect?		Significant Contributor? Weakness? Factor?
X	**Supplemental Cross-Cutting Aspects**	☐ **Yes**	☐ **No**	
X.1	Incentives, Sanctions, and Rewards	☐ Yes	☐ No	
X.2	Strategic Commitment to Safety	☐ Yes	☐ No	
X.3	Roles, Responsibilities, and Authorities	☐ Yes	☐ No	
X.4	Constant Examination	☐ Yes	☐ No	
X.5	Leader Behaviors	☐ Yes	☐ No	
H.6	Standards	☐ Yes	☐ No	
X.7	Job Ownership	☐ Yes	☐ No	
X.8	Benchmarking	☐ Yes	☐ No	
X.9	Work Process Communications	☐ Yes	☐ No	
X.10	Expectations	☐ Yes	☐ No	
X.11	Challenge Assumptions	☐ Yes	☐ No	
X.12	Accountability for Decision	☐ Yes	☐ No	

7. INDICATE for each safety culture aspect its contribution to the incident on the checklist:
   - ❑ Weakness (W)
   - ❑ Significant contributor (SC)
   - ❑ Satisfactory (S)
   - ❑ Not applicable (N) – not a factor in the incident

8. After ALL safety culture aspects have been analyzed and rated, EVALUATE each safety culture component based on the responses to each associated safety culture aspect.
   - ▸ RECORD the results of this "roll up."
   - ▸ GRADE each safety culture component using the criteria used for aspects as:
     - ❑ Weakness (W)
     - ❑ Significant Contributor (SC)
     - ❑ Satisfactory (S)
     - ❑ Not Applicable (N) – not a factor in the incident

9. In a collective review of all the weaknesses, CONSIDER the aggregate of causal factors and safety culture contributors.
   - ▸ ANSWER the following questions:
     1. Can the causal factors and contributors be assigned to the same general program or process?
     2. Can the causal factors and contributors be assigned to the same behavior category (self-checking, procedure compliance, or pre-job brief)?
     3. Can the causal factors and contributors be assigned to the same part of a work process (planning, scheduling, implementation, testing)?
   - ▸ DETERMINE if the combination of root and contributing causes points to a more fundamental, systemic, or programmatic breakdown. Examples:
     - (1) If more than one root/contributing causes is associated with procedural inadequacies, there may be a breakdown in the procedure development/review/approval process.
     - (2) If one root cause is failure to use three-part communication by an individual, and failure to follow procedure is a contributing cause by another individual, there may be a breakdown with implementation of the human performance program.
   - ▸ IF the grouping of aspects identifies an underlying theme that needs to be addressed, REVIEW the corrective actions and ensure that they address the aspects identified and any underlying themes.

10. DOCUMENT the results.
    - ▸ IDENTIFY each aspect that was assessed as a "significant contributor" and provide facts/justification for the assessment. These should be in paragraph form using the detailed information identified in Table 4-14.

Table 4-14. Safety Culture Aspect Details (adapted from Nuclear Regulatory Commission, 2013)

Code	Area/Aspect	Description
H	Human Performance	
H.1	Resources	Leaders ensure that personnel, equipment, procedures, and other resources are available and adequate to support nuclear safety.
H.2	Field Presence	Leaders are commonly seen in the work areas of the plant observing, coaching, and reinforcing standards and expectations. Deviations from standards and expectations are corrected promptly. Senior managers ensure supervisory and management oversight of work activities, including contractors and supplemental personnel.
H.3	Change Management	Leaders use a systematic process for evaluating and implementing change so that nuclear safety remains the overriding priority.
H.4	Teamwork	Individuals and work groups communicate and coordinate their activities within and across organizational boundaries to ensure nuclear safety is maintained.
H.5	Work Management	The organization implements a process of planning, controlling, and executing work activities such that nuclear safety is the overriding priority. The work process includes the identification and management of risk commensurate to the work and the need for coordination with different groups or job activities.
H.6	Design Margins	The organization operates and maintains equipment within design margins. Margins are carefully guarded and changed only through a systematic and rigorous process. Special attention is placed on maintaining fission product barriers, defense-in-depth, and safety related equipment.
H.7	Documentation	The organization creates and maintains complete, accurate and, up-to-date documentation.
H.8	Procedure Adherence	Individuals follow processes, procedures, and work instructions.
H.9	Training	The organization provides training and ensures knowledge transfer to maintain a knowledgeable, technically competent workforce and instill nuclear safety values.
H.10	Bases for Decisions	Leaders ensure that the bases for operational and organizational decisions are communicated in a timely manner.
H.11	Challenge the Unknown	Individuals stop when faced with uncertain conditions. Risks are evaluated and managed before proceeding.
H.12	Avoid Complacency	Individuals recognize and plan for the possibility of mistakes, latent issues, and inherent risk, even while expecting successful outcomes. Individuals implement appropriate error reduction tools.
H.13	Consistent Process	Individuals use a consistent, systematic approach to make decisions. Risk insights are incorporated as appropriate.
H.14	Conservative Bias	Individuals use decision-making-practices that emphasize prudent choices over those that are simply allowable. A proposed action is determined to be safe in order to proceed, rather than unsafe in order to stop.

Code	Area/Aspect	Description
P	Problem Identification and Resolution	
P.1	Identification	The organization implements a corrective action program with a low threshold for identifying issues. Individuals identify issues completely, accurately, and in a timely manner in accordance with the program.
P.2	Evaluation	The organization thoroughly evaluates issues to ensure that resolutions address causes and extent of conditions commensurate with their safety significance.
P.3	Resolution	The organization takes effective corrective actions to address issues in a timely manner commensurate with their safety significance.
P.4	Trending	The organization periodically analyzes information from the corrective action program and other assessments in the aggregate to identify programmatic and common cause issues.
P.5	Operating Experience	The organization systematically and effectively collects, evaluates, and implements relevant internal and external operating experience in a timely manner.
P.6	Self-Assessment	The organization routinely conducts self-critical and objective assessments of its programs and practices.
S	Safety Conscious Work Environment (SCWE)	
S.1	SCWE Policy	The organization effectively implements a policy that supports individuals' rights and responsibilities to raise safety concerns, and does not tolerate harassment, intimidation, retaliation, or discrimination for doing so.
S.2	Alternate Process for Raising Concerns	The organization effectively implements a process for raising and resolving concerns that is independent of line management influence. Safety issues may be raised in confidence and are resolved in a timely and effective manner.
S.3	Free Flow of Information	Individuals communicate openly and candidly, both up, down, and across the organization and with oversight, audit, and regulatory organizations.
X	Supplemental Cross-Cutting Aspects	
X.1	Incentives, Sanctions, and Rewards	Leaders ensure incentives, sanctions, and rewards are aligned with nuclear safety policies and reinforce behaviors and outcomes that reflect safety as the overriding priority.
X.2	Strategic Commitment to Safety	Leaders ensure plant priorities are aligned to reflect nuclear safety as the overriding priority.
X.3	Roles, Responsibilities, and Authorities	Leaders clearly define roles, responsibilities, and authorities to ensure nuclear safety.

Code	Area/Aspect	Description
X.4	**Constant Examination**	Leaders ensure that nuclear safety is constantly scrutinized through a variety of monitoring techniques, including assessments of nuclear safety culture.
X.5	**Leader Behaviors**	Leaders exhibit behaviors that set the standard for safety.
X.6	**Standards**	Individuals understand the importance of adherence to nuclear standards. All levels of the organization exercise accountability for shortfalls in meeting standards.
X.7	**Job Ownership**	Individuals understand and demonstrate personal responsibility for the behaviors and work practices that support nuclear safety.
X.8	**Benchmarking**	The organization learns from other organizations to continuously improve knowledge, skills, and safety performance.
X.9	**Work Process Communications**	Individuals incorporate safety communications in work activities.
X.10	**Expectations**	Leaders frequently communicate and reinforce the expectation that nuclear safety is the organization's overriding priority.
X.11	**Challenge Assumptions**	Individuals challenge assumptions and offer opposing views when they think something is not correct.
X.12	**Accountability for Decision**	Single-point accountability is maintained for nuclear safety decisions.

Table 4-15. Example (Old NRC Format) Safety Culture Component Assessment

Components Within Cross-Cutting Area	Any Concerns Within Component?		Significant Contributor? Weakness? Factor?
Human Performance	☒ **Yes**	☐ **No**	**Significant Contributor**
1. Decision-Making	☒ Yes	☐ No	Significant Contributor
2. Resources	☒ Yes	☐ No	Significant Contributor
3. Work Control	☒ Yes	☐ No	Weakness
4. Work Practices	☒ Yes	☐ No	Weakness

Problem Identification and Resolution	☒ **Yes**	☐ **No**	**Weakness**
1. Corrective Action Program	☒ Yes	☐ No	Weakness
2. Operating Experience	☒ Yes	☐ No	Weakness
3. Self and Independent Assessments	☒ Yes	☐ No	Weakness

Components Within Cross-Cutting Area	Any Concerns Within Component?		Significant Contributor? Weakness? Factor?
Safety Conscious Work Environment	☐ **Yes**	☒ **No**	**Not a Factor**
1. Willingness to Raise Concerns	☐ Yes	☒ No	Not a Factor
2. Preventing and Detecting Retaliation	☐ Yes	☒ No	Not a Factor

Other Safety Culture Components	☒ Yes	☐ No	Weakness
1. Accountability	☒ Yes	☐ No	Satisfactory
2. Continuous Learning Environment	☒ Yes	☐ No	Weakness
3. Organizational Change Management	☒ Yes	☐ No	Significant Contributor
4. Safety Policies	☒ Yes	☐ No	Satisfactory

(Old NRC Format) The NRC changed its inspection manual criteria in December 2013. This example is from the criteria the NRC was using from 2011 through most of 2013. The criteria were found in NRC Inspection Manual Chapter 0310. Nuclear Regulatory Commission (2011).

Looking Forward

As a result of the work you have done up to this point in the investigation, you should have identified and documented the following:

- ▶ Factors that triggered (released) the incident.
- ▶ Factors that made the situation worse.
- ▶ Exposure factors (holes in defenses).
- ▶ Factors that prevented the incident from being worse than it was.

The set of tools and techniques you will learn about in Step 5 (Validate Underlying Factors) will take the factors you determined to be causal in Step 4 through a deep analysis to pinpoint the latent weaknesses of the business. You will determine the underlying factors and provide the organization with the physical, human, and latent roots of the incident.

Questions for Understanding

1. What is a contributing factor? Describe a contributing factor associated with an incident your business has experienced.
2. Why is a cause and effect tree an effective tool?
3. What is the purpose of a difference analysis (change analysis)?
4. When is defense analysis (barrier analysis) most effective?
5. What tools are specialized types of structure trees?

Questions for Discussion

1. It is usually fairly easy for key decision makers to see how actions directly cause or trigger an incident or accident. It is not the same with the indirect causes. How would you go about helping management see how an inaction or condition allowed a circumstance or aggravated a situation and therefore should be considered causal?
2. In this section quite a bit of information was presented. If you are facilitating an investigation team, how would you assure team members gather the type of information you know is needed to have a complete assessment?

References

Avatar International Inc. (1985). *Problem solving and improvement process.* Atlanta, GA: Avatar International Inc.

Department of Defense (DOD). (2000). *Standard practice for system safety.* (MIL-STD-882D). Wright-Patterson AFB, OH: Department Of Defense.

Department of Energy (DOE). (1992). *DOE guideline: Root cause analysis guidance document.* (DOE-NE-STD-1004-92). Washington, DC: US Department of Energy.

Department of Energy (DOE). (2012). *DOE handbook: Accident and operational safety analysis: Volume I: Accident analysis techniques.* (DOE-HDBK-1208-2012). Washington, DC: US Department of Energy.

Livingston, A. D., Jackson, G. & Priestley, K. (2001). *Root cause analysis: Literature review.* Retrieved from http://www.hse.gov.uk/research/crr_pdf/2001/crr01325.pdf

Muschara, T. (2007, August). INPO's approach to human performance in the United States commercial nuclear power industry. *IEEE Xplore Digital Library.* Retrieved from http://ieeexplore.ieee.org/xpl/login.jsp?tp=&arnumber=4413179&url= http%3A%2F%2Fieeexplore.ieee.org%2Fxpls%2Fabs_all.jsp%3Farnumber%3D4413179 (Complete text of document may be accessed only by purchase from the publisher.)

Muschara, T. (2010). *A risk-based approach to managing the human risk.* Retrieved from http://www.slideshare.net/muschara/managing-human-risk

Nuclear Regulatory Commission (NRC). (1993). *Development of the NRC's human performance investigation process (HPIP): Investigator's manual.* (NRC NUREG/CR-5455, S1-92-101, Vol. 2). Washington, DC: US Government Printing Office.

Nuclear Regulatory Commission (NRC). (2001). *The human performance evaluation process: A resource for reviewing the identification and resolution of human performance problems.* (NUREG/CR-6751). Washington, DC: Office of Nuclear Regulatory Research.

Nuclear Regulatory Commission (NRC). (2006). *Information on the changes made to the reactor oversight process to more fully address safety culture.* (Regulatory Issue Summary 2006-13). Washington, DC: Office of Enforcement.

Nuclear Regulatory Commission (NRC). (2011). *Components within the cross-cutting areas.* (NRC Inspection Manual Chapter 0310). Washington, DC: US NRC Office of Nuclear Reactor Regulation.

Nuclear Regulatory Commission (NRC). (2011). *Inspection for one or two white inputs in a strategic performance area.* (NRC Inspection Procedure 95001). Washington, DC: US NRC Office of Nuclear Reactor Regulation.

Nuclear Regulatory Commission (NRC). (2013). *Aspects within the cross-cutting areas.* (NRC Inspection Manual Chapter 0310). Washington, DC: US NRC Office of Nuclear Reactor Regulation.

Tosti, D. T. (2007, January 8). Aligning the culture and strategy for success. *Performance Improvement.* Retrieved from http://onlinelibrary.wiley.com/doi/10.1002/pfi.035/pdf (Document may be accessed only by purchase or rental from the publisher.)

For Further Reading

American Institute of Chemical Engineers (AIChE). (1992). *Guidelines for investigating chemical process incidents.* New York, NY: Center for Chemical Process Safety of the American Institute of Chemical Engineers.

Bloch, H. P. & Geitner, F. K. (1997). *Machinery failure analysis and troubleshooting: Practical machinery management for process plants.* Houston, TX: Gulf Publishing Company.

Buys, R. J. & Clark, J. L. (1978). *Events and causal factors charting.* (DOE 76-45/14, SSDC-14). Idaho Falls, ID: Idaho National Engineering Laboratory.

Department of Energy (DOE). (1999). *DOE workbook: Conducting accident investigations.* Washington, DC: US Department of Energy.

Hartley, R. S., Swaim, D. J., & Corcoran W. R. (2008). *Causal factors analysis: An approach for organizational learning.* Amarillo, TX: Babcock and Wilcox (B&W) Technical Services Pantex LLC.

Nuclear Regulatory Commission (NRC). (2010). *Primer on lean six sigma.* (NUREG/BR-0470). Washington, DC: Office of Executive Director for Operations.

Perrow, C. (1984). *Normal accidents: Living with high-risk technologies.* New York, NY: Basic Books.

Reason, J. & Hobbs, A. (2006). *Managing maintenance error: A practical guide.* Burlington, VT: Ashgate Publishing Company.

Step 5

Validate Underlying Factors

**Chance is a word void of sense;
nothing can exist without a cause.**

— Voltaire (Francois-Marie Arouet), Philosopher

Every effect has a cause, and Step 5, Validate Underlying Factors, explores that relationship. This step will instruct you in the importance of not only asking "why" but also asking "why" in a logical manner. The author and historian Edward Hodnett is frequently quoted as remarking, "If you don't ask the right questions, you don't get the right answers."

There is a systematic way to investigate causes of behaviors by analyzing what comes before and after the behavior. As an investigator, when you understand the consequences of an action, you will understand the behaviors. It is the behaviors that will lead you to the underlying causes and help you with your cause analysis.

The purpose of your cause analysis is to identify the basic set of conditions that, if eliminated or modified, would minimize the likelihood of the same and similar incidents from happening again.

As you are looking for correctable causes for the incident, assure that you:

- ☑ Determine the *physical* roots and validate (for equipment-related incidents).

- ☑ Determine *human* roots and validate.

- ☑ Determine *organizational* roots and validate.

A root cause will fully explain the equipment failure or the human performance difficulty. If no other cause can be found, or if corrective actions are outside the control of the organization or are cost-prohibitive, you have most likely determined the root cause(s) of the incident.

Be sure to use internal and external operating experience to:

  ▸ Determine the extent of the undesired condition and the extent of the causes for the incident being investigated.
  ▸ Provide a sanity check of the contributing factors, after determined.
  ▸ Identify how applicable past lessons learned are applied to the current problem.
  ▸ Avoid corrective actions that have not worked in the past.

You will have asked "why" a lot of times by this point in the investigation. Asking "why" is a good thing. However, Daniels, Daniels, and Abernathy (2006) suggest that, in order to understand why people do what they do, beyond asking, "Why did they do that?" ask, "What happens to them when they do that?" When you understand the real or perceived consequences of a behavior, you are able to understand the behavior better. So by asking **"What happens to them when they do that?"** the investigator will be able to find out whether a *desired* behavior is perceived by the job performer as rewarding or punishing. Also the investigator will be able to discover whether *undesired* behaviors are rewarded or corrected in that job performer's perception.

The key word in the previous paragraph is *perception*. The job performer's perception is the key to explaining his or her behavior. The individual's supervisor may have a totally different perception. But the perception of the individual's supervisor does not explain the worker's behavior. The differences in perception may point out gaps in the values and mental models between the worker and the supervisor that need to be addressed by some type of intervention.

Step 5 contains a variety of logical and structured tools (listed by section number) that can be used to ensure you find correctable causes for the incident you are investigating. Use Table 5-1 as a checklist to guide you through Step 5 of the investigation.

  5.1   Support/Refute Methodology
  5.2   WHY Factor Staircase
  5.3   Root Cause Test
  5.4   Cause Evaluation Matrix
  5.5   Extent of Cause Review

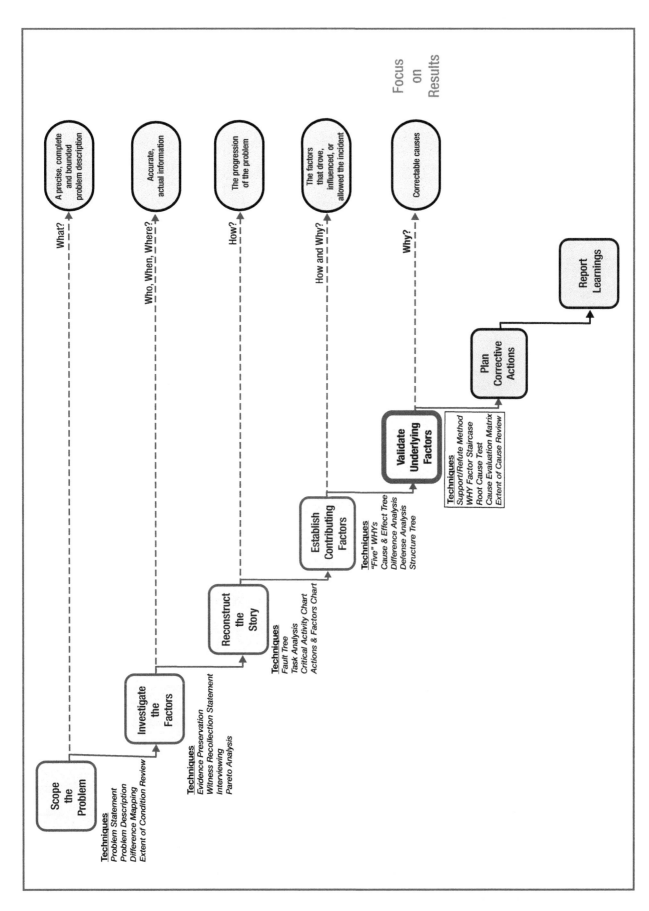

Figure 5-1. Step 5 Validate Underlying Factors

Table 5-1. Step 5 Jump Start Checklist

☑ Behaviors [Sub-Tasks]	Tools/Techniques	Required		
☐ Complete mapping the cause [C] and effect [E] relationships.	*Cause and Effect Tree*	RC	AC	AD
☐ *Make visible the team's systematic method(s) used to identify cause(s) and contributing cause(s). Show all on-lookers that structured investigative tools and techniques are being used with quantitative information on the team's actions and factors chart, timeline, process map, etc.*	*Actions and Factors Chart*	RC	AC	
	Structure Tree	RC		
☐ FOR each contributing [causal] factor, find correctable causes.	*Support/Refute Methodology*	RC	AC	
	Cause Evaluation Matrix	RC	AC	
☐ Determine physical roots and validate.	*Fault Tree*	RC	AC	
☐ *Identify the equipment failure and degradation mechanisms (if applicable).*		RC	AC	
☐ *Identify reasons for the failure of engineered barriers.*		RC		
☐ Determine human roots and validate. *Ensure all inappropriate actions have been evaluated to a level of detail matching the incident's significance. Include active errors and latent errors.*	*Task Analysis* *Actions and Factors Chart* *Structure Tree*	RC	AC	
☐ *Evaluate each triggering factor (release factor, initiating action).*		RC	AC	
☐ *Evaluate each exacerbating factor (error precursor).*		RC	AC	
☐ *Evaluate each flawed defense (exposure factor). Administrative and programmatic controls.*		RC	AC	
☐ Determine organizational roots and validate. *Identify the latent organizational weaknesses influencing or permitting the human performance difficulty or the equipment failure. Did any aspect of safety culture contribute?*	*WHY Factor Staircase*	RC		
☐ *Identify reasons for the failure of error reduction (R_e) strategies.*		RC		
☐ *Identify reasons for the failure of managing defense (M_d) strategies.*		RC		
☐ *Identify reasons for the failure of oversight controls.*		RC		
☐ *Identify reasons for the failure of cultural controls.*	*Root Cause Test*	RC		
☐ Complete the extent of condition review and include plans to correct any new adverse conditions that were identified.	*Extent of Condition Review*	RC	AC	AD
☐ Complete an extent of cause review once causes are determined and include plans to address any new adverse conditions that were identified.	*Extent of Cause Review*	RC	AC	
☐ *Consider potential common cause(s) of the problem and safety culture.*		RC		
☐ Review internal operating experience. Assure prior occurrences are considered.		RC	AC	
☐ *Evaluate the failure of the original corrective actions and use this as a causal factor in identifying new corrective actions.*		RC	AC	
☐ *Evaluate effectiveness of the original corrective actions and provide feedback to strengthen them.*		RC		

☑ **Behaviors [Sub-Tasks]** (continued)				
☐ Review external operating experience and consider knowledge of prior operating experience.			RC	AC	
☐ Provide evidence/basis for rejecting possible causes.	*Cause Evaluation Matrix*	RC	AC	
☐ Critical action completed. Involve responsible management.		RC		

RC = Root Cause Analysis; **AC** = Apparent Cause Analysis; **AD** = Adverse

☑ **Results** Required [R]/Desired [D]			
☐ Correctable cause(s) with written justification for addressing.	RC$_R$	AC$_R$	
☐ Correctable extended adverse condition(s) with written justification for addressing (IF detected).	RC$_R$	AC$_R$	
☐ Correctable extended cause(s) with written justification for addressing (IF detected).	RC$_R$		
☐ Written justification for rejecting or not addressing possible causes.	RC$_R$		

5.1   Support/Refute Methodology

What is it?

The *support/refute methodology* is a systematic matrix-based technique for side-by-side comparisons of how multiple items of evidence support or refute multiple hypotheses. Heuer (2007) indicates an investigation process must identify competing causal factors by organizing and analyzing facts to logically eliminate possible causal factors until one or more causal factors cannot be refuted and are substantiated by the evidence. Heuer also recommends trying to disprove any hypothesis you may be proposing first rather than trying to prove your hypothesis.

Why is it useful?

Horman (1997) states that, "A persistent problem in accident investigation has been the failure to verify and validate all findings and conclusions reached by the investigators. What may have been evident and clear to the investigators is not so evident and clear to those reading the report of the investigation. This failure comes from a lack of correlating the investigative analysis to the facts given

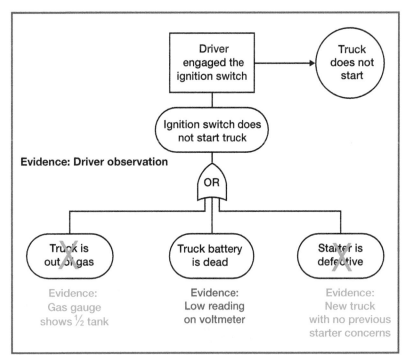

Figure 5-2. Support/Refute Example

in the report, not providing all the necessary facts to justify the analysis, not correlating findings and conclusions back to the analysis, and other similar oversights...."

The methodology aids in the logical completion of the four basic steps needed to validate (or invalidate) a factor as either a contributing cause or a root cause:

1. Identify and define the problem (using the symptoms of the incident). Evidence collection and preservation begin here.
2. List the obvious reasons (i.e., probable causes) of the incident.
3. Create a hypothesis (i.e., select the most likely reason for the incident).
4. Prove the hypothesis (verify or refute what you know through the application of the investigative techniques).

The comparison of evidence begins a process of eliminating from further consideration factors that are refuted by the evidence.

When is it used?

Supporting and refuting hypotheses may start in Step 1 (Scope the Problem) of the problem solving process. Because minimal evidence is available at the start of an investigation, care must be taken in not "jumping to conclusion." Supporting and refuting thinking is critical throughout the process, but is crucial in Step 5 (Validate Underlying Factors). The output of Step 5 — correctable causes — is the basis for Step 6 (Plan Corrective Actions).

How is it done?

1. IDENTIFY THE POSSIBLE HYPOTHESES (i.e., the probable causes) to be considered. Use Table 5-2. Identify as many potential failure modes and causal factors as possible. These suppositions will either be disproven or will change to findings and conclusions as information is gathered.
2. MAKE A LIST of all supporting and contrary evidence and arguments for and against each hypothesis (supposition). Organize the available objective evidence to determine which potential failure modes and causal factors are supported or refuted.
3. PREPARE A MATRIX with evidence across the top and hypotheses down the side. This step may be the most critical step in this methodology. Show where each piece of evidence originated (source).
4. ANALYZE the perceived helpfulness of the evidence and arguments in judging the relative likelihood of the hypothesized factors.
5. REFINE the matrix. Reconsider the hypotheses and delete evidence and arguments that have no investigative value. Give enough detail that you will not have to depend on memory.
6. INCLUDE any comments or remarks that would be beneficial to decision-makers.
7. DRAW TENTATIVE CONCLUSIONS about the relative likelihood of each hypothesis.
   - Look for evidence that enables rejection of the hypothesis.
   - Tentatively accept only those that cannot be refuted.

8 PROCEED by trying to **disprove** the hypotheses rather than prove them.
9. ANALYZE how sensitive your conclusion is to a few critical items of evidence.
   - Consider the consequences for your analysis if that evidence were wrong, misleading, or subject to a different interpretation.
   - Are there questionable assumptions underlying the interpretation?
   - Are there alternative explanations?

10. REPORT conclusions to decision-makers.

Table 5-2. Support/Refute Matrix

CR Number:_____ Date: _____				
Problem Description:				
Hypothesis (Failure Mechanism/ Potential Cause)	**Supporting Evidence**	**Refuting Evidence**	**Sources of Evidence**	**Actions Required to Refute/Support (Comments)**
Action Plan:				

5.1.1   Truck Will Not Start Example

Table 5-3. Truck Will Not Start Support/Refute Matrix

CR Number: 1995-0654 Date: June 6, 1995				
Problem Description: Truck would not start when driver engaged the ignition switch.				
Hypothesis (Failure Mechanism/ Potential Cause)	**Supporting Evidence**	**Refuting Evidence**	**Sources of Evidence**	**Actions Required to Refute/Support (Comments)**
1. Truck is out of gas.		Gas gauge shows $1/2$ tank of gas.	Observation	
2. Truck battery is dead.	Low reading on voltmeter		Voltmeter Observation	Charge battery. If truck starts, supports hypothesis.
3. Truck starter is defective.		New truck with no previous starter concerns.	Observation	
Action Plan: Re-charge battery. If still dead, have new truck dealer replace battery.				

5.1.2   Crane Incident Example

Table 5-4. Crane Incident Support/Refute Matrix

CR Number: 1976-0837   **Date:** August 7, 1976

Problem Description: Crane dropped gear box.

Hypothesis (Failure Mechanism/ Potential Cause)	Supporting Evidence	Refuting Evidence	Sources of Evidence	Actions Required to Refute/Support (Comments)
1. Brake failed	Maintenance & inspection less than adequate.	OK in 3 uses in 3 weeks.	Interview Log book	
	Icing possible.	30 minute warm up, powered up & down 3 times with brake press.	Interview	
		Load held @ 2' stop OK in test & inspection.	Log book	
	Mfr's rep: "Looser than I'd like to use."		Interview	
2. Foot slipped or pressure released	No requalification program	"Most experienced & reliable operator."	Interview	

Conclusion: Combination of human error and an error-likely situation.

Action Plan: Fix the crane and the system. No disciplinary action is recommended because of the error-likely situation the worker was in.

5.2   WHY Factor Staircase

What is it?

Corcoran (2007, p. 237) recommends a factor staircase approach to identify the underlying causes of incidents. Similar to the "five" WHYs technique (discussed earlier in this book), the *WHY factor staircase* technique consists of describing the incident in very specific terms; then asking why it happened successive times until the questions no longer yield any useful information. The WHY factor staircase technique is an advanced "five" WHYs technique because the questions the investigator is asking are aimed at digging down to the underlying organizational and cultural issues. It starts with the effect or symptom and the major group of causes, by step or category. Consider each step as a set of questions. With five steps to the staircase, you would have five general sets of questions — each set with a specific purpose. See Figure 5-3.

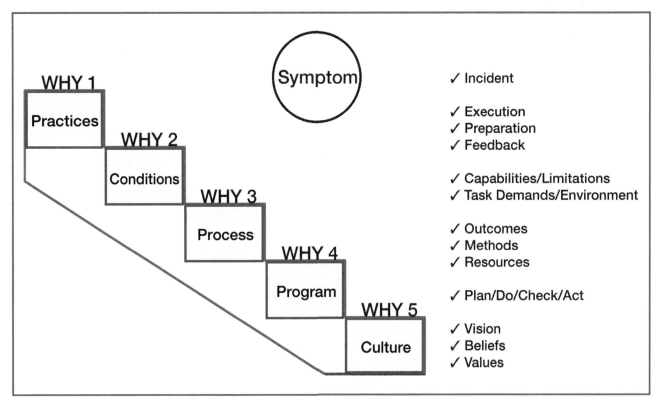

Figure 5-3. WHY Factor Staircase Objectives

Why is it useful?

The WHY factor staircase technique is useful for determining what about an organization drove, influenced, or allowed an equipment failure or a human performance difficulty that resulted in a business incident or accident. By asking the question "why" with a defined purpose, the investigator can peel away the layers of symptoms which can lead to the root causes — the latent programmatic and organizational weaknesses that permitted the incident. Very often the apparent reason for a problem will lead you to another question and deeper understanding of the incident's "set-up."

When is it used?

The quest for explanations and the reasons that drove or allowed the incident or accident began in Step 1 (Scope the Problem) and continues here in Step 5 (Validate Underlying Factors).

How is it done?

Although there are several ways to construct a cause and effect analysis using the WHY factor staircase, the steps of construction are essentially the same as a "five" WHYs. The steps to complete the WHY factor staircase are:

1. WRITE down a specific problem description. Writing the issue helps formalize the problem and helps describe the concern completely. It also helps a team focus on the same problem. Problems that are too large or too vague can bog down the process.

2. Using the data that has been collected, ASK "WHY" the problem happened. (There may be multiple answers.)

   ▶ The first set of WHY questions should be focused on the work practices of the job performers during the preparation, execution, and feedback phases of the task.

▶ The second set of WHY questions is used to determine the conditions the job performer was experiencing either internally (personal capabilities and limitations) or externally (the demands of the task and the work environment).

▶ Assuming the job performer's task was part of a process (procedure), the third set of WHY questions is aimed at finding weaknesses in the basic work plan (the expected outcome, the method used, and resources applied).

▶ The fourth set of WHY questions is looking for programmatic issues (concerns in the management control elements for planning, doing, checking, and acting associated with the work).

▶ Finally, the fifth set of WHY questions looks for cultural concerns (flawed mental models, misguided beliefs, and misplaced values).

3. WRITE the answer(s) down below the problem so decision-makers can see line of sight back to the original issue.

5.2.1   Lost Time Away Injury Example

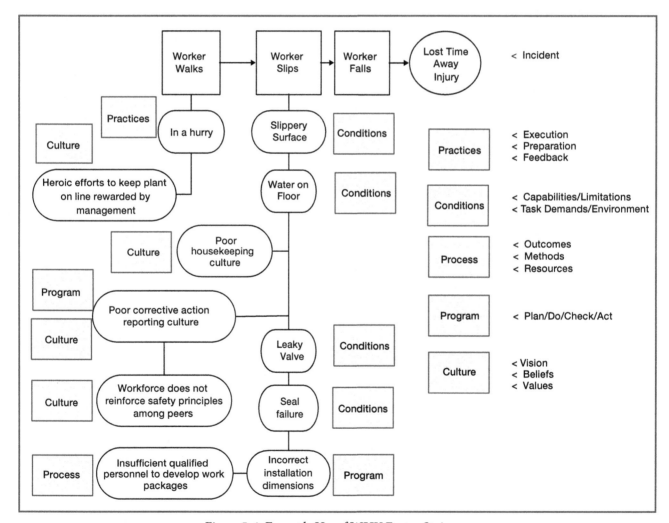

Figure 5-4. Example Use of WHY Factor Staircase

5.2.2   Criticality Incident Example

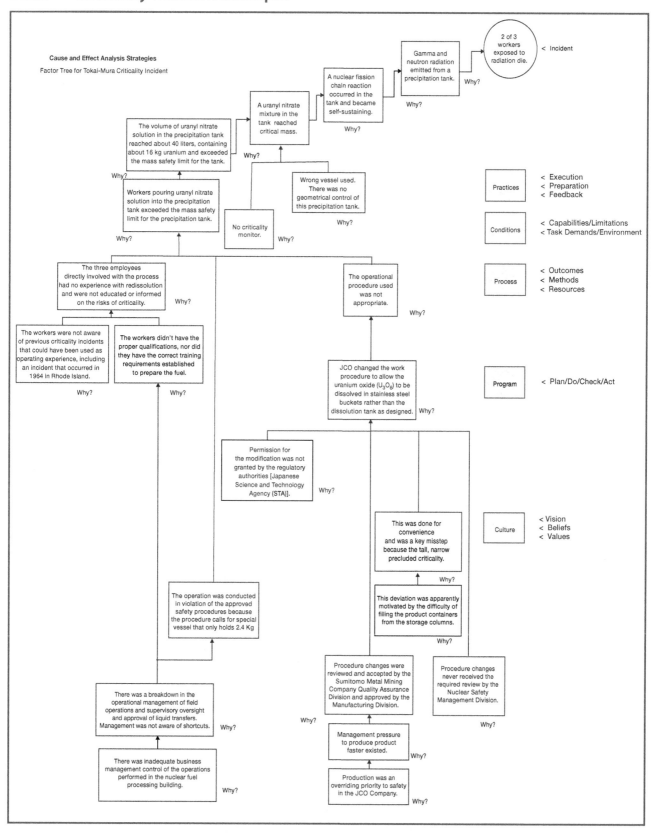

Figure 5-5. WHY Factor Staircase of Japan Tokai-Mura Incident

5.2.3 Broken Back Example

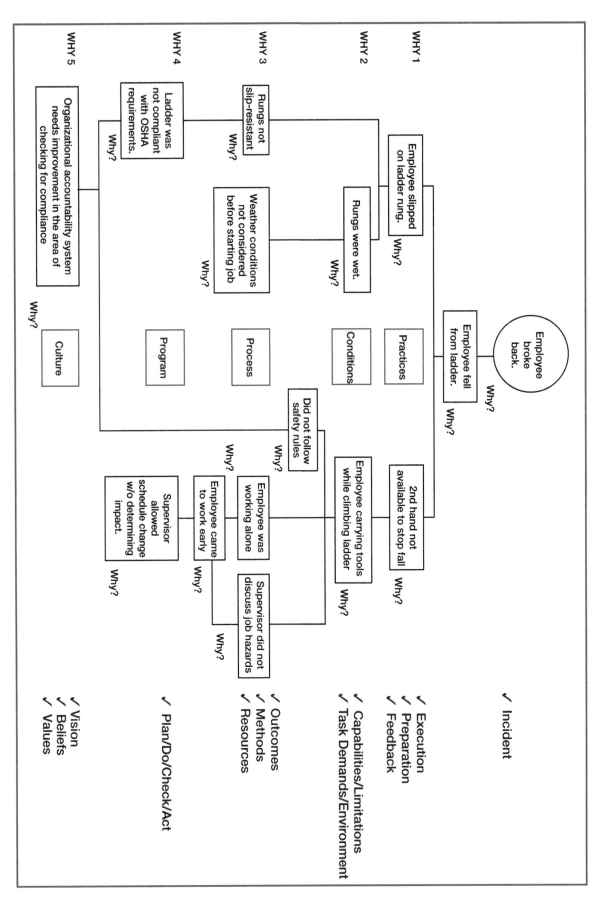

Figure 5-6. WHY Factor Staircase of Broken Back Incident

5.3   Root Cause Test

There is a mighty big difference between good, sound reasons and reasons that sound good.

— William E. "Bill" Vaughan a.k.a. "Burton Hillis," Columnist/Author

What is it?

The *root cause test* is an evaluation to determine whether a contributing factor is a "root" cause. A "root" cause has to be supported by the evidence and has to have actually triggered or influenced the incident's consequences. The following are definitions of "root cause" you need to consider as you are doing the root cause test:

- A *root cause* is an underlying driver or reason that explains how the organizational system permitted worker actions that resulted in a harmful business incident or explains the existence of the workplace conditions of the job performer. A root cause statement will explain the actions that triggered the incident, the weak organizational controls that allowed the incident, or the conditions that intensified the consequences of the incident.
- "Root Causes are defined as the basic reasons (e.g., hardware, process, or human performance) for a problem, which if corrected, will prevent recurrence of that problem" (Nuclear Regulatory Commission, 2011, February, p. 5).
- "A root cause of a human performance problem is the set of conditions that, if eliminated or modified, would minimize the likelihood that the problem would recur as well as prevent similar problems from happening. Once you find a root cause, there may be other underlying factors but they are generally outside the control of the organization or not important enough to correct" (Nuclear Regulatory Commission, 2001, p. 5-2).

Why is it useful?

This test gives the investigator acceptance criteria for labeling an issue as a "root" cause.

When is it used?

In Step 5 (Validate Underlying Factors).

How is it done?

Method 1

Once the underlying factors ("root causes") of an incident have been identified, additional action should be taken to ensure that the correction of these underlying factors will prevent recurrence. To be validated, potential underlying factors (a.k.a. "root causes") should meet the following four criteria in relationship to the problem (i.e., the incident). Ask the following questions to determine whether the cause in questions passes the test as a "root cause":

1. Does the underlying reason (condition, set of conditions, behavior, action, or inaction) explain the existence in the organization of the triggering, aggravating, or exposure factors that resulted in the harmful incident?
2. Is it true the incident with its consequences was not the effect of a more important, deeper underlying cause?
3. Is it true that correction or elimination of the underlying factor (action, behavior, or condition) will help prevent recurrence of the same or similar incidents in the future?

If the investigator can answer all three questions "yes," then the underlying factor is a "root" cause.

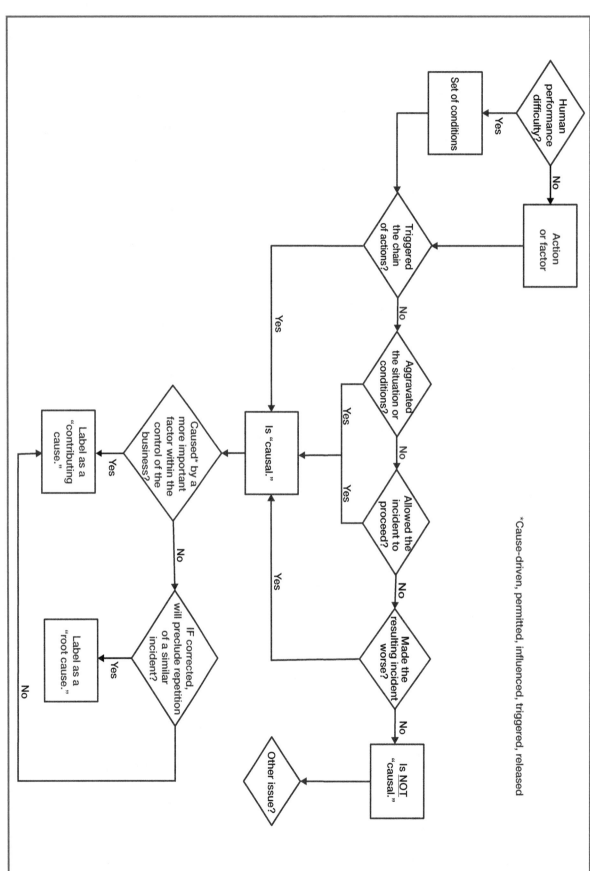

Figure 5-7. Root Cause Test Flow

5.4   Cause Evaluation Matrix

What is it?

Cause analysis is a structured search for the underlying fixable reasons for an incident. The reasons must explain why the triggering, aggravating, or exposure factors existed in the business. The goal of finding the underlying cause is so actions to preclude repetition of a similar incident can be initiated. The *cause evaluation matrix* is a decision making tool (see Table 5-5) used to evaluate several conditions or causes simultaneously (Agency for Heathcare Research and Quality, 2013). The purpose is to "narrow down" the most likely causes based on research and collected information. Another purpose is to summarize how the causes were verified, how much of the problem will be addressed, and which causes will be attacked.

Table 5-5. Cause Evaluation Matrix Template

Cause	How was the cause verified?	How much of the problem is due to this cause?	Is reducing the cause in the group's control?	Attack this cause? (Yes/No)

Why is it useful?

The cause evaluation matrix helps summarize knowledge and compare verified causes. The matrix demonstrates which causes are the more significant, risky, or costly. The remaining cause(s) should become the focus of the search for solutions.

When is it used?

After constructing a cause-and-effect diagram, use the cause evaluation matrix to help summarize the verified causes of the problem and determine which ones to attack with corrective actions. Note that more than one cause can be attacked. Ask "Which causes have the greatest impact on the problem?"

How is it done?

1. WRITE down a specific problem description. Writing the issue helps formalize the problem and describe it completely. It also helps a team focus on the same problem. Problems that are too large or too vague can bog down the process.

2. LIST the validated causes (identified as a result of their cause-and-effect analysis and then verified with data) down the left side of the matrix.

3. BRAINSTORM appropriate evaluation criteria. Possible criteria include, but are not limited to, the items in Table 5-6.

Table 5-6. Suggested Evaluation Criteria

▶ Changeability	Can the cause probably be eliminated or modified, or is it a "given" of the situation?
▶ Owner	To what extent does the particular cause affect the problem? Completely or partially? Is it sufficient or necessary, or both necessary and sufficient?
▶ Complexity	Is the causal relationship relatively straight forward and simple, or complicated?
▶ Permanence	Is any modification or elimination likely to remain, or will continued corrective action be necessary?
▶ Growth Trend	Is the cause increasing, with a likely subsequent increase in the problem, or is it stable?
▶ Multiple Impact	Is it possible that eliminating or modifying the cause will also positively affect another problem area?
▶ Measurable	Will there be some way of clearly observing whether the cause is eliminated or modified?
▶ Adverse Consequences	Is there any possibility that a modification or elimination of the cause will create an unintended, negative effect?

4. COMPLETE the remaining columns to help identify the cause(s) to be addressed in the solution.

5. DISCUSS and REFINE the list of criteria, keeping the most important items.

6. (Optional) ASSIGN a relative weight to each criterion based on how crucial that criterion is to the situation.

> **Note:** The weighting of criteria is sometimes helpful when the decision-making process seems to be getting bogged down.

7. EVALUATE each of the most probable causes against the decision-making criteria.

8. CHOOSE the root cause(s) the business and the decision-makers should address. Significant root cause(s) that are not in the control of the decision-makers should still be addressed. If this is the case, work with others to address these causes.

5.4.1   Dump Truck Example

Problem Statement:
Dump truck crash injures a nine year old boy and damages two vehicles.

Problem Description:
On Saturday, January 17, 2009, an ACME 2½ ton dump truck with a nine year old boy in its cab rolled down the hill at the condominium construction site and crashed into a parked private automobile. Both vehicles were damaged and the boy suffered minor lacerations to his arms and back.

There were several causes for the dump truck incident. In Table 5-7, four of the causes are evaluated to determine whether further corrective actions are needed.

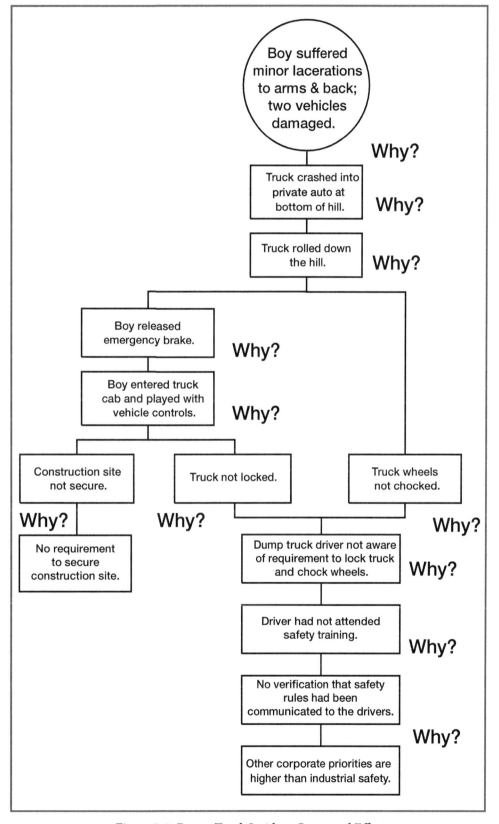

Figure 5-8. Dump Truck Incident Cause and Effect

Table 5-7. Dump Truck Cause Evaluation Matrix

Root Cause	How was the root cause verified?	How much of the problem is due to this root cause?	Is reducing the root cause in the company's control?	Attack this root cause? (Yes/No)
Construction site was not secured allowing boy to enter the truck and play with the controls. (Physical root)	Observation	Medium	Yes	No
Dump truck driver was not aware of the requirement to lock the truck and chock the wheels. (Human root)	Interview with driver. Training records	High	Yes	Yes
No verification that that safety rules had been communicated to the truck drivers. (Oversight root)	Interview with site superintendent	Medium	Yes	Yes
Other corporate priorities are higher than industrial safety. (Cultural root)	Interviews with ACME corporate management	Medium	Yes	Yes

5.5   Extent of Cause Review

What is it?

Once you have identified the more important causes of a significant incident, you need to determine the generic implications of each cause for the business. An *extent of cause review* involves putting a reasonable boundary around the population of other plant processes, equipment, or human performance jobs or tasks with the potential to be impacted by the same underlying reasons or drivers (i.e., causes) as the incident being investigated. The goal is to find other places where this same cause exists; then, correct them prior to causing an additional incident.

The extent of condition review differs from the extent of cause review in that the extent of condition review focuses on the actual condition and its existence in other places. The extent of cause review should focus more on the actual root causes of the condition and on the degree that these root causes have resulted in additional weaknesses. The extent of cause review should assess the applicability of the root causes across disciplines or departments to different programmatic activities, human performance, or different types of equipment.

The extent of cause review needs to be of sufficient breadth and depth to identify other plant equipment, processes, or human performance issues that may have been impacted by the root causes of the performance issue. For example, if an inadequate valve actuator motor torque resulted in an incident and was due to an inadequate engineering design guide for performing motor torque calculations, investigators should review other engineering design guides to assess their adequacy. The depth of the extent of cause review should be commensurate with the nature and complexity of the original performance issue (Nuclear Regulatory Commission, 2011, February).

Why is it useful?

Through investigation, the evaluator is trying to clearly define what the scope of the causes may be and what actions may be appropriate to resolve the issue. It is expected that the level of effort in determining and documenting the extent of cause is commensurate with the level of investigation and significance of the incident.

How is it done?

Method 1

Figure 5-9 is a simple flowchart showing one way an extent of cause review can be done.

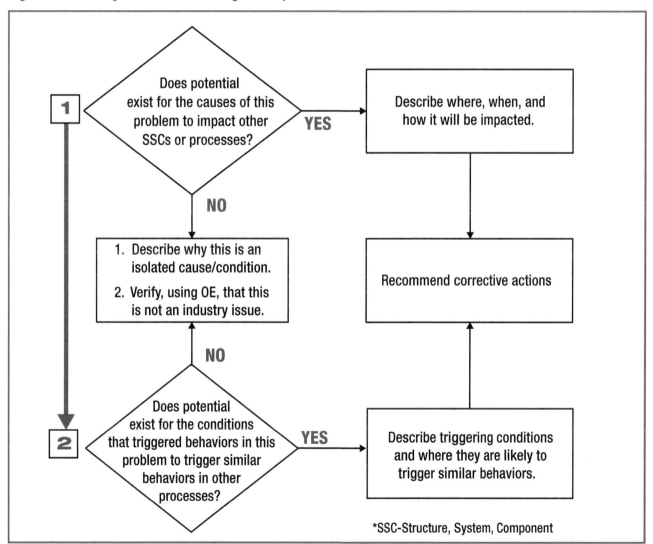

Figure 5-9. Method 1: Extent of Cause Review

Method 2

For each root cause, use the following approach:

1. RESTATE the adverse consequences (problem statement).
2. RESTATE the root cause you are reviewing for extent (underlying factor).
3. DEFINE other potential incidents with the same or similar adverse consequence(s).
4. DEFINE other potential instances of the same/similar root cause(s). Use matrices that follow. Complete same/similar possibilities using the following criteria:

   Same-Same

   ◆ Same Consequences — Same Cause

   Same-Similar

   ◆ Same Consequences — Similar Cause

   Similar-Same

   ◆ Similar Consequences — Same Cause

   Similar-Similar

   ◆ Similar Consequences — Similar Cause

5. DECIDE if action is required.

5.5.1   Example 1: Flood Protection Strategy Inadequate

(Incident) As a result of a Nuclear Regulatory Commission (NRC) inspection conducted from January 1 to June 21, 2010, the NRC determined that Fort Calhoun Station (FCS) did not have adequate procedures to protect the intake structure and auxiliary building against external flooding events.

(Cause) Unsealed penetrations were created during the installation of the original plant security system and were abandoned when the security system was replaced (approximately 1985).

(Extent of Cause Review) The penetrations for the "new" security system were appropriately sealed. Two additional conduits have been identified that are not sealed. These conduits penetrate the south wall of the auxiliary building near the transformers into Room 19 and were created as part of a station modification that was in progress at the time. An unsealed conduit (location 56E-S-43 in pull box 127) was identified that penetrates the auxiliary building into Room 56.

(Example summarized from one used in: Nuclear Regulatory Commission (NRC). (2011, May).

5.5.2   Example 2: Leak Due To Stress Corrosion Cracking

(Incident) On August 22, 2012, Three Mile Island (TMI) Unit 1 discovered a leak that could not be isolated in the upper pressurizer heater bundle diaphragm plate and shut down the reactor. The cause of the leak was primary water stress corrosion cracking.

(Extent of Condition Review) "The extent of condition is limited to Alloy 600 susceptible materials. The pressurizer is considered the highest risk because the temperature is the highest. Corrective actions to prevent recurrence (CAPRs) 1403278-15 and 1403278-16 will resolve the material issue for the pressurizer by replacing the middle bundle, which is the last external high temperature Alloy 600 location. Other Alloy 600 locations within the TMI plant are being addressed under the Alloy 600 program."

(Cause) The root cause was determined to be: "The use of Alloy 600 materials in high temperature locations was a design weakness in the construction of the TMI station."

(Extent of Cause) "New materials and designs that have not been proven through years of service are subject to failures that may not have been predicted nor expected. Appropriate NDE and monitoring techniques in accordance with the codes and standards of construction are barriers to degrading conditions causing material failures."

(Example summarized from one used in: Nuclear Regulatory Commission (NRC). (2012, October).

5.5.3   Example 3: Rental Car Flat Tire

Table 5-8. Flat Tire Extent of Cause Review

Extent of Cause Review Criteria	Deviation Statement (Adverse Consequence)	Correctable Cause (Reason/Root Cause/Underlying Factor)
Statement of Problem/Cause	The driver's side front tire on rental car parked in my driveway is flat **BECAUSE**	of a nail left by my roofing contractor when his crew spilled nails
Same-Same Identical *results* as an effect of an equivalent *underlying factor*	A tire on my pickup truck in my driveway is flat **BECAUSE**	of a nail left by my roofing contractor when his crew spilled nails
Same-Similar Identical *results* as an effect of a related *underlying factor*	A tire on my son's pickup parked in the street is flat **BECAUSE**	of sharp objects left in the driveway by my roofing contractor
Similar-Similar Comparable *results* as an effect of a related *underlying factor*	The tires on the boat trailer in my driveway are low **BECAUSE**	of sharp objects left in the driveway by my roofing contractor

Table 5-9 is an extent of cause review template that may be more useful for a more complex incident.

Table 5-9. Extent of Cause Review Template

Extent of Root Cause Review Criteria	Deviation Statement (Adverse Consequence)	Correctable Cause (Reason/Root Cause/Underlying Factor)				
Statement of Cause						
Same-Same Identical adverse consequences (results) as an effect of an equivalent *underlying factor*						
Same-Similar Identical adverse consequences (results) as an effect of a related *underlying factor*						
Similar-Same Comparable adverse consequences (results) as an effect of an equivalent *underlying factor*						
Similar-Similar Comparable adverse consequences (results) as an effect of a related *underlying factor*						

5.5.4   **Example 4: Waste Not Labeled as Required**

Table 5–10. Extent of Cause Review for Waste Not Labelled as Required

Extent of Root Cause Review Criteria	Deviation Statement (Adverse Consequence)	Correctable Cause (Reason/Root Cause/Underlying Factor)
Statement of Problem/Cause	20 gallons of hydrazine contaminated with sodium hydroxide waste was used to feed the steam generators while the plant was in Hot Standby.	An empty hydrazine drum filled with sodium hydroxide waste was not labeled per station requirements because of a willful violation (i.e., shortcut taken) on the part of the individual responsible for labeling the waste drum.
Same-Same Identical adverse consequences (results) as an effect of an equivalent *underlying factor*		Has the same individual taken shortcuts when labeling other sodium hydroxide waste drums?
		Has the same individual taken any other safety significant shortcuts while working with sodium hydroxide waste drums?
Same-Similar Identical adverse consequences (results) as an effect of a related *underlying factor*		Are other individuals in the same work group willfully violating labeling requirements for sodium hydroxide waste drums?
		Are other individuals in other work groups willfully violating labeling requirements for sodium hydroxide waste drums?
Similar-Same Comparable adverse consequences (results) as an effect of an equivalent *underlying factor*	Other contaminated chemicals were used to feed other plant systems while the plant was in any operational mode.	Has the same individual taken shortcuts when labeling other waste drums?
		Has the same individual taken any other safety significant shortcuts?
Similar-Similar Comparable adverse consequences (results) as an effect of a related *underlying factor*		Are other individuals in the same work group willfully violating labeling requirements?
		Are other individuals in other work groups willfully violating labeling requirements?

Looking Forward

By using the tools and techniques provided in Step 5, you should have found correctable causes for the incident you are investigating. Make sure you have provided key decision-makers with written justification for addressing the causes you have identified. You will be determining interventions and countermeasures for addressing the causes in Step 6, Plan Corrective Actions.

If you have identified causes that you do not recommend addressing, make sure you also provide the written justification for rejecting or not addressing possible causes.

By this time, you should have been able to put a reasonable boundary around the extent of the adverse condition you are investigating as well as the extent of the cause(s) you have identified. Again, your supervision and management will need written justification for addressing the extent of condition and the extent of cause.

Questions for Understanding

1. What are the four basic steps needed to validate (or invalidate) a factor as either a contributing cause or root cause?
2. How does the WHY factor staircase differ from the "five" WHYs technique?
3. What is a root cause test?
4. Why is an extent of cause review useful in an investigation?
5. How does the extent of condition review differ from the extent of cause review?

Questions for Discussion

1. How would you handle a situation in which you have both facts that support a potential cause and other facts that appear to refute the potential cause?
2. What are the questions you might ask yourself to determine whether a potential underlying factor is a root cause?
3. What kind of resistance do you anticipate from the organization if you were to identify a root cause that points at an underlying cultural weakness? How would you go about overcoming that resistance?

References

Agency for Heathcare Research and Quality (AHRQ). (2013, May). *Decision matrix.* Retrieved from http://healthit.ahrq.gov/health-it-tools-and-resources/workflow-assessment-health-it-toolkit/all-workflow-tools/decision-matrix

Corcoran, W. R. (2007). *The Phoenix handbook: The ultimate event evaluation manual for finding safety and profit improvement in adverse events.* Windsor, CT: Nuclear Safety Review Concepts (NSRC) Corporation.

Daniels, A. C., Daniels, J. E., & Abernathy, B. (2006, May/June). *The leader's role in pay systems and organizational performance.* Retrieved from http://aubreydaniels.com/system/files/Leaders%20Role%20in%20Pay.pdf

Heuer, R. J. (2007). *Psychology of intelligence analysis: Chapter 8: Analysis of competing hypotheses.* Retrieved from https://www.cia.gov/library/center-for-the-study-of-intelligence/csi-publications/books-and-monographs/psychology-of-intelligence-analysis/art11.html

Horman, R. L. (1997). *The use of the evidence evaluation matrix in accident investigation.* Retrieved from http://www.iprr.org/lib/qcp03.html

Nuclear Regulatory Commission (NRC). (2001, September). *The human performance evaluation process: A resource for reviewing the identification and resolution of human performance problems.* (NUREG/CR-6751). Washington, DC: Office of Nuclear Regulatory Research.

Nuclear Regulatory Commission (NRC). (2011, February). *Inspection for one or two white inputs in a strategic performance area.* (NRC Inspection Procedure 95001). Washington, DC: US NRC Office of Nuclear Reactor Regulation.

Nuclear Regulatory Commission (NRC). (2011, May). *Licensee event report 2011-003, revision 1, for the Fort Calhoun Station.* Retrieved from http://pbadupws.nrc.gov/docs/ML1113/ML111370123.pdf

Nuclear Regulatory Commission (NRC). (2012, October). *Licensee event report (LER) No. 2012-003-00: Pressurizer heater bundle leak. Retrieved from* http://pbadupws.nrc.gov/docs/ML1229/ML12298A035.pdf

For Further Reading

B&W Pantex. (2008). *High reliability operations: A practical guide to avoid the systems accident.* Amarillo, TX: Babcock & Wilcox Technical Services Pantex LLC.

Hartley, R. S., Swaim, D. J., & Corcoran W. R. (2008). *Causal factors analysis: An approach for organizational learning.* Amarillo, TX: Babcock & Wilcox Technical Services Pantex LLC.

Step 6

Plan Corrective Actions

**It is not necessary to change.
Survival is not mandatory.**

— W. Edwards Deming, Statistician

After completing the first five steps, you should have identified the causes of the incident that need to be corrected. In this section you will learn how to develop and implement a solution that will reduce or eliminate the causes. There are many techniques to use when planning your corrective actions. There are also tools to evaluate the potential effectiveness of the corrective actions you will be proposing to key decision-makers. Your action plan's top goal is to prevent recurrence of a similar incident.

**To prevent recurrence, two general types of corrective action are essential.
Your plan needs to do one of the following:**

1. Change the design of the hardware or the design of the process associated with the incident.

2. Change the behavior of job performers.

A quality corrective action plan well implemented will sustain a behavior change. Your corrective action plan will need to include some variation of the following basic steps needed to sustain a behavior change in your business:

1. Define standard/expectations. (Find out what "good" looks like by benchmarking, etc.) Get the "right" mental model.

2. Communicate standard/expectations (by training, newsletters, etc.).

3. Monitor expected behaviors and results (by observing, by performance indicators, etc.).

4. Feedback [+/-]. (Positively reinforce desired behaviors; correct inappropriate behaviors.)

If you fail to ensure each of these four steps is included in your plan, you should expect the behavior to recur and, possibly, a similar incident.

> **Note:** If you are proposing corrective actions that will adjust the defense-in-depth of your business, it is good to remember that the more reliant a defense is on human action, the weaker it will be.

Use Table 6.1 as a checklist to guide you through Step 6 of the investigation. Step 6 contains two sets of tools (listed by section number) to help plan corrective actions: 1) tools to develop an action plan, and 2) tools to determine how effective your action plan was.

6.1 Action Plan

    6.1.1 Change Management

    6.1.2 S.M.A.R.T.E.R.

    6.1.3 Barriers and Aids Analysis [Pros and Cons]

    6.1.4 Solution Selection Tree

    6.1.5 Solution Selection Matrix

    6.1.6 Contingency Plan

    6.1.7 Lessons To Be Learned Communication Plan

    6.1.8 Institutionalization/Active Coaching

6.2 Effectiveness Review

    6.2.1 Performance Indicator Development

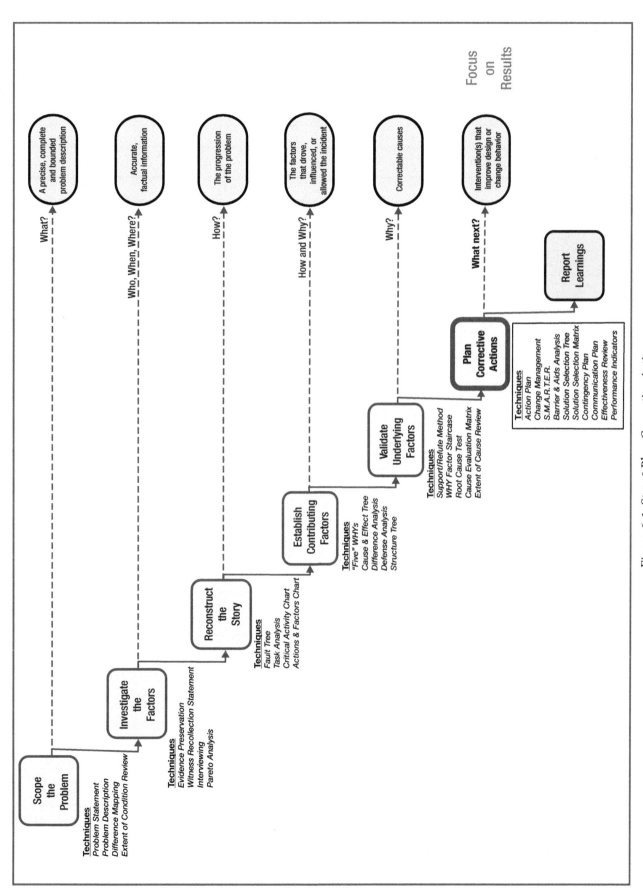

Figure 6-1. Step 6 Plan Corrective Actions

Table 6-1. Step 6 Jump Start Checklist

☑ Behaviors [Sub-Tasks]	Tools/Techniques	Required		
☐ Plan an intervention that is sustainable and will be institutionalized.	*Action Plan*	RC		
☐ Include actions to address extent of condition findings.		RC	AC	AD
☐ Include actions to address extent of cause findings.		RC		
☐ FOR each action, state WHO does WHAT by WHEN.	*Action Plan*	RC	AC	AD
☐ *Include interim, immediate, and remedial actions.*		RC	AC	AD
☐ *Goal: Develop simple and practical solutions.*	*Solution Selection Matrix*	RC	AC	AD
☐ *Goal: Correct the adverse condition (the problem, the incident).*		RC	AC	AD
☐ *Goal: Correct the cause(s).*	*Solution Selection Tree*	RC	AC	
☐ *Goal: Minimize the potential for recurrence of contributing factor(s).*	*Barrier and Aids Analysis [Pros/Cons]*	RC	AC	
☐ *Goal: Prevent recurrence of root cause(s).*	*Critical Activity Chart*	RC		
☐ *Differentiate between global and localized corrective actions.*		RC		
☐ *Address individual performance issues separate from organizational.*		RC		
☐ *Plan for unforeseen incidents or possibilities.*	*Contingency Plan*	RC		
☐ Validate the proposed corrective action plan meets **SMART[ER].**	*S.M.A.R.T.E.R.*	RC	AC	AD
☐ *Specific: State exactly what is to be done; what is expected. Focus on results.*		RC	AC	
☐ *Measurable: State the desired outcome so people can see when it's done.*	*Performance Indicator*	RC	AC	
☐ *Attainable: The physical action must be doable and realistic.*		RC	AC	
☐ *Related: FOR each cause, tie actions whose benefit is worth the cost.*	*Cost-Benefit Analysis*	RC	AC	
☐ *Time-sensitive: Set due dates before next opportunity for a problem to recur.*		RC	AC	
☐ *Effective: Assure actions are "anchored." Evaluate using safety precedence sequence.*		RC		
☐ *Reviewed: Have someone independent (a user) look for unwanted side effects.*		RC		
☐ Verify action plan meets change management policy requisites.	*Change Management*	RC		
☐ Generate a trackable activity with acceptance criteria to evaluate long-term effectiveness in preventing recurrence.	*Effectiveness Review*	RC		
☐ Write a communication plan.	*Lessons To Be Learned*	RC		
☐ Critical action completed. Involve responsible management.	*Management Sponsor*	RC		

RC = Root Cause Analysis; **AC** = Apparent Cause Analysis; **AD** = Adverse

☑ **Results** Required [R]/Desired [D]			
☐ Either a **SMART**[ER] changed, improved design (equipment/procedure) or	RC_R	AC_R	AD_R
☐ **SMART**[ER] change(s) in behavior or process (individual, leader, organizational).	RC_R	AC_D	AD_D
☐ Once corrective actions implemented, a changed/improved **SMART**[ER] organization.	RC_R	AC_D	AD_D
☐ A documented change management plan.	RC_R		
☐ A documented effectiveness review plan with measurable acceptance criteria.	RC_R		
☐ A documented communication plan.	RC_R		

6.1   Action Plan

What is it?

An *action plan* lists all the things that must be done to implement the solution or enhancement. Whatever the format, an action plan should state what steps need to be taken to implement the solution, who is responsible to complete each step, and when the step should be completed (due date).

Why is it useful?

The action plan helps explain a solution's implementation to key decision-makers, to management, and to peers. It also ensures the corrective actions are implemented methodically.

When is it used?

In Step 6 (Plan Corrective Actions), the action plan is used to explain to management how the solution will be implemented. The action plan also helps personnel implement the solution.

How is it done?

General Steps

1. WRITE the problem description at the top of the action plan (Table 6-1 or Table 6-2).

2. WRITE down each factor that contributed (i.e., direct cause, apparent cause, contributing cause, root cause) to the problem/incident.

3. DEVELOP an action step or steps (solution/intervention) to address each contributing factor.

> **Note:** The critical activity chart may be helpful in identifying these steps. A revised flowchart may assist the implementation of an improved work process.

    3.1. IDENTIFY the equipment and people needed to complete each step.

    3.2. DESIGNATE a person (owner) to be responsible for completion of each step.

    3.3. IDENTIFY a due date for completion of each step.

4. STATE the corrective actions (CA) in the following format to show the cause connection ("Line of Sight"):

The (PROBLEM STATEMENT) was caused [driven, triggered, released, influenced, permitted/allowed, aggravated] by (ROOT CAUSE STATEMENT 1) and (ROOT CAUSE STATEMENT 2) and can be prevented [fixed] by (CA PLAN STATEMENTS for RC1) and (CA PLAN STATEMENTS for RC 2).

Table 6-2. Action Plan (Style 1)

Condition Report #:	CR Creation Date:		Review Date:	
Problem Description:				
Cause/Factor/Extent Being Addressed	**Corrective Action (CA)/Deliverable**		**Responsible Owner Organization/Individual**	**Due Date**

Table 6-3. Action Plan (Style 2)

Condition Report#	CR Creation Date:		Review Date:	
Problem Description:				
Extent of Condition (EOCo)				
Direct Cause (DC)				
Root Cause 1 (RC-1)				
Root Cause 2 (RC-2)				
Contributing Factor 1 (CF-1)				
Contributing Factor 2 (CF-2)				
Extent of Cause (EOCa)				
Factor #	**Corrective Action (CA)/Deliverable**		**Responsible Owner Organization/Individual**	**Due Date**
EOCo				
DC				
RC-1				
RC-2				
CF-1				
CF-2				
EOCa				

Task: Develop a Corrective Action Plan
Initial Condition: Business has experienced a significant incident.

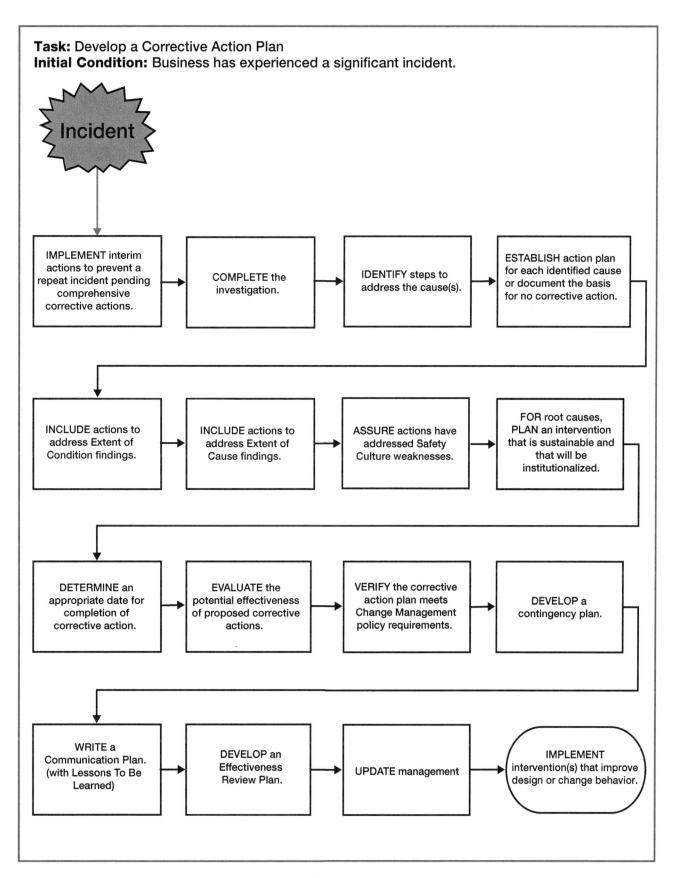

Figure 6-2. Detailed Corrective Action Planning

Detailed Steps (see Figure 6-2)

1. WHEN an incident occurs, line organizations DEFINE and IMPLEMENT the immediate actions necessary to bound, control, and mitigate the incident; restore compliance; and address the extent of condition. Record on action plan.

2. IDENTIFY interim corrective actions to prevent a repeat incident pending the root cause analysis and implementation of planned corrective actions. Record on action plan.

3. PLAN; then IMPLEMENT remedial corrective actions to fix or to restore a situation or equipment to an acceptable state or capability. Record on action plan.

4. COMPLETE the investigation including identification and analysis of causal factors.

5. WRITE the problem description at the top of the action plan.

6. WRITE down each factor that contributed (i.e., direct cause, apparent cause, contributing cause, root cause) to the problem/incident.

7. DEVELOP an action step or steps (solution/intervention) to address the contributing cause(s) and root cause(s) in order to prevent or mitigate recurrence of the incident/problem.

> **Note:** Implemented as a total package, the corrective action plan will preclude repetition of the incident, accident, or significant condition adverse to quality. With the possible exception of physical changes (i.e., engineered controls), there is no single corrective action step that resolves a human performance difficulty when there is a need to change an individual, leader, or organizational behavior.

   7.1. DEVELOP alternative actions which address the causes/underlying factors (Table 6-4).

Table 6-4. Alternative Actions for each Cause

Cause _____	↗ → ↘	Solution 1 _____ Solution 2 _____ Solution 3 _____

   7.2. EVALUATE alternative courses of action using criteria such as the following:

- Cost benefit.
- Necessary resources.
- Timeframe.
- Potential impact.
- Multiple impact.
- Likely resistance.
- Permanence.
- Complexity.
- Adverse consequences.

   7.3. DECIDE which alternatives will be recommended to management.

   7.4. ENSURE corrective actions address the causes/underlying factors.

7.5. VERIFY that the proposed corrective actions:

  ‣ Make sense when reviewed against the cause(s).

  ‣ Focus appropriately on organizational, programmatic, and individual performance issues.

  ‣ Focus correctly, showing interventions/actions that will prevent or mitigate recurrence.

7.6. VERIFY factors affecting safety significance have been identified, considered, and adequately addressed in the corrective action plan, including industrial safety, nuclear safety, radiological safety, and common mode failure.

> **Note**: The critical activity chart may be helpful to identify these steps. A revised flowchart may assist the implementation of an improved work process.

8. FOR root causes addressing significant conditions adverse to quality, PLAN an overall intervention that is sustainable and that will be institutionalized. Institutionalize the intervention (sustain the change) by including the following phases (general steps) in the plan (see Table 6-5):

8.1. OBTAIN the "right" mental model; then DEFINE the standard/expectations. (Find out what "good" looks like by benchmarking, etc.)

8.2. COMMUNICATE standard/expectations (by procedures, training, newsletters, etc.).

8.3. MONITOR expected behaviors and results (by observing, by performance indicators, etc.).

8.4. PROVIDE feedback [+/-]. (Positively reinforce desired behaviors; correct inappropriate behaviors.)

Table 6-5. General Steps to Sustain a Behavior Change

Cause Being Addressed	Corrective Action Plan	Owner	Due Date
	1. Right Picture phase		
	2. Communicate phase		
	3. Monitor phase		
	4. Feedback phase		

9. ESTABLISH an action plan for each identified cause or DOCUMENT the basis for no corrective action.

  ‣ INCLUDE actions to address extent of condition findings.

  ‣ INCLUDE actions to address extent of cause findings.

  ‣ ENSURE actions have addressed safety culture weaknesses.

9.1. IDENTIFY the equipment needed to complete each step.

9.2. DESIGNATE a person (owner) to be responsible for completion of each step. FOR each action, STATE WHO does WHAT by WHEN.

9.3. DETERMINE an appropriate target date for completion of corrective action step (as applicable) and ASSIGN based on:

  ‣ Resources available.

> ‣ Remedial actions taken to date.
> ‣ Assessment of impact on plant operation.
> ‣ Likelihood or risk of recurrence.
> ‣ Significance of recurrence.
> ‣ Safety significance of the issue.

10. STATE the corrective actions in the following format to show the cause connection ("Line of Sight"):

    The (PROBLEM STATEMENT) was caused [driven, triggered, released, influenced, permitted/allowed, aggravated] by (ROOT CAUSE STATEMENT 1) and (ROOT CAUSE STATEMENT 2) and can be prevented [fixed] by (CA PLAN STATEMENTS for RC1) and (CA PLAN STATEMENTS for RC 2). See Table 6-6 for words to avoid and use when prescribing an action.

11. PROVIDE justification for corrective action completion schedules when corrective actions will not be, or have not been, taken at the first opportunity.

Table 6-6. Action Words to Avoid and to Use

It's easy to spot weak corrective actions. They usually include verbs like:	Strong corrective actions require specific, measurable, and timely change. Try these:
☒ Analyze	✓ Install
☒ Evaluate	✓ Modify
☒ Review	✓ Revise
☒ Assess	✓ Establish
☒ Determine	✓ Implement
☒ Perform study	✓ Perform
☒ Initiate actions to…	✓ Require
☒ Consider	✓ Generate
☒ Propose	
☒ Obtain approval for…	

12. EVALUATE the potential effectiveness of proposed corrective actions and DECIDE which alternatives will be recommended to management.

    > ‣ FOR less significant issues, VERIFY the actions meet the S.M.A.R.T. criteria: Specific, Measurable, Accountable, Reasonable, Timely (International Atomic Energy Agency, 2005).
    > ‣ FOR more significant issues, VERIFY the actions meet the S.M.A.R.T.E.R. criteria: Specific, Measurable, Accountable, Reasonable, Timely, Effective, Reviewed (International Atomic Energy Agency, 2005).

13. VERIFY the corrective action plan meets change management policy requirements.

14. DEVELOP a contingency plan using the following steps:
    ‣ LIST the action steps of the action plan.
    ‣ FOR each action step, LIST any major potential problems. These problems may be identified through brainstorming, consensus, or other appropriate techniques.
    ‣ FOR each major potential problem, LIST the action that will be taken if the problem occurs.

15. WRITE a communication plan (with lessons to be learned).

16. GENERATE an effectiveness review plan — a trackable activity with acceptance criteria to evaluate long-term sustainability (see section 6.2). Include the following in the effectiveness review plan:
    ‣ Method — Describe the means that will be used to verify that the actions taken had the desired outcome.
    ‣ Attributes — Describe the particular process characteristics to be monitored or evaluated for effectiveness (e.g., process timeliness, component alignment or position, system performance).
    ‣ Success — Establish the acceptance criteria (measures and objectives) for the attributes to be monitored or evaluated.
    ‣ Timeliness — Define the optimum time to perform the effectiveness review.

> **Note:** Schedule the due date far enough in the future to allow sufficient time for corrective actions to be implemented and challenged. The timing of the review should allow sufficient time for the corrective actions to be effective, but should also be performed as early as practicable to verify effectiveness before defenses implemented by the corrective actions are required to preclude recurrence of the original significant condition or incident.

17. DOCUMENT the effectiveness review plan and effectiveness review acceptance criteria.

18. UPDATE the management sponsor to ensure that management understands the interventions needed to address the contributing and root causes in order to prevent recurrence.

The following tools, tables, and techniques can be used to help ensure the overall corrective action plan prevents recurrence of the serious incident or the same significant conditions adverse to quality:

    ‣ 6.1.1 Change Management
    ‣ 6.1.2 S.M.A.R.T.E.R.
    ‣ 6.1.3 Barriers and Aids Analysis [Pros and Cons]
    ‣ 6.1.4 Solution Selection Tree
    ‣ 6.1.5 Solution Selection Matrix
    ‣ 6.1.6 Contingency Plan
    ‣ 6.1.7 Lessons To Be Learned Communication Plan
    ‣ 6.1.8 Institutionalization/Active Coaching

Table 6-7. Action Plan Example to Ensure Better Cause Analyses

Action Plan (Style 1)			
Condition Report #: 2011-1998	CR Creation Date: 4/4/2011		Review Date: 5/12/2011
Problem Description: Cause evaluations have frequently focused on specific events or groups involved and have not adequately assessed broader vulnerabilities to similar events. The narrow cause evaluation scope has resulted in corrective actions that were not effective in preventing repeat or similar events.			
Cause/Factor/Extent Being Addressed	**Corrective Action (CA)/Deliverable**	**Responsible Owner Organization/Individual**	**Due Date**
1. Interim action for inappropriately focused root cause analyses.	Send an e-mail to department heads who have the potential to become management sponsors for Level A CRs and to trained root cause analysts to make them aware of problems with inappropriately focused root cause analyses as documented in CR 2011-1998. The interim actions that sponsors and analysts need to take are summarized as follows: ☐ Insist on a clear charter and a thorough pre-job brief for your root cause analysis. ☐ Use a structured root cause analysis process. Try the WHY factors staircase technique. ☐ Insist that your management get involved at critical steps of the root cause analysis. ☐ Use the guidance on the report template to help "show your work."	Root Cause Analysis Coordinator	Complete 4/11/2011
2. (Resource allocation) Management is not consistently supporting the corrective action program with resources (mostly people and time) dedicated to resolving the problem.	All site department managers will designate one individual to be trained in root cause analysis and then perform root cause analysis as a core job function.	Chief Nuclear Officer	6/1/2011
	Train designated department personnel in root cause analysis techniques.	Root Cause Analysis Coordinator	7/1/2011
3. (Proficiency) Individuals performing or evaluating the analyses have insufficient skills and proficiency.	Train designated department personnel in root cause analysis techniques.	Root Cause Analysis Coordinator	7/1/2011
	Train designated corrective action review board members in what "good" root cause analyses look like.	Performance Improvement peer	7/15/2011
4. (Procedure improvements) Guidance provided in the Corrective Action Program (CAP) procedure and in the Root Cause Manual (RCM) is not sufficient to compensate for the lack of management understanding and, thereby, ensure the appropriate depth of analysis is identified and documented.	Benchmark industry best practices for management review of cause evaluations.	Root Cause Analysis Coordinator	6/14/2011
	Revise CAP procedure and RCM to reflect industry best practices for management review of cause evaluations.	Performance Improvement Department Manager	6/28/2011
	Incorporate industry best practices for management review of cause evaluations into corrective action review board training.	Performance Improvement Department Manager	7/6/2011
	Train designated corrective action review board members on industry best practices for management review of cause evaluations.	Performance Improvement peer	7/15/2011

6.1.1   Change Management

What is it?

Every corrective action plan is developed to bring about change. The *change management* checklist below will help an investigative team include key elements in an intervention that is aimed at improving hardware design or changing behavior for a sustained period of time. Table 6-8 includes some of the ramifications of leaving out one of the elements of bringing about a sustained change. The table contains a simple checklist of key elements for sustaining change and what happens to people when an element is not sufficiently addressed.

Table 6-8. Change Management Elements

Key Elements	Definitions	Without Key Element, there is …
☐ **WII-FO***	Business Case, Gaps to Plug, Need Recognized	No Sense of Urgency
☐ **Right Picture**	Mental Model, Vision, Desired Future State	Ambiguity
☐ **Communication**	Message Sent and Received, Stakeholder Consultation	Misunderstanding
☐ **Action Plan**	Outcomes, Methods, Resources, Schedule	Sputtering Starts
☐ **Resources**	Time, People, Money, Equipment	Frustration
☐ **WII-FM****	Motivation, Rewards, Recognition, Celebration	Slow Progress
☐ **Skills**	Training, Practice, Preparation	Apprehension

* WII-FO: What's In It For the Organization
** WII-FM: What's In It For Me

Why is it useful?

To preclude a problem from recurrence depends on effective change management. When managers make complex and far-reaching changes, the chance for error is high. A structured approach to planning and implementing change reduces the potential for error by managers and supervisors.

When is it used?

In the beginning of Step 6 (Plan Corrective Actions), change management elements must be given consideration.

How is it done?

Consider each of the attributes. If one is missing, decide what will be done (if anything) but understand fully the risk of omission of the element. The following change process is one of many, but is suggested here as it specifically relates to human performance improvement (Learning Point Associates, 2011):

- (WII-FO) ESTABLISH a sense of urgency. Identify and discuss the actual or potential crisis or major opportunities, persuading "leaders" and managers to personally do something about it. This was a serious business incident; so there has to be a business case.

- (Right Picture) DEVELOP a clear vision and strategy. Paint a clear picture of the desired future state of human performance and develop a deliberate approach to achieving that future state. Eliminate inconsistencies with the vision.

- (Communication) COMMUNICATE the vision and goals. Align the leadership team. Obtain agreement and commitment from the members of the senior managers of the organization to support the change as a team.

- (Action Plan) DEVELOP a change management action plan, completing the following steps in order:

    1. (Outcomes) State the desired results (i.e., the vision). WHAT?

    2. (Methods) When a clear vision of what must be achieved is at hand then the possible approaches that would lead to that goal are considered. Ingrain the new methods in the culture. Leaders clearly connect new values, beliefs, and behaviors with organizational success. Reinforce people whose performance is consistent with the new culture. HOW?

    3. (Resources) The time, people, and money that it would require are considered after selecting the method that would result most successfully (not just quickly or cheaply) in the desired outcome. WHEN? WHO? HOW MUCH?

- (WII-FM) EXPLAIN to personnel "what's in it for them" using various forums, especially face to face. Show people how they personally fit into the new vision. Engage the workforce for broad-based action. Seek buy-in from the workforce, working with them in a spirit of teamwork, giving and receiving feedback. Generate short-term wins and consolidate gains. Plan for and build on visible successes, openly celebrating and rewarding those successes when achieved. Show commitment to the change by revising key policies and processes.

- (Skills) TRAIN personnel on the vision and clear measurable goals.

6.1.2   S.M.A.R.T.E.R.

What is it?
Short (2012) suggests testing the quality of the corrective actions you are recommending to management using *S.M.A.R.T.E.R.* criteria. S.M.A.R.T.E.R. criteria are used to test corrective actions to preclude repetition that comes out of the root cause analyses of more significant incidents. S.M.A.R.T.E.R. stands for Specific, Measurable, Attainable, Related, Time-sensitive, Effective, Reviewed.

> **Note:** S.M.A.R.T. criteria would be used to test the quality of corrective actions that are the result of apparent or basic cause analysis for less significant incidents or problems.

Why is it useful?
Using the S.M.A.R.T.E.R. technique helps an investigator recommend corrective actions that have an excellent chance of preventing the incident or a similar incident from happening again. This technique ensures the corrective action is within the control of the organization and will provide reasonable value for the cost of implementing and sustaining.

When is it used?
In Step 6 (Plan Corrective Actions), the S.M.A.R.T.E.R. checklist criteria are used after root causes are identified and whenever actions are being developed to prevent or mitigate future occurrences of a similar incident or adverse condition.

How is it done?

Test each corrective action being recommended using the S.M.A.R.T.E.R. checklist criteria on the form (Table 6-9). Document the conclusion (Yes ☐ No ☐) about each of the seven aspects of the corrective action.

Table 6-9. Checklist for Evaluating Each Corrective Action Using S.M.A.R.T.E.R.

Specific	☐ Does action step describe exactly (clearly) what is expected to be done when? ☐ Does action step begin with an action verb (such as revise, install, modify)? ☐ Does the action step AVOID words like analyze, review, evaluate, consider? ☐ Is there one action per corrective action (i.e., multiple tasks not grouped together)?	**Specific?** Yes ☐ No ☐

Measurable	☐ Can the desired outcome be seen physically?
	☐ Does action have a verifiable end point or end product (i.e., is it closeable)?
	☐ Action avoids use of terms such as all, ongoing, continue, and improve?
	☐ Are quantitative criteria defined for measuring success? Standard measurement parameters include:
	  ▸ Safety (dose, safety monitor risk, first aid incidents, recordables)
	  ▸ Quality (score card results, housekeeping, rework)
	  ▸ Quantity (person-hours, incident rate, number of CRs)
	  ▸ Frequency (observations per week)
	  ▸ Timeliness (outage duration, tardies)
		Measurable?
		Yes ☐ No ☐

Attainable	☐ Is desired outcome actionable? ☐ Are correct (qualified/available) individuals assigned to perform the action item? ☐ All criteria agreed to by stakeholder(s)/responsible individuals? ☐ Do responsible individuals accept due dates for completing the action item? ☐ Is desired outcome achievable? ☐ Is the corrective action good business? Makes good business sense? ☐ Has the cost/benefit ratio been calculated? ☐ Has the return on investment been calculated? ☐ Are required resources available?	**Attainable?** Yes ☐ No ☐
Related	☐ Identifies the performance gap (the difference between desired and present condition) that is being closed. ☐ Is there a logical tie (line of sight) between the performance gap and the causes? ☐ Is there a logical tie between the causes and the corrective actions?	**Related?** Yes ☐ No ☐
Time-sensitive	☐ Will we be able to operate the facilities/use the process before all corrective actions are implemented? ☐ Does the due date allow sufficient time for proper implementation of the corrective action? ☐ Are corrective action due dates set before the next opportunity for a problem to occur in this area? ☐ Do the due dates allow sufficient time to implement training and monitor for sustained performance? ☐ Are the due dates timely considering the significance of the incident? ☐ Is the timeframe for evaluation of effectiveness considered?	**Timely?** Yes ☐ No ☐
Effective	☐ Is the corrective action fixing the underlying factor (root cause) sustainable? ☐ Will the corrective action be anchored (institutionalized) in the business? ☐ Do the corrective actions address extent of condition and extent of cause? ☐ Has a physical fix been considered instead of using human intervention (safety order of precedence)?	**Effective?** Yes ☐ No ☐
Reviewed by customer/SME*	☐ Has an independent individual (a user or subject matter expert) looked for unwanted side effects? ☐ Has the corrective action been reviewed for negative results (unintended consequences) that should reasonably be expected?	**Reviewed?** Yes ☐ No ☐

*SME: Subject Matter Expert

6.1.2.1 Safety Precedence Sequence
(Hierarchy of Corrective Action Effectiveness)

When developing corrective actions, consider a simple hierarchy of corrective action effectiveness (Department of Defense, 2012). Identify potential mishap risk mitigation alternatives and the expected effectiveness of each alternative or method. Mishap risk mitigation is an iterative process that culminates when the residual mishap risk has been reduced to a level acceptable to the appropriate authority. The system safety design order of precedence for mitigating identified hazards is:

1. **ELIMINATE hazards through design selection.**

   If unable to eliminate an identified hazard, reduce the associated mishap risk to an acceptable level through design selection. Appropriate design/hardware changes are the most foolproof ways to prevent recurrence of undesirable incidents. The human element is virtually removed, and reliance on safety devices, procedures, training, and judgment is minimal. **(The cost vs. the benefit must be considered.)**

2. **INCORPORATE safety devices.**

   If unable to eliminate the hazard through design selection, reduce the mishap risk to an acceptable level using protective safety features or devices. This is the next most effective type of corrective action. Again, human involvement is minimal, since safety devices are automatic, reducing dependence on training, judgment, etc. (Of course, these devices must be properly designed, installed, and maintained.)

3. **PROVIDE warning devices.**

   If safety devices do not adequately lower the mishap risk of the hazard, include a detection and warning system to alert personnel to the particular hazard. The third most effective type of corrective action involves the use of warning devices, such as alarms, sirens, and lights. These are considered automatic, in that they require no human action for their activation, but their potential effectiveness is less than the previous two types of corrective action due to the need for a proper human response to the warning device in order for the corrective action to be completed.

4. **USE procedures and administrative controls.**

   Where it is impractical to eliminate hazards through design selection or to reduce the associated risk to an acceptable level with safety and warning devices, incorporate special procedures and training. Procedures may include the use of personal protective equipment. For hazards assigned catastrophic or critical mishap severity categories, avoid using warning, caution, or other written advisory as the only risk reduction method. Reliance on procedures and other administrative controls is considered to be the weakest form of corrective action due to the total dependence on the proper human response. (People are the weakest link.)

Safety precedence sequence number (see Figure 6-3) is a tool that can be used to manage risk.

1. Extreme risk: Design for minimum hazard. Include fail-safe features and redundancy.

2. High risk: Control hazards to an acceptable risk level with safety devices.

3. Important: Provide devices that warn targets of hazards.

4. Moderate: Develop procedures to reduce and control hazards.

5. Uneconomic: Select, train, supervise, and motivate personnel to work safely in presence of hazard.

6. Negligible: Identify residual hazards, and accept the risks at the proper management level.

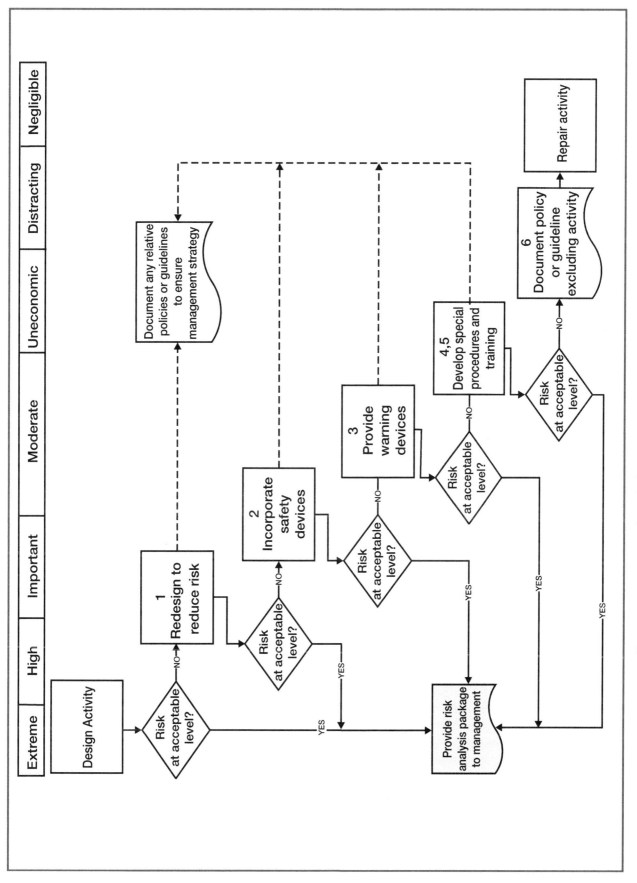

Figure 6-3. Manage Risks with the Safety Order of Precedence (Another View)

6.1.3　Barriers and Aids Analysis (Pros and Cons)

What is it?

Barriers and aids analysis identifies factors that resist a change or corrective action (barriers) or facilitate change (aids).

Why is it useful?

This technique pinpoints the driving and restraining forces of ideas or options; then helps develop strategies to overcome inherent barriers and to make maximum use of available aids.

How is it done?

Steps to barriers and aids analysis (Tables 6-10 and 6-11):

1. IDENTIFY the objective, task, or concern (i.e., pose the idea or option).

2. LIST barriers (forces challenging change).

3. LIST aids (forces facilitating change).

Tables 6-10. Example of Barriers and Aids

Examples of barriers (-)	Examples of aids (+)
☐ Higher cost compared with other corrective actions. ☐ No support from other employees. ☐ May be difficult to communicate. ☐ Does not fully address the cause.	☐ Low cost corrective action. ☐ Increases awareness of competition issues. ☐ Successfully implemented in other departments/at other sites. ☐ Improves safety of the workplace.

4. RANK listed items as high, medium, or low.

5. MATCH aids which balance or overcome barriers.

6. LIST matching barriers and aids.

7. LIST non-matching barriers and identify (brainstorm) any offsetting aids.

8. LIST non-matching aids and identify any offsetting barriers.

9. IDENTIFY items needing group action using your rankings (high, medium, or low).

10. DEVELOP the corrective action plan.

Table 6-11. Cost-Benefit Form

Consequences of not changing ($) _____

Alternative	Cost of Changes ($)	Benefits ($)	Cost/Benefit Ratio	Payback Period
A				
B				
C				
D				
E				

6.1.4   Solution Selection Tree

What is it?

A *solution selection tree* (Figure 6-4) is a barriers and aids analysis diagram used to show the relationship between an incident, its causes, and potential corrective actions. It also identifies the pros and cons for each potential corrective action to determine the practicality of implementing that action as part of the resolution for the incident.

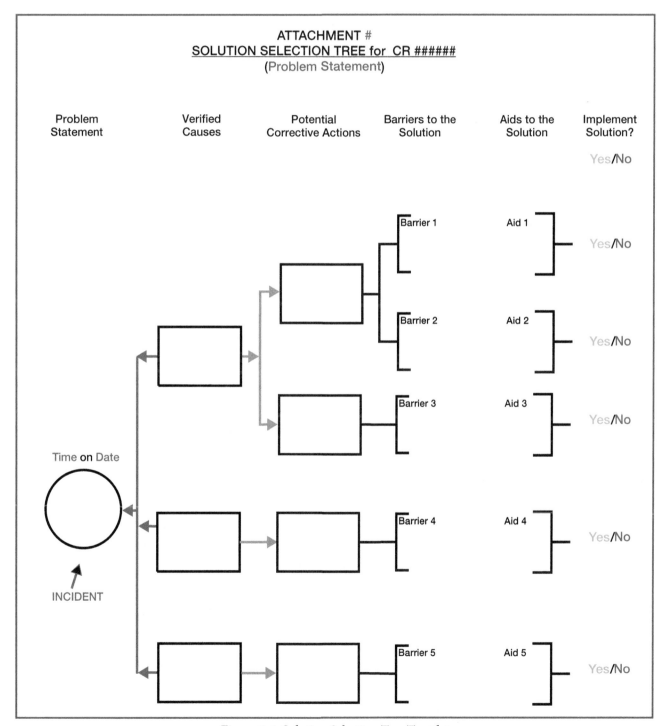

Figure 6-4. Solution Selection Tree Template

Why is it useful?

The tree shows decision-makers a clear "line of sight." Use the solution selection tree to link each potential corrective action with the incident and its cause(s). Ultimately the solution selection tree will help the organization decide on the best corrective action(s).

When is it used?

Use the solution selection tree in Step 6 (Plan Corrective Actions) to evaluate a list of corrective actions to determine those which should be implemented to preclude repetition of a similar incident or adverse condition.

How is it done?

1. DOCUMENT the problem statement in the circle (the reason for the investigation).

2. In the next column, DOCUMENT the verified cause(s) for the incident.

3. From the list of potential interventions, LIST the solutions that will address each cause. Realize the same corrective action may be listed for more than one cause.

4. IDENTIFY the barriers and aids for each solution. Barriers are factors that will challenge the effective implementation of the solution. Aids are factors that facilitate the solution. Try to identify the three or four largest barriers and aids for each solution.

5. Considering the barriers and aids for each potential corrective action, IDENTIFY the solutions to implement.

6.1.5   Solution Selection Matrix

What is it?

The *solution selection matrix* (Agency for Healthcare Research and Quality, 2013) shows factors affecting possible improvement actions or problem solutions. To help choose the best solution, the decision-making matrix can be used with the headings shown or similar criteria. Be creative. Develop a matrix suitable to your situation (Tables 6-12 and 6-13).

Table 6-12. Solution Selection Matrix

Possible Corrective Actions	Cost to Implement (High/Low)	Tangible and Intangible Savings	# of Person Days to Apply	Who Has Commitment to This Solution?	Summary
# 1					
# 2					
# 3					

Why is it useful?

It is a proven technique for organizing information for decision-makers as well as comparing possible corrective actions and identifying information gaps.

How is it done?

1. DEVELOP alternative corrective actions which address the causes/underlying factors.

2. EVALUATE alternative courses of action using criteria such as the following:

   ▸ **Adverse consequences:** Is there any possibility that the corrective action will create an unintended, negative effect?

   ▸ **Complexity:** Is the corrective action relatively straightforward and simple, or complicated? How much change is involved?

   ▸ **Cost benefit:** Will the corrective action pay for itself over time? How soon?

   ▸ **Likely resistance:** Will the corrective action be accepted by decision-makers and the people who must implement it and live with it?

   ▸ **Measurable:** Is there some way of clearly observing whether the corrective action has an impact?

   ▸ **Multiple impact:** Will the corrective action also positively affect another problem area?

   ▸ **Necessary resources:** Are the resources (people, time, materials, and money) available to implement the corrective action?

   ▸ **Permanence:** Is the corrective action likely to remain? Or will continued follow-up action be necessary?

   ▸ **Potential impact:** To what extent will this corrective action prevent recurrence of a similar incident or adverse condition? Completely or partially?

   ▸ **Timeframe:** How long will the corrective action take to implement? How soon will results be known, even on a preliminary basis?

3. DECIDE which alternatives will be recommended to management.

4. ENSURE corrective actions address the causes/underlying factors.

Table 6-13. Solution Selection Matrix Template

Possible Corrective Actions	Cost to Implement (High/Low)	Tangible and Intangible Savings	# of Person Days to Apply	Who Has Commitment to This Solution?	Summary
# 1					
# 2					
# 3					
# 4					
# 5					

6.1.6   Contingency Plan

What is it?

A *contingency plan* is an extension of the corrective action plan. The plan maps out major potential problems that could occur during each step of the corrective action plan (Figure 6-5). The plan is then used to develop actions to take if these potential problems happen.

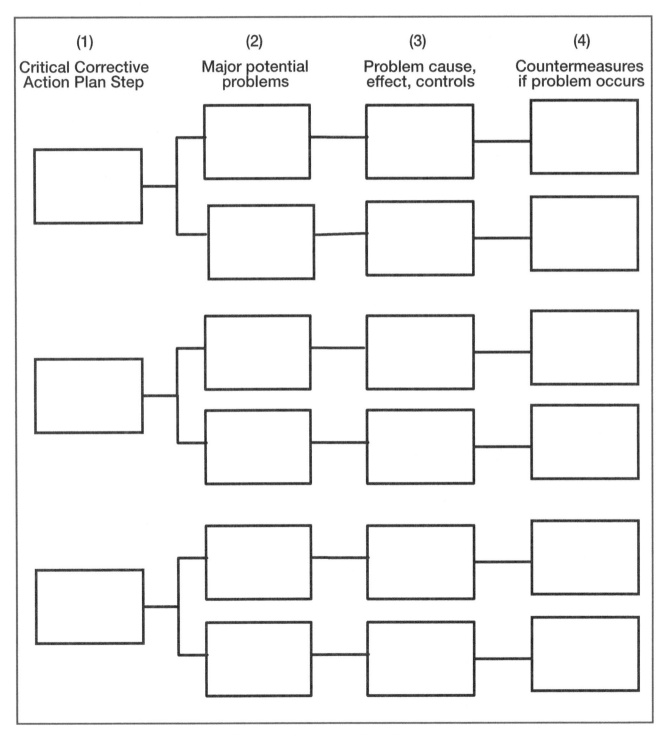

Figure 6-5. Contingency Plan Template

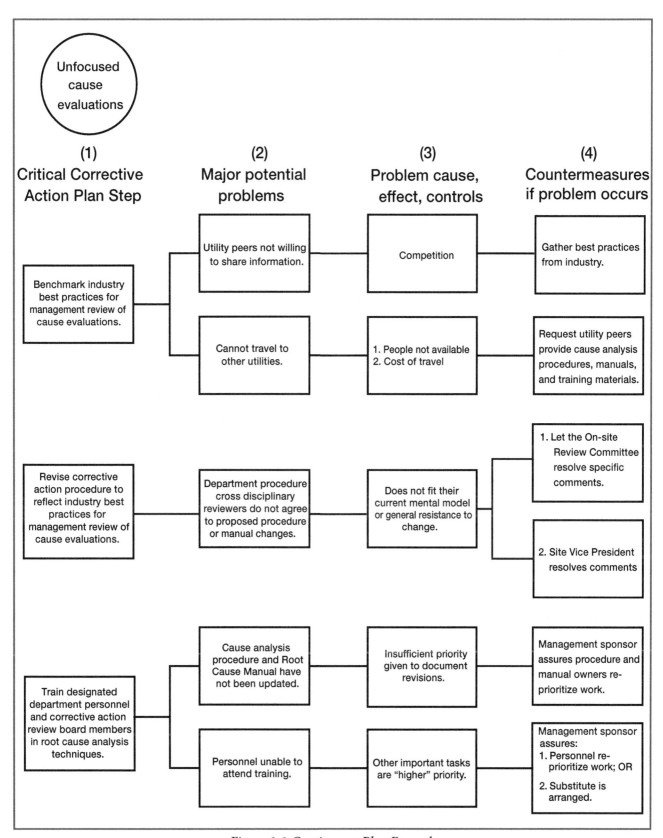

Figure 6-6. Contingency Plan Example

Why is it useful?

A contingency plan helps to anticipate problems in advance, analyze their potential consequences, and identify possible actions to reduce the risk of failure of the change. The contingency plan is especially helpful for complex implementations.

When is it used?

During Step 6 (Plan Corrective Actions), a contingency plan is developed after the corrective action plan. Simple corrective actions and small improvements may not require a contingency plan.

How is it done?

A contingency plan is developed in the form of a structure tree diagram (Figure 6-6). The following steps should be used to develop a contingency plan:

1. LIST the corrective action plan steps critical to the success of the proposed change or that are at risk because of the change.
2. FOR each action step, LIST the major potential problems that could arise. Ask "What could go wrong?"
3. IDENTIFY the effects, causes, and current controls for each potential problem.
4. FOR each major potential problem, LIST the countermeasure(s) that will be taken to reduce the risk of the problem occurring.

6.1.7   Lessons To Be Learned Communication Plan

What is it?

The *lessons to be learned communication plan* template is a form used to report the important phases of an investigation into a significant incident to the rest of the organization.

Why is it useful?

One of the most important factors in the prevention of future incidents is communication. The template is used so other organizations are informed about the causes of the significant incident so those causes can be addressed in other parts of the organization, if they exist. Also, other parts of the organization can replicate applicable corrective actions to prevent significant incidents before they occur.

When is it used?

The lessons to be learned communication plan template should be used when a significant incident has occurred within your business or within your industry. The communication plan should be developed and sent out to the organization as soon as management has approved the corrective action plan for implementation.

How is it done?

1. IDENTIFY your target audience.
2. FILL out each section of the template using the guidance on the template.
3. RECORD a concise version of each of the following important phases of the investigation in a manner that helps other people learn from the investigation:
   ‣ The problem (incident).
   ‣ The cause(s).
   ‣ The resolution (corrective action plan).
4. ENSURE the information is accurate, concise, and coherent.

Month Day, Year

Cause Analysis for **CR ####**	**Problem Statement:** *State the gap (object/deviation)*

Problem Description: *State the details of the incident. This should typically be specified in terms of what, when, where, who, consequences, and significance.*

Causes and Resolutions

Cause:

Statements of the causes of the incident or adverse condition.

Resolution:

State the planned corrective actions.

Lessons To Be Learned

State any critical precursors identified and missed opportunities. State the changes in thinking that the organization and its leadership need. State the work practices that need to be changed.

Figure 6-7. Communication Plan Template

October 12, 1999

Cause Analysis for **CR 1999-0123**	**Problem Statement:** Three workers preparing fuel for an experimental reactor received high doses of radiation; two of these workers exposed to radiation died.

Problem Description: On September 30, 1999, at 10:35 a.m. (Japanese Standard Time) three workers preparing fuel for an experimental reactor at Tokai, Japan's small fuel preparation plant of the Japan Nuclear Fuel Conversion Company (JCO), received high doses of radiation estimated at 1 to 4.5 gray equivalent (GyEq), 6.0 to 10 GyEq, and 16 to 20 GyEq respectively. The incident was classified by the Japanese authorities as Level 4 on the International Atomic Energy Agency (IAEA) International Nuclear Event Scale (INES), indicating an event without significant off-site risk.

Causes and Resolutions

Causes:

- JCO workers exceeded the mass safety limit for the precipitation tank because the JCO operational procedure used was not appropriate.
- JCO's management of field operations and supervisory oversight and approval of liquid transfers broke down.
- JCO failed to establish the proper technical management control over the preparation and approval of technical manuals and instructions.
- JCO had inadequate business management control of the operations performed in the nuclear fuel processing building.
- Japan's regulatory authority failed to perform adequate oversight to ensure compliance with the safety rules.

Resolution:

- JCO improved disaster-management facilities and coordination difficulties between the national, local, and municipal governments.
- Japan's regulatory authority performed a reassessment of the nuclear disaster prevention policy which omitted facilities like JCO.
- JCO addressed the problems encountered with communications from both the company and regulatory authorities and with notification of offsite responders that the accident was a nuclear accident.

Lessons To Be Learned

The accident resulted primarily from human error and serious breaches of safety principles. The accident had implications for the regulatory regime, safety procedures, and safety culture at the JCO facility. Three areas identified as requiring an extensive investigation are: (1) the JCO facility, including its safety-related design aspects, managerial provisions, and operational matters, (2) regulatory control, including licensing and inspection; and (3) emergency preparedness and response.

6.1.8   Institutionalization/Active Coaching Plan

What is it?

This technique institutionalizes fixes involving changes in behavior for latent organizational weaknesses (LOWs) as follows:

- Define standard/expectations. (Find out what "good" looks like by benchmarking, etc.) Get the "right" mental model.

- Communicate standard/expectations (by training, newsletters, etc.).

- Monitor expected behaviors and results (by observing, by performance indicators, etc.).

- Feedback [+/-]. (Positively reinforce desired behaviors; correct inappropriate behaviors.)

See Figure 6-8.

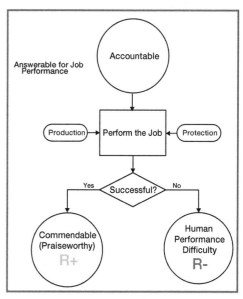

Figure 6-8. Accountability

Why is it useful?

This technique facilitates the establishment of clear accountability and alignment for production and protection. To assure proper alignment of any mental model in an organization, the corrective action plan needs to anchor the individual, leader, and organizational behaviors that will be changing. See Figure 6-9. Visions, beliefs, and values will need to change to bring about the behavior change.

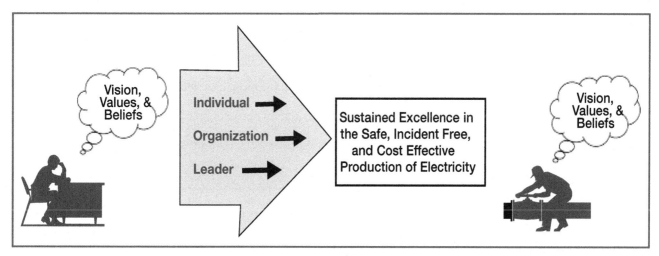

Figure 6-9. Alignment

When is it done?

During Step 6 (Plan Corrective Actions) while the overall corrective action plan is being developed.

How is it done?

FOR root causes addressing significant conditions that are adverse to quality, PLAN an overall intervention that is sustainable and that will be institutionalized (Figure 6-10). Institutionalize the intervention (sustain the change) by including the following phases (general steps) in the plan (Table 6-14):

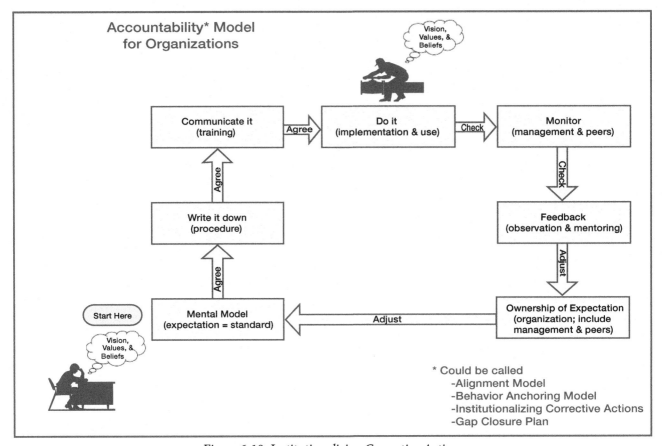

Figure 6-10. Institutionalizing Corrective Actions

1. FIND the "right" mental model; then DEFINE the standard/expectations.
   (Determine what "good" looks like by benchmarking, subject matter expert, etc.)

2. COMMUNICATE standard/expectations (by procedures, training, newsletters, etc.).

3. MONITOR expected behaviors and results (by observing, by performance indicators, etc.).

4. PROVIDE feedback [+/-]. (Positively reinforce desired behaviors; correct inappropriate behaviors.)

Table 6-14. General Institutionalization Plan

Cause Being Addressed	Corrective Action Plan	Owner	Due Date
	1. Right Picture phase		
	2. Communicate phase		
	3. Monitor phase		
	4. Feedback phase		

Active Coaching

A period of *active coaching* time needs to be designated in which a concentrated (i.e., not routine) effort will be made to actively monitor opportunities for the change in behavior (step 5 below) and provide feedback based on the observed behavior. The steps to ensure alignment and accountability are listed below and should be included in the plan:

1. TELL the job performer what you want.
   - Ensure there is a clear agreement.
   - Anticipate problems/remove barriers.

2. ENSURE job performer is skilled enough.

3. GIVE proper authority for the task.

4. PROVIDE access to needed resources.

5. BE there (location, location, location).

6. HELP the job performer make future choices.
   - Recognize accomplishments (positive reinforcement).
     - Never let great work go unnoticed.
     - When you see it, say it.
   - Maintain self-esteem when correcting/challenging.
     - Never let poor work go unnoticed.
     - Make it private and make it positive.

Essential Actions for Giving Recognition

1. IDENTIFY an occasion for giving recognition.

2. DESCRIBE the behavior immediately and as specifically as possible.

3. STATE how the behavior made a difference to you and to the organization.

Essential Actions for Correcting or Challenging Undesired Behavior

Challenge and correct undesired behaviors to help your coworkers perform better or to completely turn performance around.

1. STATE what you witnessed.

   You state: "This is what I saw…"

2. WAIT for a response.

   You wait for a response from your coworker.

3. REMIND him or her of the expectation.

   You state: "This is what I need to see….."

4. ASK for a specific resolution.

   You ask: "What can we do to make sure this happens?"

5. AGREE together.

   You restate: "So we agree……"

(Tables 6-15 and 6-16) Institutionalize fixes for latent organizational weaknesses (LOW's) as follows:

1. DEFINE standard/expectations. (Find out what "good" looks like by benchmarking, etc.)
2. COMMUNICATE standard/expectations (by training, newsletters, etc.).
3. MONITOR expected behaviors and results (by observing, by performance indicators, etc.).
4. FEEDBACK [+/-]. (Positively reinforce desired behaviors; correct inappropriate behaviors.)

Table 6-15. Institutionalization Plan Template

Factor Being Addressed	Corrective Action Plan Step	Institutionalization				Owner	Due Date
		1. Right Picture	2. Communicate	3. Monitor	4. Feedback		
		✓					
			✓				
				✓			
					✓		

Table 6-16. Evaluate Institutionalization Plan vs. S.M.A.R.T.E.R.

Factor Being Addressed	Corrective Action Plan Step	Specific	Measurable	Attainable	Related	Time-sensitive	Effective	Reviewed	Owner	Due Date
	1. Right Picture									
	2. Communicate									
	3. Monitor									
	4. Feedback									

S.M.A.R.T.E.R.

Institutionalization Plan

6.2   Effectiveness Review

What is it?
This tool outlines a strategy (Figure 6-11) for developing corrective actions; then conducting *effectiveness reviews* to determine whether corrective actions have been successful in precluding repetition of incidents (International Atomic Energy Agency, 2005).

Why is it useful?
The effectiveness review plan identifies and defines the management organization, guidelines, and key personnel necessary to plan, conduct, and document effectiveness reviews on corrective action plans intended to preclude repetition of significant problems to provide a high level of confidence that one of the following occurs:

▶   Causes are eliminated so that the same or similar incidents are not repeated.

▶   The probability of occurrence of similar incidents is significantly reduced.

▶   The consequences of a repeat occurrence are mitigated where the root causes of an incident have not been positively established.

When is it done?
Effectiveness review plans are developed during Step 6 (Plan Corrective Actions). Effectiveness reviews are done after an organization has developed and executed a corrective action plan to preclude repetition of a problem. Effectiveness reviews are scheduled for a due date far enough in the future to allow sufficient time for corrective actions to be implemented and challenged.

How is it done?
General Steps
Develop the effectiveness review plan completing each of the four attributes of a simple acronym called **M.A.S.T.**, defined as follows:

1.   METHOD – Describe the method that will be used to verify that the actions taken had the desired outcome.
2.   ATTRIBUTES – Describe the process attributes to be monitored or evaluated.
3.   SUCCESS – Establish the acceptance criteria for the attributes to be monitored or evaluated.
4.   TIMELINESS – Define the optimum time to perform the effectiveness review.

Detailed Steps

> **Note**: Steps 1 to 3 are completed by the investigator/team.

1.   DEVELOP an effectiveness review plan to evaluate the long-term effectiveness of the corrective action plan to preclude repetition (i.e., a repeat occurrence). An effectiveness review plan contains the following elements, at a minimum:
     ▶   METHODS: INCLUDE a description of the method(s) that will be used to verify effectiveness (e.g., performance testing, self-assessments, work observations, facility tours, performance indicators, documentation reviews, or interviews).
     ▶   ATTRIBUTES: INCLUDE the attributes (critical dimensions) to be measured which should demonstrate eradication, mitigation, or regulation of the root causes of the incident.

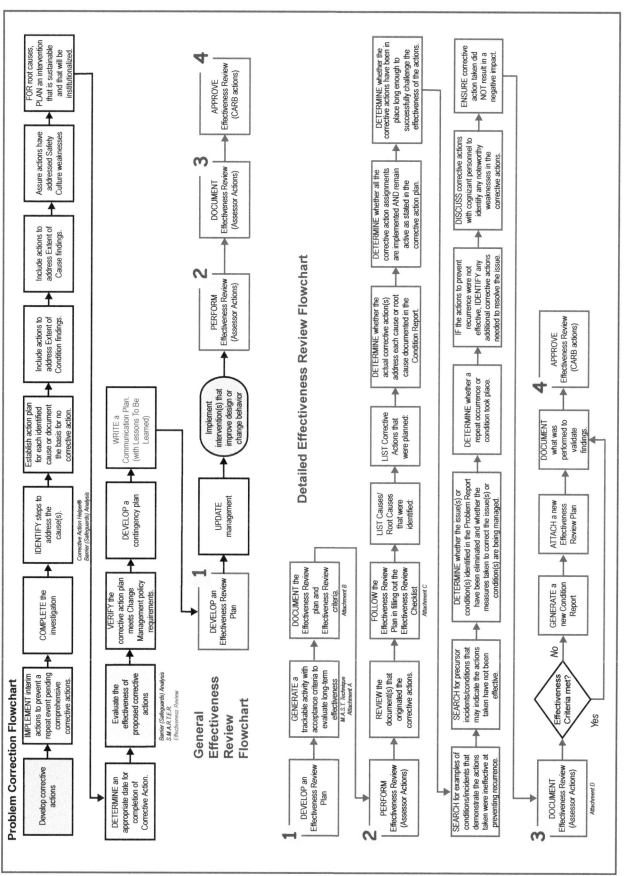

Figure 6-11. Planning Corrective Actions and Evaluating Effectiveness

> ‣ SUCCESS: DETERMINE the discrete value that will identify successful accomplishment of any particular attribute. Each attribute must have its own success criteria, which may be either quantitative or qualitative. The attributes would include the criteria, targets, or indicators that will be used in that determination. This can be either qualitative, such as performance assessments; quantitative, such as performance indicators; or a combination of the two.

> ‣ TIME: DETERMINE an appropriate date for completion of the evaluation based on the completion of the corrective action plan, including presentation of the plan results to the review committee. Be sure to allocate enough time to preclude repetition and allow for an adequate period of observation.

2. DOCUMENT the effectiveness review plan and effectiveness review acceptance criteria.

3. UPDATE the management sponsor to ensure that management understands the interventions needed to address the contributing and root causes in order to preclude repetition.

> **Note**: Steps 4 to 6 are completed by the reviewer/assessor.

4. PERFORM effectiveness review to determine success of corrective action in preventing the same OR similar incidents using criteria developed (M.A.S.T.).

   4.1. REVIEW the document(s) that originated the corrective actions.

   4.2. FOLLOW the effectiveness review plan in filling out the needed documentation.

   4.3. IDENTIFY the corrective actions to be evaluated.

   4.4. DETERMINE whether the actual corrective action(s) address each cause or root cause documented in the condition report.

   > ‣ IF "Yes," DESCRIBE how this was verified.

   > ‣ IF "No," INDICATE changes, deletions, and, reasons why the changes were made.

   4.5. DETERMINE whether all the corrective action assignments are implemented AND remain active as stated in the corrective action plan.

   > ‣ IF "Yes," STATE the corrective action assignment and describe what was actually done for each assignment.

   > ‣ IF "No," STATE the corrective action assignment(s) that was not completed. If the assignment(s) was completed, but not as stated, describe what was actually done.

   > ‣ If deviations from the original corrective action plan were not properly justified or approved, INITIATE a condition report.

   4.6. DETERMINE whether the corrective actions have been in place long enough to successfully challenge the effectiveness of the actions.

   > ‣ IF "Yes," INDICATE how this was verified.

   > ‣ IF "No," INDICATE how this was established. Initiate a tracking document to complete another review in an appropriate timeframe. Stop the review at this point. Inform management.

   4.7. PERFORM an internal operating experience review and ENSURE the following are acceptable (as applicable):

   - ✓ Equipment operating performance
   - ✓ Equipment reliability performance
   - ✓ Human performance
   - ✓ Program and process performance

- SEARCH for examples of conditions/incidents that demonstrate the actions taken were ineffective at preventing recurrence.
- SEARCH for precursor incidents/conditions that may indicate the actions taken have not been effective.

4.8. DETERMINE whether the issue(s) or condition(s) identified in the condition report have been eliminated and whether the measures taken to correct the issue(s) or condition(s) are being managed.

- IF "Yes", DOCUMENT how this was verified.
- IF "No", DOCUMENT why, INITIATE a new condition report, and EXTEND the due date of the effectiveness review.

4.9. DETERMINE whether a repeat occurrence or condition took place.

- IF "Yes", DOCUMENT how this was verified, INITIATE a new condition report, and EXTEND the due date of the effectiveness review. (Yes, a recurrence of this condition or a condition sufficiently similar indicates the problem still exists.)
- IF "No", DOCUMENT how this was established. (No, a repeat event or condition has not occurred and the measures that are in place to prevent repeat events or conditions are sustainable.)

4.10. IF the actions to preclude repetition were not effective, IDENTIFY any additional corrective actions needed to resolve the issue. Possible areas to evaluate include:

- The root causes were incorrectly identified.
- The root causes were correctly identified, but the corrective actions were incorrectly identified.
- The corrective actions were not fully implemented or not implemented as intended.
- The corrective actions were not implemented in a timely manner.
- The corrective actions created new or different problems.
- The corrective actions were implemented and then eliminated or defeated.
- The organization does not understand the issue or accept ownership.

4.11. DISCUSS corrective actions with cognizant personnel to identify any noteworthy weaknesses in the corrective actions and CONSIDER interviewing the following:

- Personnel who are directly involved with programs, processes, OR procedures related to the original nonconformance.
- Personnel who were negatively impacted by original nonconformance.

4.12. ENSURE corrective action taken did NOT result in a negative impact to plant operations, programs, OR equipment:

- DISCUSS with cognizant personnel to ensure that implemented corrective action did NOT result in any new performance problems.
- IF necessary, PERFORM an internal operating experience review to ensure implemented corrective action did NOT result in any new performance problems.

5. DOCUMENT the results of the effectiveness review.

5.1. IF criteria in the effectiveness review is met (i.e., corrective action in original underlying condition report precluded repetition), COMPLETE the following:

- DOCUMENT what was performed to validate findings.
- ENSURE the documented effectiveness review is attached to the condition report.

5.2. IF criteria in the effectiveness review is NOT met (i.e., corrective action in original underlying condition report was NOT effective in preventing recurrence), PERFORM the following:

- DOCUMENT in the effectiveness review what was performed to validate findings.
- GENERATE a new condition report to determine why the original corrective action(s) were ineffective.
- ATTACH a new effectiveness review plan to the newly generated condition report.
- ENSURE the effectiveness review and new condition report cross reference each other; then CLOSE the original effectiveness review.

6. OBTAIN approval of the effectiveness review.

    6.1. PRESENT effectiveness review conclusions to the management sponsor and the review board.

> **Note**: Steps 7 to 10 are completed by the review board.

7. DISPOSITION effectiveness review results as one of the following, as applicable:

- Approved.
- Approved as modified.
- Disapproved.

8. IF the effectiveness review is "approved," CLOSE the effectiveness review action and ENSURE the effectiveness review is included in the condition report.

9. IF effectiveness review condition report is "approved as modified," PERFORM the following:

    9.1. PROVIDE review board comments directly to the condition report lead.

    9.2. CREATE a review board action with comments to condition report lead.

    9.3. INFORM condition report lead to CLOSE the action when comments are addressed.

    9.4. ENSURE the effectiveness review checklist is included in the condition report.

10. IF the effectiveness review is "disapproved," perform the following:

    10.1. PROVIDE review board comments directly to condition report lead.

    10.2. CREATE a review board action with comments to condition report lead.

    10.3. WHEN revisions to the condition report are complete, INFORM condition report lead to perform the following:

- CONTACT the review board coordinator to schedule a review board review.
- GENERATE a condition report documenting the adverse condition.

6.2.1   Performance Indicator Development

What is it?

Performance indicators help us understand, manage, and improve what a business does. A performance indicator is a tool used to tell us something important about an organization's products or services (output) and the processes that produce them (Wilmoth, Prigmore, & Bray, 2002). See Figure 6-12. Performance indicators are quantitative measures of the products or services of a process or system (Department of Energy, 1995).

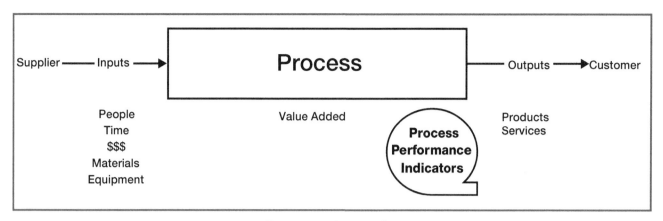

Figure 6-12. Process Flow

Why is it useful?

Performance indicators help us understand our work processes and help show where improvements need to be made. Sound performance indicators assure the monitoring of the right things and help identify performance gaps that should be analyzed and eliminated.

When is it used?

In cause analysis, the most likely use of this tool is during Step 6 (Plan Corrective Actions) because often your recommended resolution will be to change an existing process. You need indicators of how the process was performing before the process was changed and, once the process is changed, you need a way of demonstrating whether the process has improved and its effectiveness. An effectiveness review after process improvements have been implemented should include measurable elements such as performance indicators.

How is it done?

> **Note:** Use Table 6-17 as a job aid as you develop performance indicators.

Table 6-17. General Performance Indicator Development

Organizational Outcome/Output: *Step 1* Process Outcome/Output: *Step 2* Process Purpose: *Step 3*				
Outcome/Output	**Dimension**	**Measure**	**Goal**	**Performance Level**
Step 4	*Step 5*	*Step 6*	*Step 7*	*Step 8*

Step 1:   IDENTIFY; THEN RECORD the business outcome/output.

Step 2:   IDENTIFY the process flow (Figure 6-12), including its outputs; THEN RECORD the process outcome/output.

Step 3:   IDENTIFY; THEN RECORD the process purpose.

Step 4:   IDENTIFY; THEN RECORD the most important outputs of the process.

Step 5:   IDENTIFY critical steps of the process and dimensions of process performance (Table 6-18). Dimensions should be derived from both the needs of the customers who use the products or services and the financial needs of the business (Rummler & Brache, 1995).

Table 6-18. Examples of Dimensions

Quality	Productivity	Cost
▸ Accuracy ▸ Fit for use ▸ Ease of use ▸ Novelty ▸ Reliability ▸ Ease of repair ▸ Appearance	▸ Quantity ▸ Rate ▸ Timeliness	▸ Labor ▸ Materials ▸ Overhead ▸ Capital ▸ Fuel
Efficiency	**Effectiveness**	**Timeliness**
▸ Schedule adherence ▸ Proficiency ▸ Competency	▸ Dependability ▸ Success ▸ Reliability	▸ Meets schedule ▸ Promptness

Step 6:   DEVELOP; THEN RECORD the measure for each dimension. You may find you can measure a dimension in more than one way.

Step 7:   DEVELOP; THEN RECORD goals for each measure. Goals must be informative and **SMART** (Department of Energy, 1995):

   S — Specific — what will be accomplished, using limiting factors, and identifying the range of acceptable change from the present to the proposed condition.

   M— Measurable — the present and proposed output must be able to be calculated either qualitatively or quantitatively.

   A — Achievable/Attainable — are doable and feasible within a designated time period.

   R — Related/Relevant — related in all instances to the business plan goals and relevant to current management practices.

   T — Time-sensitive — goals must be trackable over time and must include a definite timeframe for achievement, monitoring, and evaluation.

Step 8:   DEFINE; THEN RECORD the specified levels of success using annunciator windows which indicate whether the desired results have been achieved (Table 6-19). In order to maintain consistency for performance indicators, the following set of objective window colors and definitions should be used.

Table 6-19. Performance Level Definitions for Window Colors

GREEN	Performance exceeding the expected target level, industry standards, and/or management expectations.
WHITE	Acceptable performance at a level meeting expectations and industry standards.
YELLOW	Performance requiring action to return to an acceptable level.
RED	Unacceptable performance at a level requiring corrective actions to return to an acceptable performance level.

Table 6-20. Performance Indicator Development Example

Business Outcome/Output: Performance improvement
Process Outcome/Output: Problem reporting
Process Purpose: Self-identify problems for timely correction.

Outcome/Output	Dimension	Measure	Goal	Performance Level
1. A direct and open means of raising nuclear safety concerns is available to all employees.	Participation Openness	Self-identification ratio. Self-identified condition reports vs. self-revealing condition reports (including those identified by outside organizations).	75-80%	**Green** **> 80 %** **White** **75 – 80 %** **Yellow** **70 - 75 %** **Red** **< 70 %**
2. Incidents are investigated promptly to preserve information and physical evidence.	Timeliness	Time it takes to conduct an incident review.	1-2 days	**Green** **<1 day** **White** **1-2 days** **Yellow** **3-5 days** **Red** **> 5 days**
	Timeliness	Time elapsed before an incident investigation begins.	24 - <48 hours	**Green** **< 24 hours** **White** **24 – < 48 hours** **Yellow** **48 – < 72 hours** **Red** **> 72 hours**

Looking Forward

With the use of the tools in this section, you should have the following ready for your management:

1. A plan to address each root and contributing cause you found during the investigation.
2. An action plan to change and improve behavior or to improve a process or equipment design.
3. A documented change management plan.
4. A documented effectiveness review plan with measurable acceptance criteria.
5. A documented communication plan (lessons to be learned).

Your corrective action plan should help the organization take effective corrective actions to address issues in a timely manner commensurate with their safety significance. You are now ready to provide a formal report to the organization's decision-makers (Step 7, Report Learnings).

Questions for Understanding

1. Why is an action plan useful?
2. What is the purpose of a solution selection tree?
3. What is a contingency plan?
4. What four steps should be used to develop a contingency plan?
5. What is the purpose of a performance indicator?

Questions for Discussion

1. What might a consequence be if you used the S.M.A.R.T.E.R. technique before you had established what your root cause is?
2. If you were asked to develop a solution selection matrix, what might be some of the questions that you would need to ask?
3. What does the "right" mental model mean to you?

References

Agency for Healthcare Research and Quality (AHRQ). (2013, May). *Decision matrix.* Retrieved from http://healthit.ahrq.gov/health-it-tools-and-resources/workflow-assessment-health-it-toolkit/all-workflow-tools/decision-matrix

Department of Defense (DOD). (2012, May). *Standard practice: System safety.* (MIL-STD-882E). Wright-Patterson Air Force Base, OH: Headquarters Air Force Materiel Command/SES.

Department of Energy (DOE). (1995, October). *How to measure performance: A handbook of techniques and tools.* (DOE DP-31 and EH-33). Washington, DC: US Department of Energy.

International Atomic Energy Agency (IAEA). (2005, July). *Effective corrective actions to enhance operational safety of nuclear installations.* (IAEA-TECDOC-1458). Vienna, Austria: Operational Safety Section, International Atomic Energy Agency.

Learning Point Associates. (2011, August). *Secondary school for journalism: Final report.* Retrieved from http://www.p12.nysed.gov/accountability/School_Improvement/Reports/1011/15K463_Secondary SchoolforJournalismESCA_Final

Rummler, G. A. & Brache, A. P. (1995). *Improving performance: How to manage the white space on the organization chart.* San Francisco: Jossey-Bass Publishers.

Short, J. C. (2012). *Investigation articles: Writing S.M.A.R.T.E.R. recommendations.* Retrieved from http://www.jcshort.com/Articles/SMARTER-Recommendations.htm

Wilmoth, F. S., Prigmore, C., & Bray, M. (2002). HPT models: An overview of the major models in the field. *Performance Improvement. 41*(8), 18.

Step 7

Report Learnings

Information is not knowledge.

— Albert Einstein, Physicist

Reporting what you have learned throughout your investigation helps facilitate the creation of an accurate, auditable, and defensible record. Reviewing the incident and showing the details of your work will produce a strong report that your management should approve. Most of all, your report should help decision-makers make good decisions.

You may need to provide an oral report to key decision-makers not only during the investigation but also at the conclusion of the investigation. The presentation may be informal or formal but, in any case, the oral report needs focus.

7.1   Preparing to Create Your Report

The success of an investigation depends not only on how well the report is written but also on how well you and your team can talk about the findings of the investigation. Expect to provide the following **general** information:

- What was expected   (anticipated consequences)
- What has happened   (real consequences)
- What could have happened   (potential consequences)
- Cause and effect relations   (symptom, contributing cause, root cause)
- Faulty/failed technical elements   (structures, systems, or components)
- Inappropriate actions   (human, leader, organizational)
- Failed or missing defenses   (barriers, controls)

The report should also document answers to the following **specific** questions:

- What triggered this? What released it?
- How long did the issue exist?
- Did the business have prior opportunities to identify?
- What was the job performer focused on?
- Could the job performer do the job if his or her life depended on it?
- Would an equally qualified person be likely to make the same error?
- What made it as bad as it was?
- What set up the business for this?
- What kept the incident from being a lot worse?
- What happens to workers when they do what they do?

You are writing the report for three audiences and therefore the report has three major parts:

1. The executive summary: for top management and to communicate general lessons to be learned by the organization.
2. The body: for the organizations that need to understand the basis for the action plan they will be implementing.
3. The attachments: consist of the details which may never be read by the groups in 1 and 2 (above), but will be scrutinized by regulators and by posterity — should the incident recur.

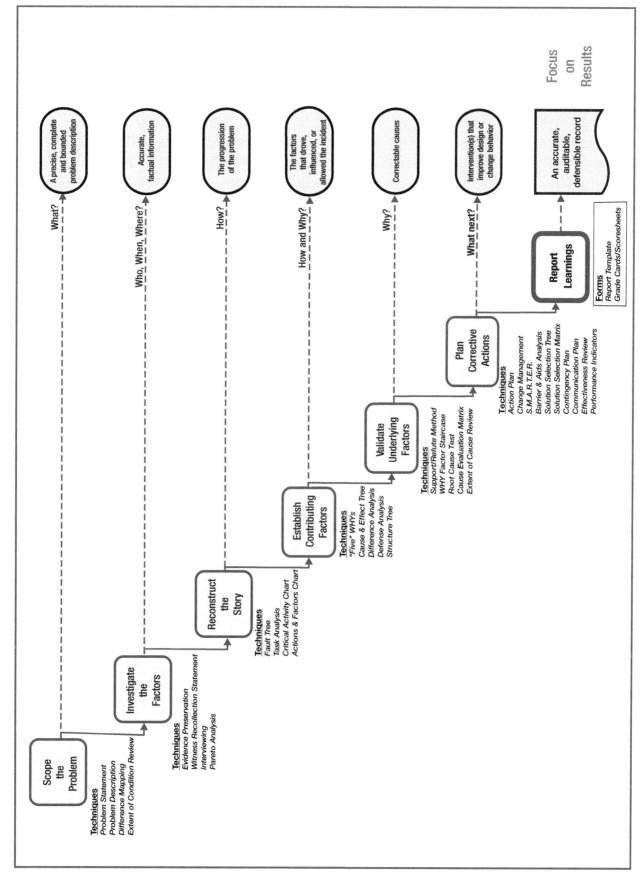

Figure 7-1. Step 7 Report Learnings

Table 5-1. Step 5 Jump Start Checklist

Use Table 7-1 as a checklist to guide you through Step 7 of the investigation. You will learn about the following tools (listed by section number):

7.2 Report Template

7.3 Grade Cards/Scoresheets

Table 7-1. Step 7 Jump Start Checklist

☑ Behaviors [Sub-Tasks]	Tools/Techniques	Required		
☐ Use the copy of the report template you saved.	*Report Template*	RC	AC	AD
☐ Document as you go.		RC	AC	
☐ Support concusions with facts.		RC	AC	
☐ Show all work, in the form of a complete, written analysis.		RC	AC	
☐ Document findings to provide a permanent auditable record.		RC	AC	
☐ Provide retrievable information for subsequent trending, problem solving, and corrective action review.		RC	AC	
☐ Critical action completed. Involve responsible management.	*Grade Cards/Scoresheets*	RC		

RC = Root Cause Analysis; **AC** = Apparent Cause Analysis; **AD** = Adverse

☑ Results Required [R]/Desired [D]			
☐ A permanent, auditable, defensible record.	RC_R	AC_R	AD_R
☐ Retrievable information for subsequent trending, problem solving, and corrective action review	RC_R	AC_R	AD_R
☐ A unified, coherent document that answers the following questions for management:	RC_R		
What happened? *The Problem Description*	RC_R		
What are the problems? *The Causal Factors*	RC_R		
What caused the problems? *The Underlying Factors ("Root Causes")*	RC_R		
How can we keep it from happening again? *The Corrective Action Plan*	RC_R		
What do we need to learn? *The Communication Plan*	RC_R		
☐ FOR significant conditions adverse to quality, include:	RC_R		
☐ *The identification/description of the significant condition adverse to quality.*	RC_R		
☐ *The identification/description of the cause(s) of the condition(s).*	RC_R		
☐ *A corrective action plan which, when implemented as a total package, will preclude repetition of the incident, accident, or significant condition adverse to quality.*	RC_R		

7.2   Report Template

What is it?

An incident analysis *report template* includes the sections you should include in order to document the results of your investigation.

Why is it useful?

The report template provides a standard template that follows the structured problem solving process and gives decision-makers a consistent format for the delivery of the findings of the investigation.

When is it done?

The report template should be retrieved during Step 1 of the investigation. The various sections of the report should be filled in as you are able to verify and validate facts during Steps 1 to 6 of the investigation. The report is finished in Step 7.

How is it done?

1. The following sections are recommended for your report:
   - Executive Summary
   - Problem Description
   - Issue Background
   - Safety Significance Implications and Business Impact
   - Extent of Condition
   - Remedial Actions Taken
   - Assessment Process
   - Incident Narrative
   - Operating Experience Review
   - Analysis Results
   - Corrective Action Plan to Preclude/Minimize Repetition
   - Effectiveness Review Plan
   - Information Sources
   - Attachments
     - A. Fault Tree
     - B. Timeline/Actions and Factors Chart
     - C. Causal Factor Tree

2. Use the template that follows on the next few pages.

3. Some of the information on the template is for guidance and to help jog your memory. This information can be deleted when it has served its purpose.

7.2.1   Sample Incident Analysis Report Template

Incident Analysis Report

DRAFT Report No. IAR YY- ###

Incident Summary Statement

Select date:

MM/DD/YYYY

Prepared by:

Isadore N. Vestigate

Submitted to:

[Enterprise Name]

[Street or P.O. Box Address]

[City, ST Zip]

Preparer:

_____

I. N. Vestigate

Table of Contents

Revision	Review Date	Summary of Revisions
0	MM/DD/YYYY	Initial Issue Team Leader: Team Members: Management Sponsor:

Executive Summary

Note: Information in BLUE is for guidance and should be deleted from the final report.

Enter the description of the activities that were in progress at time of incidents (paraphrased from the associated CORRECTIVE ACTION DOCUMENT and investigation).

Things to Consider for Executive Summary

Keep the summary simple. Ideally, the summary will fit on the first page. In no case should the summary be more than a page and a half.

Suggestion: Write the executive summary *after* writing the remainder of the report (i.e., write down the details first, then summarize).

First paragraph
- Occurrence date.
- Optimally, a single sentence describing the activity in progress at the time of or immediately preceding the incident.
- Optimally, a single sentence describing what happened.
- Optimally, a single sentence describing the significance of the incident.

Second paragraph
- Optimally, a single sentence describing the direct cause (i.e., the initiating action) of the incident.
- Optimally, a single sentence describing the immediate actions taken, and the safety significance.

Third paragraph
- Optimally, the paragraph has one sentence for each root cause in the body of the report.
- Generally, not in bullet or list format.

Fourth paragraph
- Optimally, the paragraph has one sentence for each corrective action in the body of the report. Generally, not in bullet or list format.

Problem Description

Issue Background

Safety Significance Implications and Business Impact

Nuclear Safety Impact
Actual Impact:

Potential Impact:

Radiological Safety Impact
Actual Impact:

Potential Impact:

Industrial Safety Impact
Actual Impact:

Potential Impact:

Business or Other Impact
Actual Impact:

Potential Impact:

Extent of Condition

Remedial Actions Taken (for Condition/for EOCo)

Assessment Process

The following steps were followed in this investigation:

1. Identify Performance Gaps

2. Discover Causes of Gaps

3. Recommend Strategies for Improving Performance

Incident Narrative

Operating Experience Review

Internal OE

External OE

Conclusions

Analysis Results

The primary investigative techniques used (☒) during this cause analysis were:

☐ Interviewing	☐ Actions and Factors Chart
☐ Pareto Analysis	☐ Difference [Change] Analysis
☐ Fault Tree Analysis	☐ Defense [Barrier] Analysis
☐ [Job] Task Analysis	☐ Causal Factor Tree (e.g., MORT)
☐ Critical [Human] Activity Chart	☐ WHY Factor Staircase
☐ [Other]	☐ [Other]

Performance Gaps/Causal Factors

Causes

Worker Practice
In work preparation, the following concerns were identified:

In work performance, the following concerns were identified:

In work feedback, the following concerns were identified:

Organization Processes
In engineered barriers, the following concerns were identified:

In administrative defenses, the following concerns were identified:

In oversight defenses, the following concerns were identified:

In cultural defenses, the following concerns were identified:

Extent of Cause

Corrective Action Plan to [Preclude/Minimize] Repetition

STATE the corrective actions in the following format to show the cause connection ("Line of Sight"):

The (DEVIATION STATEMENT) was caused [driven, triggered, released, influenced, allowed, aggravated] by (ROOT CAUSE STATEMENT 1) and (ROOT CAUSE STATEMENT 2) and can be precluded [fixed] by (CA PLAN STATEMENTS for RC1) and (CA PLAN STATEMENTS for RC 2).

- ☐ Immediate and interim actions are identified and address short term vulnerabilities.
- ☐ At least one corrective action clearly addresses each identified root and contributing cause or the basis for no corrective action is clearly documented.
- ☐ The corrective actions will correct the identified root cause.
- ☐ Corrective actions address extent of condition and extent of cause as necessary.
- ☐ Corrective actions are SMARTER.
- ☐ Completed actions are clearly documented.

Action(s) to Correct the Condition

Problem Description — Describe *WHAT* was found or happened (incident or undesired condition) in *object/defect format* (this information should be copied from applicable portions in the analysis).

Corrective Action For Undesired Condition — Describe SMART actions taken or required to be taken to correct the condition (insert rows for more actions).

Group: _____   **Assignee:** _____   **Concurrence:** _____

Assigned the CA   Individual responsible for corrective action   Individual giving concurrence for assignment

Expected Due/Completion Date — Include adequate detail to ensure traceability (indicate if complete).

Committed?   No ☐   Yes ☐   **Committed Date:** _____

Corrective Action for Extent of Condition — SMART actions taken or required to be taken to correct the extent of condition, if applicable (insert rows for more actions).

Group: _____   **Assignee:** _____   **Concurrence:** _____

Assigned the CA   Individual responsible for corrective action   Individual giving concurrence for assignment

Expected Due/Completion Date — Include adequate detail to ensure traceability (indicate if complete).

Committed?   No ☐   Yes ☐   **Committed Date:** _____

Action(s) to Correct the Cause(s)

Problem Description — Describe *WHAT* was found or happened (incident or undesired condition) in *object/defect* format (this information should be copied from applicable portions in the evaluation).

(**Note:** Copy the information boxed in below for *each* separate cause. Some of the information will repeat because the goal is for the reader to be able to trace "line of sight" from the WHY back to the HOW and then back to the WHAT.)

Factors That Influenced Human/Equipment Performance
Describe HOW the condition occurred, i.e., the performance gap.

Cause — Describe a validated reason WHY the incident occurred or the undesired condition existed.

  Cause Type: Root: ☐ Contributing Cause/Causal Factor: ☐

  Root Cause or Contributing Cause Number: _____ **Cause Code:** _____

  Organization Involved: _____

Corrective Action For Extent of Cause — SMART[ER] actions taken or required to be taken to correct the cause (insert rows for more actions).

Group: _____ **Assignee:** _____ **Concurrence:** _____
Assigned the CA   Individual responsible for corrective action   Individual giving concurrence for assignment

Expected Due/Completion Date — Include adequate detail to ensure traceability (indicate if complete).

Committed? No ☐ Yes ☐   **Committed Date:** _____

(**Note**: Copy the information boxed in below for each separate extent of cause.)

Extent of Cause — Describe a validated boundary of a "root cause". (May also be a "contributing cause.")

  Cause Type: Root: ☐ Contributing Cause/Causal Factor: ☐

  Root Cause or Contributing Cause Number: _____ **Cause Code:** _____

  Organization Involved: _____

Corrective Action For Extent of Cause — SMART[ER] actions taken or required to be taken to correct the cause (insert rows for more actions).

Group: _____ **Assignee:** _____ **Concurrence:** _____
Assigned the CA   Individual responsible for corrective action   Individual giving concurrence for assignment

Expected Due/Completion Date — Include adequate detail to ensure traceability (indicate if complete).

Committed? No ☐ Yes ☐   **Committed Date:** _____

Enhancement(s) ("ENHN")

(**Note:** Copy the information boxed in below for each separate review action.)

Action (ENHN) — Identify action(s) to address an aspect of a condition that is not undesired but can be improved upon (insert rows for more actions).

Group: _____　**Assignee:** _____　**Concurrence:** _____
Assigned the CA　　　　　　Individual responsible for corrective action　　　　Individual giving concurrence for assignment

Expected Due/Completion Date — Include adequate detail to ensure traceability (indicate if complete).

Committed?　　　No ☐　Yes ☐　　　　　**Committed Date:** _____

Effectiveness Review Plan

Establish criteria to measure success of the corrective action plan using the M.A.S.T. technique.

Method
☐　*Describe the means that will be used to verify that the actions taken had the desired outcome.*

Attributes
☐　*Describe the process characteristics to be monitored or evaluated.*

Success
☐　*Establish the acceptance criteria for the attributes to be monitored or evaluated.*

Timeliness
☐　*Define the optimum time to perform the effectiveness review.*

Effectiveness Review(s) ("EREV")

(**Note:** Copy the information boxed in below for each separate review action.)

Action (EREV) — Include M.A.S.T. from the evaluation above (insert rows for more EREV assignments, such as interim effectiveness reviews).

Group: _____　**Assignee:** _____　**Concurrence:** _____
Assigned the CA　　　　　　Individual responsible for corrective action　　　　Individual giving concurrence for assignment

Expected Due/Completion Date — Include adequate detail to ensure traceability (indicate if complete).

Committed?　　　No ☐　Yes ☐　　　　　**Committed Date:** _____

page viii

Information Sources

Team members

Documents Reviewed

Individuals Contacted

Attachments

A. Fault Tree

B. Timeline/Actions and Factors Chart

C. Causal Factor Tree

Attachment A: Fault Tree

Example Generalized Fault Tree Analysis

Attachment B: Timeline/Actions and Factors Chart

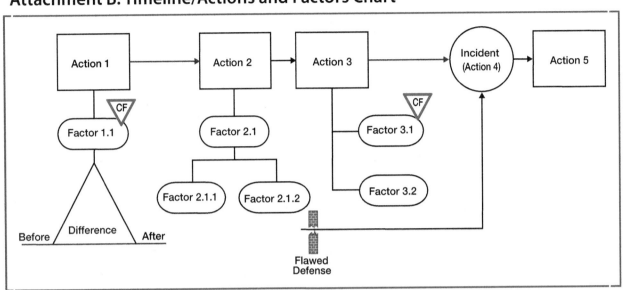

Example Generalized Actions and Factors Chart

Attachment C: Causal Factors Tree

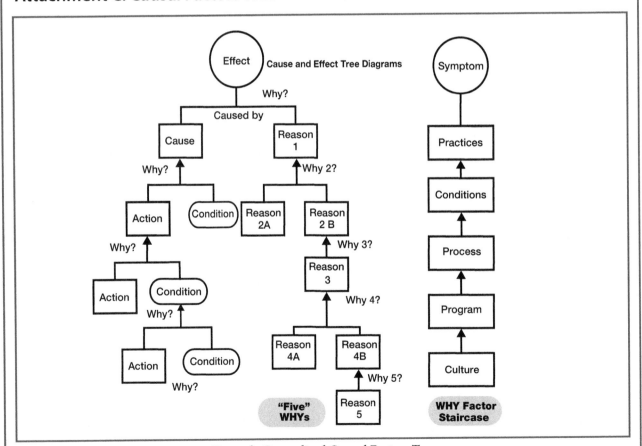

Example Generalized Causal Factors Tree

7.3   Grade Cards/Scoresheets

What is it?

Grade cards and *scoresheets* are used to evaluate an investigation report against established problem identification and resolution criteria. The following are requirements found in the Nuclear Regulatory Commission's (NRC) Inspection Procedure 95001 and 95002 (Nuclear Regulatory Commission, 2011a and 2011b).

02.01 **Problem Identification**

a. Determine that the evaluation documented who identified the issue (i.e., licensee-identified, self-revealing, or NRC-identified) and under what conditions the issue was identified.

b. Determine that the evaluation documented how long the issue existed and prior opportunities for identification.

c. Determine that the evaluation documented the plant-specific risk consequences, as applicable, and compliance concerns associated with the issue.

02.02 **Root Cause, Extent of Condition, and Extent of Cause Evaluation**

a. Determine that the problem was evaluated using a systematic methodology to identify the root and contributing causes.

b. Determine that the root cause evaluation was conducted to a level of detail commensurate with the significance of the problem.

c. Determine that the root cause evaluation included a consideration of prior occurrences of the problem and knowledge of prior operating experience.

d. Determine that the root cause evaluation addressed the extent of condition and the extent of cause of the problem.

e. Determine that the root cause, extent of condition, and extent of cause evaluations appropriately considered the safety culture components as described in IMC 0305.

02.03 **Corrective Actions**

a. Determine that appropriate corrective actions are specified for each root and contributing cause or that the licensee has an adequate evaluation for why no corrective actions are necessary.

b. Determine that corrective actions have been prioritized with consideration of risk significance and regulatory compliance.

c. Determine that a schedule has been established for implementing and completing the corrective actions.

d. Determine that quantitative or qualitative measures of success have been developed for determining the effectiveness of the corrective actions to prevent recurrence.

e. Determine that the corrective actions planned or taken adequately address a Notice of Violation (NOV) that was the basis for the supplemental inspection, if applicable.

Why is it useful?

The grade card on the following pages is derived from regulatory expectations for investigations found in NRC Inspection Procedures 95001 and 95002. If your investigation fulfills the requirements on the grade sheet, your investigation should satisfy your regulator and your management.

When is it done?

The grade card should be used by a mentor or peer to evaluate your report prior to going to key management decision-makers. A mentor or peer can give you an objective evaluation of the quality of your report prior to going to an upper management review committee. This gives you an opportunity to fill in any gaps and to correct any mistakes. The grade card should be used by the upper management review committee so reports receive consistent evaluation.

How is it done?

1. Use the guidance on Sheets 2 and 3 of the grade card to evaluate each of the 13 questions.

2. Assign a grade from 1 to 5 that coincides with the criteria on Sheets 2 and 3. A grade of 4 is passing for an objective. Grades of 1 to 3 indicate the objective has not been met and more investigation must be done or more findings must be documented to attain the passing grade of 4. A grade of 5 signifies a standard that has been exceeded.

7.3.1   Root Cause Analysis — Sample Organizational Learning Scoresheet

Sheet 1 of 3

CR #_____   Management Sponsor _____   Date Reviewed _____

Performance Standard/Criteria [NRC Inspection Procedures 95001/95002] Score of 4 is the Performance Standard. Score of 4 or 5 designates Approval. Score of 1, 2, or 3 Disapproves Report	Addresses?		Reviewer _____ Comments
	Yes	**No**	
	☐5 ☐4	☐3 ☐2 ☐1	
Problem Identification and Extent of Condition Evaluation [02.01]	Yes	No	
A. Evaluation documents who identified the issue and under what conditions, how long the issue existed, prior opportunities for identification, and plant-specific risk consequences. [02.01.a,b,c]	☐5 ☐4	☐3 ☐2 ☐1	
B. The extent of condition is documented, considers safety culture, and is addressed adequately by corrective action plan. [02.02.d,e]	☐5 ☐4	☐3 ☐2 ☐1	
Root Cause Evaluation and Extent of Cause Evaluation [02.02]	Yes	No	
C. Structured visible investigative tools and techniques were used with quantitative information to develop the incident narrative and cause analysis (timeline, process map, change analysis, defense analysis, WHY factor staircase, etc.). All statements are qualified and quantified, not based on opinion or assumptions. [02.02]	☐5 ☐4	☐3 ☐2 ☐1	
D. The evaluation identified the error precursors, the flawed defenses, and the latent organizational weaknesses and considered safety culture. [02.02.b,e]	☐5 ☐4	☐3 ☐2 ☐1	
E. (Only applies to a recurring problem) The investigation evaluates the failure of the original corrective actions and uses this as a causal factor in identifying new corrective actions. [02.02.c]	☐5 ☐4	☐3 ☐2 ☐1	
F. Internal and external operating experience was researched and lessons learned incorporated clearly documenting applicability. Non-applicability was well documented. [02.02.c]	☐5 ☐4	☐3 ☐2 ☐1	
G. Root cause(s) were identified that addressed the stated problem and were well supported by the facts of the investigation. Contributing causes were identified. [01.01]	☐5 ☐4	☐3 ☐2 ☐1	
H. The extent of cause (generic implications) is documented for each root cause and addressed adequately by the corrective action plan. Considers safety culture. [02.02.d,e]	☐5 ☐4	☐3 ☐2 ☐1	
Corrective Action Plan [02.03]	Yes	No	
I. The corrective actions are focused appropriately on organizational, programmatic, and individual performance issues. [02.03.a]	☐5 ☐4	☐3 ☐2 ☐1	
J. The corrective actions addressed all of the identified causes and are S.M.A.R.T.E.R. (specific, measurable, achievable, relevant, time-sensitive, effective, reviewed). [02.03.a]	☐5 ☐4	☐3 ☐2 ☐1	
K. The safety significance factors were considered and identified, and the corrective actions were appropriate. [02.03.b]	☐5 ☐4	☐3 ☐2 ☐1	
L. Schedule for corrective action implementation is timely, commensurate with the safety significance of the issue. [02.03.c]	☐5 ☐4	☐3 ☐2 ☐1	
M. The effectiveness review plan contains a method for verifying acceptable quantitative recurrence thresholds or qualitative measures of success after an optimal time period. [02.03.d]	☐5 ☐4	☐3 ☐2 ☐1	
☐ Approved	☐ Approved as Modified (minor editorial).	☐ Disapproved. Discuss with Team Lead. Direct Team Lead to perform needed changes.	Average_____

Root Cause Analysis Review Criteria [NRC IP 95001/95002]
Organizational Learning Worksheet
Sheet 2 of 3
Problem Identification and Extent of Condition Evaluation [02.01]

A. Evaluation documented who identified the issue, how long the issue existed, and the plant specific risk consequences.
1. Documentation missing on who identified the issue, how long the issue existed, prior opportunities for identification, and the plant-specific risk consequences.
2. Evaluation does not document more than one of the following: who identified, how long issue existed, prior opportunities for identification, or plant-specific risk consequences.
3. Evaluation does not document at least one of the following: who identified, how long issue existed, prior opportunities for identification, or plant-specific risk consequences.
4. Evaluation documents who identified the issue and under what conditions, how long the issue existed, prior opportunities for identification, and plant-specific risk consequences.
5. In addition to 4 above, the issue was self-identified and *potential* plant-specific risk consequences were documented.

B. Determine that the root cause evaluation addresses the extent of condition. [02.02.d,e]
1. The extent of condition evaluation was not identified or documented in the report.
2. The extent of condition was tentatively identified, but a documented evaluation was missing from the report or was not completely relevant to incident condition.
3. The extent of condition is addressed for the incident, but is narrowly focused (for example, ignores one or more organization, process, component, or safety culture aspect).
4. The extent of condition issue(s) is documented, considers safety culture, and is addressed adequately by the corrective action plan.
5. In addition to 4 above, the extent of condition is addressed at high standards (i.e., documentation was accurate, thorough, comprehensive, exhaustive, systematic).

Root Cause Evaluation and Extent of Cause Evaluation [02.02]

C. Problem was evaluated using a systematic method(s) to identify root cause(s) and contributing cause(s). [02.02.a]
1. It was not readily apparent that the problem was evaluated using a systematic method(s) to identify root cause(s) and contributing cause(s).
2. A structured approach was barely visible (generally limited to comfortable techniques such as brainstorming and interviewing).
3. Simplistic (i.e., one-dimensional) tools such as the "five"WHYs (a.k.a. cause mapping), fishbone analysis, or gap analysis formed the sole basis for conclusions.
4. Structured visible investigative tools and techniques were used with quantitative information to develop the incident narrative and cause analysis chart, timeline, process map, difference analysis, defense analysis, WHY factor staircase, etc.). All statements are qualified and quantified, not based on opinion or assumptions.
5. In addition to 4 above, the critical data is verified with an independent source (interviews, surveys, etc.) and findings are validated using alternative methods of analysis.

D. Evaluation was conducted to a level of detail commensurate with the significance of the problem. [02.02.b,e]
1. The evaluation did not go much beyond the inappropriate human action or the equipment failure symptoms.
2. The evaluation identified some flawed defenses, but focused on error precursors or the equipment failure and degradation mechanisms.
3. The evaluation identified some organizational weaknesses, but focused on flawed defenses and on equipment degradation influences or human-machine interface concerns.
4. The evaluation identified the error precursors, the flawed defenses, and the latent organizational weaknesses and considered safety culture.
5. The evaluation thoroughly integrated all error precursors, flawed defenses, and latent organizational weaknesses with safety culture considerations. Also mitigating factors.

E. Evaluation considered prior occurrences of the problem. (Only applies to a recurring problem.) [02.02.c]
1. The same corrective actions were used for recurring problems that were used for the original incident.
2. The investigation does not evaluate why the original corrective actions did not work and should have done so.
3. The investigation evaluates the failure of the original corrective actions but does not factor those results into proposed corrective actions.
4. The investigation evaluates the failure of the original corrective actions and uses this as a causal factor in identifying new corrective actions.
5. In addition to 4 above, the investigation provides feedback to strengthen effectiveness of the original corrective actions.

F. Evaluation considered knowledge of prior operating experience. [02.02.c]
1. Operating experience was not evaluated and documented.
2. Either internal or external operating experience was not searched (based on a documented evaluation missing from the report).
3. Internal and external operating experience was researched adequately; however, applicability or non-applicability was not well documented.
4. Internal and external operating experience was researched and lessons learned incorporated, clearly documenting applicability. Non-applicability was well documented.
5. In addition to 4 above, the internal and external operating experience was shared with the industry.

G. Root causes and contributing causes of risk significant performance issues are understood. [01.01]
1. No root cause was identified and should have been. Or only direct or apparent causes were identified.
2. Root or contributing causes did not match the stated problem or only addressed a small part of the problem. The difference was not resolved.
3. Root cause(s) were identified that addressed most, but not all, of the stated problem; or no clear root cause was identified and sufficient justification was not provided.
4. Root cause(s) were identified that addressed the stated problem and were well supported by the facts of the investigation. Contributing causes were identified.
5. In addition to 4 above, the root causes of the contributing causes were also identified.

Sheet 3 of 3

H. Determine that the root cause evaluation addresses the extent of cause of the problem. [02.02.d,e]
1. An extent of cause review was not performed (i.e., generic implications were not considered).
2. The extent of cause (generic implications) is addressed, but not completely relevant to incident root causes.
3. The extent of cause (generic implications) is addressed for the incident, but narrowly focused.
4. The extent of cause (generic implications) is documented for each root cause and addressed adequately by the corrective action plan. Considers safety culture.
5. In addition to 4 above, the extent of cause (generic implications) is addressed at high standards and is thorough; that is, extents of contributing causes are also addressed.

Corrective Action Plan [02.03]

I. Corrective actions are focused correctly, addressing the root cause(s) identified and will prevent recurrence. [02.03.a]
1. The corrective actions are too narrowly focused or significantly inappropriately focused. Global (programmatic) corrective actions are used based on a limited analysis of a single incident, or no corrective actions are used to repair the existing damage identified in the root cause analysis.
2. The corrective actions are narrowly focused or inappropriately focused. Localized programmatic corrective actions are used for individual performance issues, or individually focused corrective actions are used for localized programmatic issue.
3. The corrective actions are focused primarily on individual and programmatic concerns, not organizational weaknesses, and should have been.
4. The corrective actions are focused appropriately on organizational, programmatic, and individual performance issues.
5. The corrective actions are focused on programmatic concerns with differentiation between global and localized issues; individual performance issues are appropriately separated. Corrective actions, when implemented, will provide a high degree of confidence that the problem will not recur.

J. Proposed corrective actions make sense when reviewed against the cause(s). [02.03.a]
1. No corrective actions were assigned, yet they appear to be required. No justification was provided.
2. The corrective actions did not address the identified cause. No justification was provided.
3. The corrective actions for the identified causes are at best only S.M.A.R.T. (specific, measurable, attainable, related, time-sensitive), not reviewed, potentially ineffective.
4. The corrective actions addressed all of the identified causes and are S.M.A.R.T.E.R. (specific, measurable, attainable, related, time-sensitive, effective, reviewed).
5. In addition to 4 above, the corrective actions were validated using a structured tool or technique (e.g., solution selection matrix, economic analysis, cost-benefit analysis).

K. Factors affecting safety significance have been considered, including industrial safety, nuclear safety, radiological safety, and common mode failure. [02.03.b,e]
1. Some of the safety significance factors were not considered or documented.
2. One of the safety significance factors was not considered and identified.
3. The safety significance factors were considered and identified, but the corrective actions were not completely appropriate.
4. The safety significance factors were considered and identified, and the corrective actions were appropriate.
5. The safety significance factors evaluations were far reaching and took into account similar equipment and impact on other departments or processes.

L. The corrective action implementation plan appears timely. [02.03.c]
1. Schedule for corrective action implementation is clearly unacceptable based on impact on plant operation.
2. Schedule for corrective action implementation appears to be untimely based on significance of the issues.
3. Schedule for corrective action implementation is adequate, but does not "stretch" us to be a performance leader.
4. Schedule for corrective action implementation is timely commensurate with the safety significance of the issue.
5. Schedule for corrective action implementation will correct problem before opportunity for recurrence (proactive).

M. Quantitative or qualitative measures of success have been developed for determining the effectiveness of the corrective actions to prevent recurrence. [02.03.d]
1. An Effectiveness Review Plan is not provided (Note: Must be documented in the report — reference to a CR number is not appropriate).
2. An Effectiveness Review Plan is provided, but does not contain an effective verification method **and** does not establish acceptable recurrence thresholds.
3. An Effectiveness Review Plan is provided, but either does not contain an effective verification method **or** does not establish acceptable recurrence thresholds.
4. The Effectiveness Review Plan contains a method for verifying acceptable quantitative recurrence thresholds or qualitative measures of success after an optimal time period.
5. In addition to 4 above, the Effectiveness Review Plan establishes both short and long term recurrence thresholds for the identified causes and corrective actions to prevent recurrence.

CR: _____	Avg. Score: _____	

Excellent	>=4.5	**Green**
Acceptable	>=4.0 and <4.5	**White**
Needs Improvement	>=3.5 and <4.0	**Yellow**
Unacceptable	<3.5	**Red**

Incident: _____

Sponsor: _____   Investigator: _____

Grader: _____   Date: _____

Looking Forward

Once you've completed the report, you may be called on to present your findings to management or you may have to defend the investigator to your regulator. If you've followed the structured process laid out in this manual, you should have a lot of confidence in your product.

Use the executive summary when you talk to your upper management — people who need to know about what you learned, but may not need to get into the details. Use the body of the report for the individuals who have to fix the problem and implement the corrective actions you and your team are recommending.

The detailed attachments are for posterity. The details will help you remember what you were thinking months and years after completing the report. You will not always be called on to defend or explain your findings immediately. It may be a year or more before your regulator calls on you to discuss the logic of your investigation.

Questions for Understanding

1. What are the six questions management should expect you to answer during the course of your investigation?
2. What should you consider bringing to any formal presentation?
3. What determines the success of an investigation?

Questions for Discussion

1. What possible consequences might arise if you did not report what you learned during your investigation?
2. Discuss the ramifications of taking information "off the record."

References

Nuclear Regulatory Commission (NRC). (2011a, February). *Inspection for one or two white inputs in a strategic performance area.* (NRC Inspection Procedure 95001). Washington, DC: US NRC Office of Nuclear Reactor Regulation.

Nuclear Regulatory Commission (NRC). (2011b, February). *Inspection for one degraded cornerstone or any three white inputs in a strategic performance area.* (NRC Inspection Procedure 95002). Washington, DC: US NRC Office of Nuclear Reactor Regulation.

Appendix A

Creating Working Definitions

What is a working or operational definition?

During investigations, you will discuss various ideas with a variety of people. Some concepts will be truly new and ambiguous. And, while other terms may seem familiar, the concepts can be misunderstood during discussions. A word may be concrete and tangible, like *door* or *pump*, or abstract and intangible, like *quality* or *trust*. A *working definition* is a description agreed upon by a group in order to translate a concept into either a qualitative or quantitative concept of some kind so your discussions can move on. Working definitions may already be available in procedures or job descriptions. Often, needed definitions have not been developed. Sometimes, when definitions do exist, they have not been communicated to employees.

Why is it useful?

A working definition is a vital instrument which will help you use all the other tools in this manual successfully (US Navy, 1996). During the investigation, you may find that people are supposedly speaking the same language but that some words or terms may be confusing. For example, if people misunderstand one term in a problem description, there is a good chance the real problem will be misunderstood. A working definition will help to ensure people are speaking the same language.

In the case where standard definitions are not available, this technique can greatly facilitate your problem-solving effort. An investigation can become bogged down while people debate vague or confusing terms such as *rigor*, *culture*, or *accountability*. A glossary, dictionary, or standard operating procedure definition may help achieve clarity.

When is it used?

This technique can be used during any step of the problem-solving effort whenever it appears there is confusion during any form of communication. You may need to use the working definition technique several times during an investigation.

How is it done?

> **Note:** If a definition is available in a dictionary, procedure, or job description, use it (at least as a starting point). A glossary is provided at the end of this manual to help define terms frequently encountered in incident investigations.

1. RECORD each controversial word or term on the working definition form. See Table A-1.

2. RECORD each critical concept associated with the word or term.

   (The concept may be an object, a process, or a quality.)

3. For each object, process, or quality, ASK:
   - If we see it, how would we know it?
   - What indicates it is happening?
   - What does it mean?

4. WRITE down indicators and measures for each critical concept.

5. TRANSLATE the indicators and measures into a definition.

6. AGREE among the people involved that this is a definition everyone can work with.

Table A-1. Working Definition Form

Word/Term: _____		
Critical Concept(s)	**Indicator(s)**	**Measure(s)**
(1) _____	_____	_____
	_____	_____
	_____	_____
	_____	_____
	_____	_____
	_____	_____
	_____	_____
(2) _____	_____	_____
	_____	_____
	_____	_____
(3) _____	_____	_____
	_____	_____
	_____	_____
(4) _____	_____	_____
	_____	_____
	_____	_____
Definition: _____		

Working Definition of "Promptly" Example

Word/Term: Incidents are investigated **promptly** to preserve information and physical evidence.

	Critical Concept(s)	Indicator(s)	Measure(s)
(1)	Promptly	Timeliness	Time it takes to conduct an incident review: 1-2 day.
			Time elapsed before an incident investigation begins: $\leq$ 24 hours.

Definition: "**promptly**" Started within 24 hours and reviewed within 48 hours.

Working Definition of "Quality" Example

Juran (1979, pp. 2-1 – 2-9) provides an extensive discussion of the term *quality*. This example uses that discussion to come up with a definition of the word *quality*.

Word/Term: **Quality** is built into each of our products.

	Critical Concept(s)	Indicator(s)	Measure
(1)	Design	Marketing Research	Customer satisfaction (qualitative). Competitor performance (qualitative).
		Concept	Fitness for customer use (qualitative).
		Specification	Completeness (qualitative). Correctness (qualitative).
(2)	Conformance	Technology	Meets all valid specification targets. Meets all valid specification tolerances.
		Manpower	Proficiency (qualitative). Competency (qualitative).
		Management	Schedule adherence. Time spent observing work.
(3)	Availability	Reliability	$\dfrac{uptime}{uptime + downtime}$
		Maintainability	Mean time to repair. Mean time for scheduled maintenance.
		Logistical Support	Labor cost. Material cost.
(4)	Field Serivce	Promptness	Meet schedule. Time between service call and service.
		Competence	Fixed right the first time. No rework.
		Integrity	Arrived at agreed to time (+/-) one minute. Dependability (qualitative).

Definition: "**quality**" Fit for the customer's use and conforms to customer's specifications.

Questions for Understanding

1. When would you need to use a working definition during an incident investigation?

2. What sources do you have available to get a working definition?

Questions for Discussion

1. Why should you and your team go through the rigorous exercise of developing a working definition for a term?

2. Think of situations you have encountered in which it was obvious people did not understand each other. How was the misunderstanding resolved?

References

Juran, J. M. (1979). *Quality control handbook.* St. Louis, MO: McGraw-Hill.

US Navy (USN). (1996). *Handbook for basic process improvement. Appendix 1: The basic tools for process improvement. Module 1: Operational definitions.* Retrieved from http://www.au.af.mil/au/awc/awcgate/navy/bpi_manual/mod1-opdef.pdf.

Appendix B

Common Factor Analysis

What is it?

The Nuclear Regulatory Commission (NRC) (2011) defines a *common cause* as multiple failures (i.e., two or more) of plant equipment or processes attributable to a shared cause. *Common factor analysis* (CFA) is a diagnostic tool that provides a systematic method for evaluating a group of adverse conditions for possible common cause or shared weaknesses or factors. A common factors analysis is performed with the intent of identifying those factors that generally lead to an adverse condition or significant incident.

Why is it useful?

Significant incidents are typically preceded by low-level precursor incidents that share the same causal factors or weaknesses. By connecting the dots from multiple low-level incidents, we can pinpoint the vulnerable areas and address them before they find us.

When is it used?

CFA is the tool of choice whenever we are analyzing a group of adverse conditions together. Use it to find the driving factors behind a known problem area or to "mine" low-level corrective action documents for hidden problem areas.

How is it done?

Use the flowchart in Figure B-1 to guide the analysis.

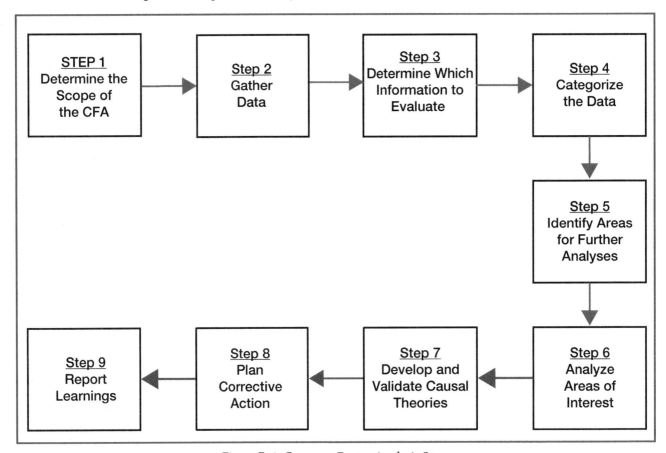

Figure B-1. Common Factor Analysis Steps

Step 1: Determine the Common Factor Analysis Scope. Develop a clear statement of purpose, scope, and desired outcome of the common factor analysis. In conjunction with the sponsoring manager, identify the population of documents to evaluate.

▸ Interest area.

  ◆ *Tools dropped from heights.*

  ◆ *Qualifications of supplemental personnel.*

▸ Applicable organization(s).

  ◆ *Conditions reports involving all site personnel.*

  ◆ *Conditions reports involving chemistry personnel only.*

▸ Timeframe.

  ◆ *Conditions reports issued during the last outage.*

  ◆ *Conditions reports issued since a process was changed.*

Step 2: Gather Data. Determine the data to be used in the analysis. Assemble data in the form of condition reports, work orders, and other performance information. Data to be considered might include:

- Cause analysis reports.
- Self-assessments.
- Independent assessments.
- Regulatory performance.

Using keywords or trend codes or other means, identify condition reports and other documents that fall within the scope. Exclude any that:

- Occurred before the period of interest (but are just now being discovered).
- Involve contractor/vendor activities performed off-site.
- Involve personnel, organizations, or activities outside the scope.

Step 3: Determine Which Information to Analyze. Up front, settle on what information to glean from the condition reports, such as:

- A specific type of human performance difficulty.
  - *Component placed in wrong position.*
  - *Procedure step skipped.*
- Responsible organization/sub-organization.
- Work process being followed when the inappropriate action occurred.

For technical issues:

- Identify the hardware loss of function in terms of failure mode, failure mechanism (direct cause of loss of function), and degradation influences.
- Identify failure precursors — conditions that allowed the degradation influences to exist. These would typically be decisions about run to failure; maintenance practices; assembly, installation, or repair methods; operation practices; service conditions; design; manufacture; or material specification.
- Identify flawed defenses such as preventive maintenance, predictive maintenance, post-mod/maintenance testing, in-service testing, trending, receipt inspection, maintenance work instructions, and previous corrective action effectiveness.

For human issues:

- Identify error precursors.
  - Task demands.
  - Individual capabilities.
  - Work environment.
  - Human nature.
- Identify flawed defenses.
  - Jobsite conditions.
  - Individual or team behaviors.
  - Organization process and values.
  - Leadership weaknesses.

For all issues:

‣ Look for influences that were both identified in the incident evaluation and those that could be drawn but were not explicitly identified in the evaluation.

‣ For recurring issues, determine why previous corrective actions were not fully effective.

Step 4: Categorize the Data. Catalogue the data by using a model and developing a matrix of incidents and causal information. Populate the matrix with developed causal information.

‣ Choose one or more models to use to plot the data. Be creative. See examples in Figures B-2 through B-9.

‣ Develop a matrix, spreadsheet, or model, listing information categories determined in Step 3.

‣ Record each factor separately on the template (a single report may document multiple factors).

‣ For each contributing factor, record information on the template.

Example 1: Industrial Safety Incidents by Time of Day

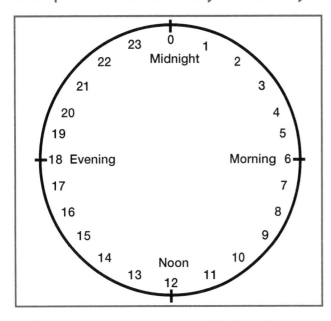

Figure B-2. 24-Hour Clock

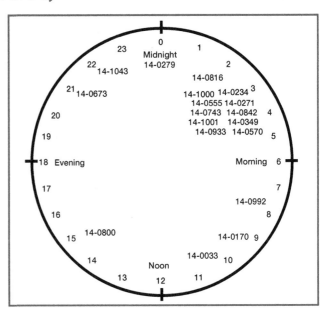

Figure B-3. Time Incident Occurred

Example 2: Multiple Procedure Quality Issues

The NRC (1993) developed the criteria diagrammed in Figure B-4 to assess the quality of an organization's written instructions. Figure B-5 is an example of an assessment using the NRC's criteria to establish exactly where an organization's procedure quality issues were concentrated. In this example, this organization needs to ensure a procedure includes all the relevant information a user needs.

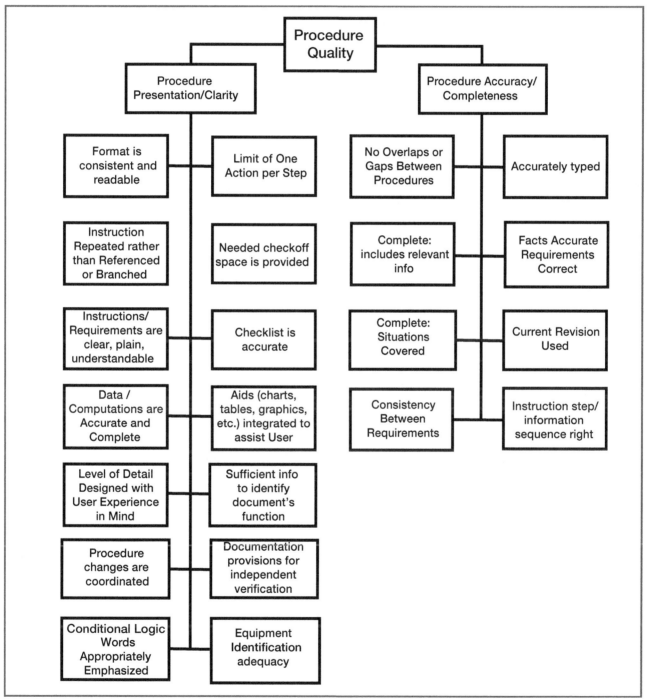

Figure B-4. Drivers of Procedure Quality

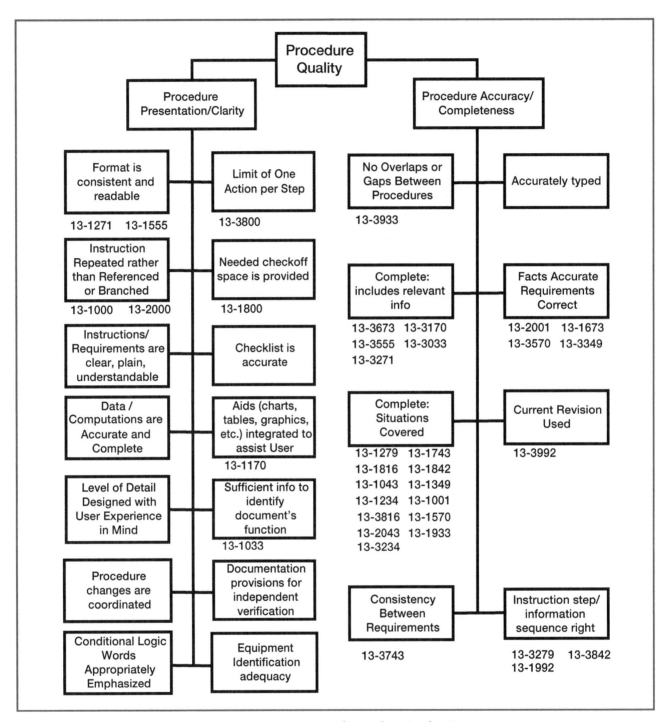

Figure B-5. Categorization of Procedure Quality Issues

Example 3: Procurement Process Issues

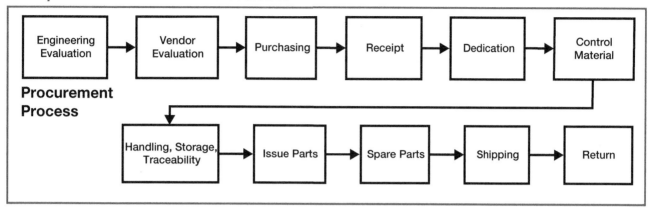

Figure B-6. Procurement Process

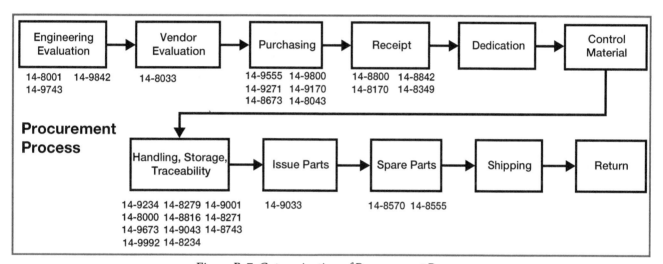

Figure B-7. Categorization of Procurement Process

Example 4: Repeat Occurrences Plotted on Organizational Chart

According to the NRC (2011) repeat occurrences are defined as two or more independent conditions which are the result of the same basic cause(s).

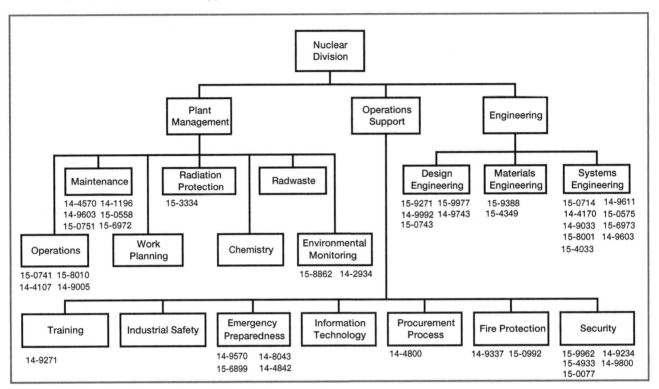

Figure B-8. Categorization of Repeat Occurrence by Department

Example 5: Weaknesses in Safety Culture Aspects

The NRC (2014) uses a defined set of characteristics to assess the cultural values and beliefs an organization has toward safety.

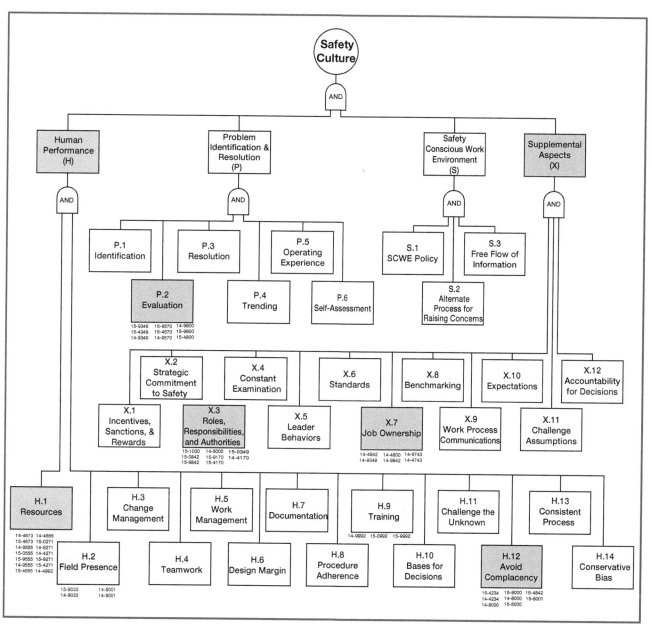

Figure B-9. Categorization of NRC Safety Culture Issues

Step 5: Identify Areas for Further Analysis. Analyze for common behaviors, conditions, and causes. Develop problem descriptions for identified common failure modes. These will now be the areas for further analysis. Evaluate data for issues that appear to stand out, for example:

▸ Data that appears significant when compared to the rest of the data set.
  ◆ *Most errors are occurring on nightshift!*
  ◆ *We're making a lot of knowledge-based errors!*

▸ Data that represents a noteworthy decline in performance.
  ◆ *Documentation errors on work packages increased since the last self-assessment!*

▸ Data that represents a generic concern affecting multiple organizations, programs and/or processes.
  ◆ *The number of site-wide procedure violations is high!*

▸ Data which represents a level of performance below management expectations.
  ◆ *We've had eight cases where work was done on the wrong train!*

Examples
From the models displayed after Step 4, these are the areas that should be selected for further analysis:

▸ 24-Hour Clock: the time period from 2 a.m. to 5 a.m. needs more analysis (Figure B-3).
▸ Procedure Quality Issues: completeness situations covered and relevant information included (Figure B-5).
▸ Procurement Process Issues: handling, storage, and shipping along with purchasing (Figure B-7).
▸ Repeat Occurrence by Department: engineering, maintenance, and security (Figure B-8).
▸ Weaknesses in Safety Culture Aspects (Figure B-9):
  ◆ Resources.
  ◆ Avoiding complacency.
  ◆ Problem evaluation.
  ◆ Roles, responsibility, and authority.
  ◆ Job ownership.

Note: Steps 6 through 9 of common factor analysis are roughly the same as cause analysis Steps 4 through 7. As such, the techniques introduced in cause analysis Steps 4 through 7 can be used to complete the remainder of the steps of common factor analysis.

Step 6: Analyze Areas of Interest. Commensurate with the significance of the issue, drill into the common failure modes (the areas of interest) to identify causes. Having identified data that appears to stand out, it is time to begin considering why that is the case. Consider special circumstances that may explain the data.

▸ A sudden rise in the number of procedure violations may be due to increased management emphasis on procedure compliance.
▸ An increase in the number of personal safety issues could be due to the fact that more workers are present during outage periods.

Step 7: Develop and Validate Causal Theories. Document analyses of common failure modes and causes. Validate cause conclusions.

▸ Develop theories regarding causes for recurring difficulties.

- Look beyond the difficulties to identify organizational weaknesses.
- Perform verification and validation of causal theories using:
  - ◆ Interviews.
  - ◆ Internal evaluations.
  - ◆ External inspections.
  - ◆ Field observations.
  - ◆ Documents reviews.
- Eliminate those that cannot be supported.

Step 8: Plan Corrective Actions. Recommend corrective/improvement actions and interventions.

- Once common causes are validated, develop a corrective action plan.
- Discuss conclusions and corrective action recommendations with the sponsoring manager.

Step 9: Report Learnings. Document the results of the common factor analysis.

- Prepare a report documenting the results of the analysis and final corrective action plan.
- Common factor analysis performed as part of an investigation of a significant condition adverse to quality should be documented in accordance with corrective action program procedures.

> **Note:** Figure B-10 shows how common factor analysis is integrated into a cause analysis investigation.

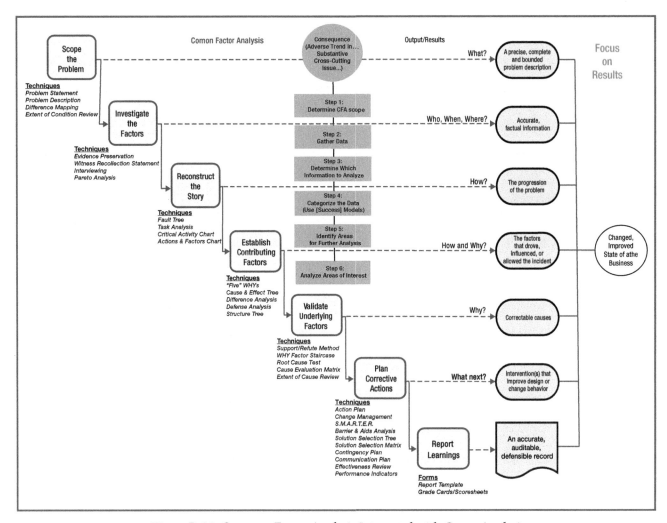

Figure B-10. Common Factor Analysis Integrated with Cause Analysis

Questions for Understanding

1. What is the primary intent of a common factor analysis?
2. What documents or data would you exclude from a common factor analysis?

Questions for Discussion

1. When you are analyzing a series of low-level incidents, what does the success of your analysis depend upon?
2. Discuss some of the models you might use to put structure to a problem you are analyzing.

References

Nuclear Regulatory Commission (NRC). (1993, October). *Development of the NRC's human performance investigation process (HPIP): Investigator's manual.* (NRC NUREG/CR-5455, S1-92-101). Washington, DC: US Government Printing Office.

Nuclear Regulatory Commission (NRC). (2011, February). *Inspection for one degraded cornerstone or any three white inputs in a strategic performance area.* (NRC Inspection Procedure 95002). Washington, DC: US NRC Office of Nuclear Reactor Regulation.

Nuclear Regulatory Commission (NRC). (2014, December). *Aspects within the cross-cutting areas.* (NRC Inspection Manual Chapter 0310). Washington, DC: US NRC Office of Nuclear Reactor Regulation.

Glossary

The following definitions provide for a common language, aid in understanding, and promote consistency in the use of words, terms, and phrases used in this document.

ACA Apparent cause analysis.

accident An unwanted transfer of energy or an environmental condition that, due to the absence or failure of barriers or controls, produces injury to persons, damage to property, or reduction in process output.

accountability The expectation that an individual or an organization is answerable for results; to explain its actions, or be subject to the consequences judged appropriate by others; the expectation that individuals accept responsibility for the consequences of their actions, including the rewards or sanctions.

action A real-time happening or occurrence. A discrete, relevant deed or event that preceded or followed the incident being investigated.

actions and factors charting A graphical depiction of the chronology of a logical series of events and related conditions that precede an incident or accident.

active error Action (behavior) that changes equipment, system, or plant state, triggering immediate undesired consequences.

administrative defense or control The policies, procedures, training, work practices, processes, managerial controls, and expectations that direct people's activities so that they are predictable and safe and limit their exposure to hazards, especially for work performed in and on the facility. Altogether, such controls help people anticipate and prepare for problems. Written instructions specify what, when, where, and how work is to be done, and what personal protective equipment workers are to use. The rigor with which people follow and perform work activities according to correctly written procedures, expectations, and standards directly affects the integrity of this line of protection.

adverse condition Any item or activity that does not conform to requirements. *Adverse condition* is synonymous with terms such as *failure, malfunction, deficiency, deviation, defective material, defective equipment,* and *non-conformances.*

adverse trend A tendency or movement in a negative direction requiring further investigation.

aggravating factor A behavior, inaction, or condition which makes a situation or consequence more severe. Undesirable prior conditions or workplace circumstances can provoke an error or drive errant behaviors or reduce the opportunity for successful behavior at the job site. Roughly equivalent to an *error-inducing condition. See also* exacerbating factor, error precursor.

a.k.a. Also known as.

alignment The extent to which the values, processes, management, and existing factors within an organization influence human performance in a complementary and non-contradictory way. Facilitating organizational processes and values to support desired safe and productive behavior.

analysis Investigating the facts and evaluating the factors associated with a project. The use of methods and techniques for arranging data to (1) assist in determining what additional data are required; (2) establish consistency, validity, and logic; (3) establish necessary and sufficient events for causes; and (4) guide and support inferences and judgments.

anatomy of an incident A cause-and-effect illustration of the active and latent origins (linkages) of business accidents or mishaps initiated by human action.

apparent cause A probable reason for the existence of an adverse condition.

assumption A condition taken for granted or accepted as true without verification of the facts.

at-risk practice A behavior or habit that tends to diminish the effectiveness of a human performance tool or increases the chance for error during an activity, generally adopted for expedience, comfort, or convenience.

attitude An unobservable state of mind, or feeling, toward an object, person, or subject.

barrier Any means used to control, prevent, or impede energy flows. Anything used to control, prevent, or impede a hazard from reaching a target. Anything that protects equipment or people from a hazard whether natural, physical, administrative, or human in nature. The administrative or physical controls designed to detect, prevent, or inhibit an inappropriate act or equipment malfunction. A.k.a. *safeguard. See also* defense.

barrier analysis An analytical technique used to identify energy sources and the failed or deficient barriers and controls that contributed to an accident. An investigative technique used to identify hazards associated with an accident and the controls (defenses/safeguards) that should have been in place to prevent the hazard from reaching a target. The evaluation determines what could have prevented the incident or significantly mitigated its consequences.

behavior The physical, observable actions executed to produce a result. The mental and physical efforts to perform a task; observable (movement and speech) and non-observable (thought, decisions, and emotional response) activity by an individual. Generally, observable behavior is treated as measurable and controllable.

belief Acceptance of or faith in the truth, existence, or validity of something (e.g., vision, mental model, principle, or rule) including suppositions or assumptions about what will be successful.

benchmarking A process of comparing products, processes, and practices against the best in class, the toughest competitors, or those companies recognized as industry leaders; a method of discovering innovative thinking or approaches.

CAP Corrective action program.

causal factor An occurrence or condition in the accident sequence necessary and sufficient to produce or contribute to the unwanted result. An action, condition, or event which directly or indirectly influences or permits the outcome of a situation or problem. An action, event, condition, situation, or circumstance that could have produced the incident, prevented the incident, permitted the incident, or lessened the incident's severity. *See also* contributing factor or contributing cause.

cause Anything that contributes to an accident or incident. An action, situation, or condition which directly produces or indirectly shapes or contributes to an effect (result/consequence). In an investigation, the use of the word *cause* as a singular term should be avoided. It is preferable to use it in the plural sense, such as *causal factors*, rather than identifying *the cause*.

cause analysis An investigation and evaluation used to identify reasons for performance problems or adverse conditions with the purpose of developing associated corrective or preventive actions to resolve the situation.

CFR Code of Federal Regulations.

change Stress on a system that was previously in a state of equilibrium, or anything that disturbs the planned or normal functioning of a system.

change analysis An analytical technique used for accident investigations, wherein accident-free reference bases are established, and differences relevant to accident causes and situations are systematically identified. In change analysis, all changes are considered, including those initially considered trivial or obscure. *See also* difference analysis.

change management A methodical planning process to establish the direction of change, align people and resources, and implement the selected modifications throughout an organization, large or small.

checking The act of confirming the actions of a job performer are correct, without error.

coaching The process of facilitating changes in behavior of another person through direct interaction, feedback, collaboration, and positive relationships. *See also* feedback.

common cause Multiple failures (i.e., two or more) of plant equipment or processes attributable to a shared cause. A reason for problems shared by or attributed to multiple (i.e., two or more) incidents or failures of plant equipment or processes.

common factor analysis A diagnostic tool that provides a systematic method for collectively evaluating a group of issues and difficulties experienced in a defined area for possible shared causes. A.k.a. *common cause evaluation.*

common mode failure A specific condition that has the potential to cause multiple failures by the same failure mechanism. When multiple redundant features fail due to the same defect or adverse trend, it is called a *common cause.*

compensatory (corrective) action An interim measure used until final correction to resolve the condition is complete.

complacency Self-satisfaction accompanied by unawareness of actual dangers, hazards, or deficiencies; being unconcerned in a hazardous environment.

conclusions Significant deductions derived from analytical results. Conclusions are derived from and must be supported by the facts, plus results from testing and analyses conducted. Conclusions are statements that answer two questions the accident investigation addresses: *What happened?* and *Why did it happen?* Conclusions include concise recapitulations of the causal factors (direct, contributing, and root causes) of the accident determined by analysis of facts.

condition Any as-found state, whether or not resulting from an incident, that may have adverse safety, health, quality assurance, security, operational, or environmental implications. A pertinent situation, circumstance, or factor that may have influenced (triggered, allowed, or aggravated) a chain of events.

condition adverse to quality (CAQ) Any situation, circumstance, action, or incident in which (1) planned and systematic actions have not assured that a safety-related structure, system, or component will perform satisfactorily in service; (2) actions related to the physical characteristics of a material, structure, component, or system have not controlled the quality (fitness for use) of the safety-related material, structure, component, or system to predetermined requirements; or (3) failures, malfunctions, deficiencies, deviations, defective material and equipment, or non-conformances involve safety-related structures, systems, and components that prevent or mitigate the consequences of postulated accidents that could cause undue risk to the health and safety of the public.

consequences The actual or potential result/outcome of an incident, usually measured in terms of health/safety effects, environmental impacts, property loss/damage, or business interruption costs.

conservative decision-making Reaching conclusions by placing greater value on safety above the production goals of the business. Decisions demonstrate recognition and avoidance of activities that unnecessarily reduce safety margins.

contributing cause(s) An event or condition that collectively with other causes increases the likelihood of an accident but that individually did not directly cause the accident. *See also* contributing factor(s).

contributing factor(s) An action, event, condition, situation, or circumstance that directly triggered the incident. An action, event, condition, situation, or circumstance that indirectly influenced or allowed the incident or shaped its outcome. A clear cause that addresses the stated problem and is supported by the facts of the investigation. An action or condition that could have prevented the incident (a.k.a. a *sin of omission*).

controls (1) Barriers used to control energy flows, such as the insulation on an electrical cord, a stop sign, a procedure, or a safe work permit. (2) Administrative and engineering mechanisms that can affect the chemical, physical, metallurgical or nuclear process of a nuclear facility in such a manner as to effect the protection of the health and safety of the public and workers, or the protection of the environment. (3) Error-prevention techniques adopted to prevent error and to recover from or mitigate the effects of error; to make an activity or process go smoothly, properly, and according to high standards. Multiple layers of controls provide defense-in-depth.

correcting Providing feedback to a performer to immediately stop either an unsafe, at-risk, or unethical behavior.

corrective action Measures taken to alleviate symptoms of a problem or to eliminate or diminish causes of problems to minimize the potential for recurrence of the condition. Includes measures to restore an item to an acceptable condition or capability. Includes phrases *compensatory action, immediate action*, and *remedial action.*

corrective action review board (CARB) A group of senior management personnel that meets to review the classification, assignment, and completed evaluations of selected condition reports.

corrective action to prevent recurrence (CATPR) or (CAPR) Measure(s) implemented to preclude another occurrence of the root cause of a significant adverse condition. Steps which eliminate or mitigate most probable root cause(s) to keep problem from happening again. A specific, implementable activity necessary to address a root cause of an incident or adverse trend.

CR Condition report.

critical step A procedure step, series of steps, or action that, if performed improperly, will cause irreversible harm to equipment, people, or the environment. A step in the process where potential threats could interact with the hazard that could be released. For accident analysis, the absence of hazards or threats in a process step makes it a *non-critical step.*

cross-cutting area Fundamental performance attributes that extend across all of the US National Regulatory Commission's Reactor Oversight Process (ROP) cornerstones of safety. These areas are human performance (HU), problem identification and resolution (PI&R), and safety conscious work environment (SCWE).

cross-cutting aspect A performance characteristic of a finding that is the most significant causal factor of the performance deficiency.

culpability The amount of personal responsibility one would expect to accept for an act (behavior) judged on intended purpose and knowledge.

cultural defense or control The assumptions, values, beliefs, and attitudes and the related leadership practices that encourage either high standards of performance or mediocrity, open or closed communication, or high or low standards of performance. Personnel in highly reliable organizations practice error-prevention rigorously, regardless of their perception of a task's risk and simplicity, how routine it is, and how competent the performer. The integrity of this line of defense depends on people's appreciation of the human's role in safety, the respect they have for each other, and their pride in the organization and the facility.

culture An organization's system of commonly held values and beliefs that influence the attitudes, choices, and behaviors of the individuals of the organization. *See also* safety culture.

defense Means or measures taken to prevent or catch human error, to protect people, plant, or property against the results of human error, and to mitigate the consequences of an error. *Defense* is a term used in much of the human performance literature. A.k.a. *safeguard. See also* barrier, controls.

defense analysis A set of questions to identify tools or barriers for error-likely situations and worst-case consequences, controls and safeguards important for task completion, and missing or flawed controls or barriers.

defense-in-depth The set of redundant and diverse controls, barriers, and safeguards to protect personnel and equipment from human error, such that a failure with one defense would be compensated for by another defensive mechanism to prevent or mitigate undesirable consequences.

degradation influence Adverse conditions involving concerns with human-machine interfaces that must be present in order for equipment, components, materials, or human performance to degrade to the point of failure. Examples are faulty design, material defects, fabrication or manufacturing errors; assembly or installation defects; off-design or unintended service conditions; improper operation; and maintenance deficiencies. The degradation influences are the roots of the physical problem with the equipment; however, more analysis must be done to discover the human and latent roots of the incident.

degradation mechanism The process or physical phenomena involved in the equipment failure. Generally, the mechanism involves force (transient, cyclic, steady, or voltage), reactive environment (chemical or nuclear), time (aging), or temperature (heat or cold). These mechanisms either alter material dimensions or inhibit component operation, and are induced by degradation influences.

difference analysis An analytical technique used for accident investigations, wherein accident-free *reference bases* are established, and changes relevant to accident causes and situations are systematically identified. In *difference analysis*, all changes are considered, including those initially considered trivial or obscure. *See also* change analysis.

direct cause The final action or condition which brings about an incident or accident.

distractions/interruptions Conditions of either the task or work environment requiring the individual to stop and restart a task sequence diverting one's attention to and from the task at hand.

DOE Department of Energy.

E&CF Events and causal factors.

effect The result, outcome, or consequence of a preceding action, situation, or condition.

effectiveness In the corrective action context, success gauged by a significant change in one or more of these four measures: (1) the probability of the original incident recurring; (2) the frequency of the problem recurring; (3) reduction in the magnitude or severity of the problem; and (4) elimination of the original problem.

effectiveness review An assessment of conditions after corrective actions have been implemented, opportunities for recurrence have occurred, and sufficient time has elapsed to verify the measures taken were successful in preventing recurrence of the problem, issue, or incident.

emergent issue A concern that could have an immediate and direct impact on the health and safety of the general public or plant personnel, pose a significant industrial hazard, or allow the deterioration of plant conditions to a possible unsafe or unstable level.

engineered barrier or control The physical ability to protect from errors. To optimize this set of controls, equipment is reliable and is kept in a configuration that is resistant to simple human error and allows systems and components to perform their intended functions when required. Facilities with high equipment reliability, effective configuration control, and minimum human-machine vulnerabilities tend to experience fewer and less severe facility incidents than those that struggle with these issues. How carefully facility equipment is designed, operated, and maintained (using human-centered approaches) affects the level of integrity of this line of protection. *See also* control.

enhancement Actions which do *not* directly fix a problem or directly prevent its recurrence and are considered "nice to do."

error An unintentional human action which deviates from an expected behavior according to some standard. The individual may slip up, make a mistake, or unintentionally deviate from a standard.

error-likely situation A slip, lapse, or mistake about to happen which typically exists when the demands of the task exceed the capabilities of the individual or when work conditions aggravate the limitations of human nature. A.k.a. *error trap*.

error precursor Unfavorable prior conditions at the job site that increase the probability for a slip, lapse, or mistake during a specific action. Factors that influence human reliability through their effects on performance. Includes factors such as environmental conditions, human-system interface design, procedures, training, and supervision. A.k.a. *error-inducing factor*.

event An occurrence; something noteworthy and real-time that happens. An accident involves a sequence of events occurring in the course of work activity and culminating in unintentional injury or damage.

events and causal factors charting *See* actions and factors charting.

evidence Objects or information that can be sensed and described used to infer, confirm, or refute the causation of a phenomenon. Generally, evidence is personnel (testimony), documentary, or physical.

exacerbating factor A behavior, inaction, or condition which makes a situation or consequence more severe. Undesirable prior conditions or workplace circumstances that can provoke an error or drive errant behaviors or reduce the opportunity for successful behavior at the job site. Roughly equivalent to an *error-inducing condition*. *See also* aggravating factor, error precursor.

expectation An established, explicit description of acceptable plant outcomes, business goals, process performance, safety performance, or individual behavior established by management.

exposure factor Job-site barriers/defenses that are missing, degraded, weak, or not used to prevent a hazard from reaching a target. This weakness or vulnerability results in the "set-up" of situations or circumstances which can lead to an incident. Roughly equivalent to *failed barriers*. *See also* flawed defenses.

extent of cause The extent to which the root causes of an identified problem have impacted other plant processes, equipment, or human performance. A reasonable boundary around the population of other plant processes, equipment, or human performance jobs or tasks with the potential to be impacted by the same underlying reasons or drivers (i.e., causes) as the concern being investigated. When a cause is discovered, it raises the question about what other similar causes could be reasonably expected. Those causes constitute the *extent of cause*. The extent of cause may cross the boundaries of disciplines, departments, or programs or for different types of structures, systems, or components.

extent of condition The extent to which the actual adverse condition exists with other plant processes, equipment, or human performance. The scope of or boundary around identical or similar *objects* with the potential to exhibit the identical or similar *defect* or *deviation*. A reasonable boundary around the population of other plant processes, equipment, or human performance jobs or tasks with the potential to exhibit the same undesired symptoms, circumstances, or effects as the concern being investigated. When an adverse condition is discovered, it raises the question about what other similar adverse conditions could be reasonably expected. Those conditions constitute the *extent of condition*.

factor Any as-found or existing state that influences the outcome of a particular task, process, or operation.

failure An unacceptable difference (gap) between expected and observed performance, behavior, or results. The condition of not having achieved the required or desired end state (outcome/result).

failure mechanism The specific type of equipment fault (the form, fit, or function shortfall) that resulted in the loss of function or capability. Generally the failure mechanisms involve deformations, fractures, surface or material changes, or displacements. Examples are broken linkage, torn diaphragm, blown fuse, valve seat leakage, scored flange, loose valve packing, loose fitting, low voltage, ground fault, short circuit, corrosion, wear, pitting, erosion, expansion, shrinkage, melting, yielding, cracking, blockage, sticking, and moisture intrusion. Failure mechanisms are induced by degradation mechanisms.

failure mode The manner in which the failure manifested (i.e., the effect). Examples are failed to open, close, regulate flow, energize, or actuate; loss of indication, cooling, heating, or pressure; tripped; over pressurized; and overheated. Failure modes are induced by failure mechanisms.

failure scenario The sequence of events that led up to a failure mode. Usually defined as a series of chronological events that starts with an initiating event and ends with an identified failure mode.

fallible/fallibility A fundamental, internal characteristic of human nature to err or to be imprecise.

fault tree analysis (1) An investigative technique that involves identifying and visually depicting possible ways that a condition could have occurred. Possible explanations are then eliminated (based upon further investigation and deductive reasoning) until only the actual failure path remains. (2) A logic diagram used to evaluate all possible failure scenarios that caused an incident. Causes which can contribute to the incident are listed and proven or refuted as appropriate. The evaluation continues until all the actions and their combinations which could cause the undesired incident have been determined. The user identifies the critical path to failure.

feedback Information about past or present behavior and results that gives a job performer or an organization the opportunity to change.

fishbone diagram Cause and effect structure that represents the relationships between a given effect and its potential causes.

fit The ability of an item to physically interface or interconnect with or become an integral part of another item.

flawed defenses Defects with engineered, administrative, cultural, or oversight controls that, under the right circumstances, fail to: protect plant equipment or people against hazards; prevent the occurrence of active errors; or mitigate the consequences of error.

form The shape, size, dimension, mass, weight, and other visual parameters which uniquely characterize an item.

function The action or actions that an item is designed to perform.

gap analysis The process of comparison of actual results or behavior with desired results or behavior, followed by an exploration of why the gap exists.

generic implication An inference that the reasons (underlying factors) for an incident are not unique to the incident but may be indicative of similar problems in multiple areas of the business.

habit An unconscious pattern of behavior acquired through frequent repetition.

hazard Any condition, situation, or activity representing a potential for adversely affecting economic values or the health or quality of people's lives. The potential for energy flow(s) to result in an accident or otherwise adverse consequence.

high reliability organization (HRO) An organization that has succeeded in avoiding catastrophes in an environment where normal accidents can be expected due to risk factors and complexity. Examples are aircraft carriers, air traffic controllers, power grid dispatch centers, nuclear submarines, airline cockpit crews, nuclear power plants, and offshore platforms.

HPES Human Performance Enhancement System.

HPIP Human Performance Investigation Process.

human error An action or behavior which unintentionally deviates from an expected standard. A phrase that generally means the slips, lapses, and mistakes of human beings.

human factors A body of scientific facts about human characteristics. The term covers all biomedical, psychological, and psycho-social considerations. Includes, but is not limited to, principles and applications in the areas of human factors engineering, personnel selection, training, job performance aids, and human performance evaluation.

human factors engineering (HFE) The application of knowledge about human capabilities and limitations to plant, system, and equipment design. Provides reasonable assurance that the design of the plant, systems, equipment, human tasks, and the work environment are compatible with the sensory, perceptual, cognitive, and physical attributes of the personnel who operate, maintain, and support the plant. *See also* human factors.

human-machine interface That part of the system through which personnel interact to perform their functions and tasks. The point of contact or interaction between the person and the physical hardware.

human nature (limitations) The bounds of being born human. Generic traits, dispositions, and limitations that may incline individuals to err under unfavorable conditions such as habit, short-term memory, stress, complacency, inaccurate risk perception, mindset, and mental shortcuts.

human performance *See* performance.

IAEA International Atomic Energy Agency.

illness/fatigue Degradation of a person's physical or mental abilities caused by a sickness, disease, or debilitating injury. Lack of adequate physical rest to support acceptable mental alertness and function.

immediate action Steps taken to promptly resolve situations involving safety or similar concerns requiring swift attention. Such measures focus on the direct cause of an identified problem. These actions could include steps addressing a deficient condition temporarily until permanent or remedial corrective actions can be implemented.

inaction The absence of a deed, usually the absence of a specific task or behavior. A.k.a. *error of omission*.

incident An unwanted, undesirable change in the state of facility structures, systems, or components or human/organizational conditions (e.g., health, behavior, administrative controls, and environment) that exceeds established significance criteria. The undesirable consequence that is the reason for an investigation. *See also* event.

independent Freedom of thought between a performer and a verifier, created by separating the actions of each individual by physical distance and time, such that audible or visual cues of the performer are not detectable by the verifier, before and while aligning a plant component.

individual An employee in any position in the organization from yesterday's new hire in the storeroom to the senior vice president in the corner office.

individual capability Unique mental, physical, and emotional characteristics of a particular person that fail to match the demands of the specific task. This involves cognitive and physical limitations. Examples are unfamiliarity with the task, unsafe attitudes, level of education, lack of knowledge, unpracticed skills, personality, inexperience, health and fitness, poor communication practices, fatigue, and low self-esteem.

information Data from one source only (i.e., not independently verified).

initiating action A deed of an individual, either correct, in error, or in violation, that results in a business incident.

INPO Institute of Nuclear Power Operations.

interim actions Temporary steps or measures taken for an adverse condition pending completion of the final corrective actions.

investigation A detailed, systematic search to uncover the who, what, when, where, why, and how of an occurrence and to determine what corrective actions are needed to prevent a recurrence.

irrecoverable acts Action that, once taken, cannot be reversed without some significant delay despite best efforts. No obvious means of reversing an action.

job A combination of tasks and duties that define a particular position within the organization usually related to the functions required to achieve the organization's mission, such as control room operator.

job-site conditions The unique factors associated with a specific task and a particular individual. Factors embedded in the immediate work environment that influences the behavior of the individual during work.

just culture An environment in which those who make honest errors and mistakes are not blamed, while those who willfully violate standards and expectations are censured. Workers willingly accept responsibility for the consequences of their actions, including the rewards or sanctions. They feel empowered to report errors and near misses. *See also* accountability, control.

JTA Job task analysis.

knowledge-based performance Behavior in response to a totally unfamiliar situation (no skill, rule, or pattern recognizable to the individual). A classic problem-solving situation that relies on personal understanding of the system, the system's present state, and the scientific principles and fundamental theory related to the system.

lapse An error due to a failure of memory or recall. *See also* mistake, slip.

latent condition An undetected situation or circumstance created by past hidden errors that are embedded in the organization or production system lying dormant for periods of time doing no apparent harm. *See also* latent organizational weakness.

latent error An undetected act or decision resulting in organization-related weaknesses or equipment flaws that lie hidden or dormant until revealed either by an incident, another human error, testing, or self-assessment. *See also* latent condition.

latent organizational weakness Undetected (hidden) or uncorrected deficiencies in management control processes (e.g., strategy, policies, work control, training, and resource allocation) or group values (e.g., shared beliefs, attitudes, norms, and assumptions) creating workplace conditions that can provoke an error and/or degrade the integrity of defenses. Can be conditions or factors present in the organization that are manifested as flawed defenses and error precursors. *See also* anatomy of an incident, latent error.

leader Any individual who takes personal responsibility for his or her performance and the facility's performance and attempts to positively influence the processes and values of the organization. Managers and supervisors are in positions of responsibility and as such are organizational leaders. Some individuals in these positions, however, may not exhibit leadership behaviors that support this definition of a leader. Workers, although not in managerial positions of responsibility, can be and are very influential leaders. The designation as a leader is earned from subordinates, peers, and superiors.

leadership The behavior of an individual attempting to influence the behaviors, values, and beliefs of others. That group of employees given the positional responsibility for guiding the direction and values of the organization. *See also* management.

limited short-term memory Forgetfulness. Inability to accurately attend to more than two or three channels of information (or five to nine bits of data) simultaneously. The mind's "workbench" for problem-solving and decision-making. The temporary, attention-demanding storeroom we use to remember new information.

LTA Less than adequate.

management That group of people given the positional responsibility and accountability for the performance of the organization. *See also* leadership.

management practices Techniques, methods, or behaviors used by managers to set goals, plan, organize, monitor, assess, and control relative to the organization's mission. *See also* practices.

mental model Structured organization of knowledge a person has about how something works (usually in terms of generalizations, assumptions, pictures, or key words). A conceptual picture of the underlying way in which a system functions, helping to describe causes, effects, and interdependencies of key inputs, factors, activities, and outcomes. Sometimes referred to as *vision* or *picture*.

mindset A tendency to "see" only what the brain is tuned to see. Information that does not fit a mental vision may not be recognized or noticed.

mistake Errors committed because the intent of the act was incorrect for the work situation, typically defined by the condition of the physical plant. Incorrect decision or interpretation. *See also* error, slip.

moderating factor An action, condition, or circumstance that mitigates or prevents a situation from becoming much worse than it could be.

MORT Management oversight & risk tree. A type of defense analysis in a tree structure used to systematically deduce the causes and contributing factors of significant incidents.

motives Personal (internal) hopes, goals, needs, interests, or purposes that tend to drive, or stimulate an individual to action in order to achieve or meet them.

norm Pattern/trait observed as typical practice or behavior for a group of people.

NRC US Nuclear Regulatory Commission.

NUREG Nuclear Regulatory Commission Report.

operating experience (OE) review An assessment of relevant history from the plant's ongoing collection, analysis, and documentation of business and related industry incidents and from interviews with plant staff.

organization A group of people with a shared mission, resources, and plans to direct people's behavior toward safe and reliable operation. Organizations direct people's behavior in a predictable way, usually through processes and their value and belief systems. Workers, supervisors, support staff, managers, and executives all make up the organization.

organizational factors (1) In the task-specific sense, an existing job-site condition that influences behavior and is the result of a business process, culture, and other environmental factors. (2) In the general sense, the aggregate of all management and leadership practices, processes, values, culture, corporate structures, technology, resources, and controls that affect behavior of individuals at the job site.

OSHA Occupational Safety and Health Administration.

oversight defense or control A method for achieving accountability for personnel and facility safety, for security, and for ethical behavior in all facets of facility operations, maintenance, and support activities, achieved by a kind of *social contract* entered into willingly by workers and management where a *just culture* prevails. This *accountability* helps verify margins, the integrity of controls and processes, as well as the quality of performance. *Performance improvement* activities facilitate the accountability of line managers. The integrity of this line of defense depends on management's commitment to high levels of human performance and consistent follow-through to correct problems and vulnerabilities. *See also* accountability, control, just culture, performance improvement, performance indicator.

ownership Personal internalization of the responsibility for the quality and timeliness of the performance of a job which leads to taking action and delivering value-added results.

Pareto analysis A way of organizing data to determine the "vital few" factors responsible for a particular problem. A *Pareto chart* is a bar graph of failures ordered by frequency of failure, cost of failure, or contribution to system unavailability.

performance Any activity that has some effect on the environment. The accomplishment of work.

performance gap The difference between desired accomplishments and actual accomplishments, whether in terms of results or behavior.

performance gap analysis The process of gathering and analyzing data to determine the causes of the difference between current and desired behaviors or results.

performance improvement A systematic process of identifying and analyzing gaps in human behavior and results, followed by developing and implementing interventions or corrective actions to close the gaps between the desired behavior or result and the actual behavior or result. *See also* oversight defense, control.

performance indicator Parameters measured to reflect the critical success factors of an organization. A lagging indicator is a measure of results or outcomes. A leading indicator is a measure of system conditions or behaviors which provide a forecast of future performance. A.k.a. *metrics.*

performance mode One of three modes a person uses to process information related to one's level of familiarity and attention given to a specific activity. People will likely use multiple modes to complete a task. *See also* knowledge-based performance, rule-based performance, skill-based performance.

performance monitoring Review and comparison of accomplishments against expectations and standards using problem reporting, feedback, reinforcement, coaching, observation data, incident data, and trend data. *See also* gap analysis, performance gap, performance indicator.

performance problem A discrepancy in behaviors or results with respect to expectations or operating experience, or an opportunity to improve behaviors and results created by changes in technology, procedures, or expectations. *See also* performance gap.

PI Performance indicator.

post-job review An assessment activity conducted after task completion to solicit feedback from those involved. Usually the feedback involves a face-to-face meeting between workers and supervisors, but the method is not limited to a meeting. Post-job reviews provide workers and their supervisors with a forum to document what went well and to identify potential enhancements.

practices Behaviors or deeds usually associated with a role that can be applied to a variety of goals in a variety of settings. *See also* work practices.

pre-job brief A meeting of individuals conducted before performing a job to have an interactive discussion on the tasks involved, hazards, and related safety precautions. This meeting helps individuals to understand better what to accomplish and what to avoid. Pre-job briefings help participants avoid surprises in the field and reinforce the idea that there are no "routine" activities.

presumptive action An event or happening that is assumed because it appears logical in the sequence, but cannot be proven. It need not be proved or eliminated prior to issuing the root cause analysis (RCA), as long as no causal factors arise as a result of a presumptive event.

presumptive factor A condition, situation, or circumstance that is assumed because it appears to have been an existing condition or real action but has not been identified or substantiated yet.

principles A set of underlying truths that can be used to guide both individual performance and the management of human performance.

proactive Preemptive measures to prevent incidents or avoid error by identifying and eliminating organizational and job-site contributors to performance problems before they occur. Preventing the next incident.

problem A real or perceived gap between the existing performance (i.e., behavior or results) and the expected standard of performance.

problem statement A sentence which describes what is wrong (what *object* with what *defect*) in specific terms, avoiding hidden solutions or cause statements. The problem statement should describe the concern or issue in terms that are quantifiable and factual.

process A series of actions organized to provide a product or service. Tangible structures established to direct the behavior of individuals in a predictable, repeatable fashion as they perform various tasks.

prompt Ready and fit for use prior to or by the expected or needed time.

qualification Criterion indicating capability to perform to all aspects of license basis, including codes and standards, design criteria, and commitments.

RCA Root cause analysis.

reactive Taking corrective action in response to an incident, error, or near miss, after the fact.

readiness An individual's mental, physical, and emotional preparedness to perform a job as planned.

reinforcement The process of applying consequences to improve the chances of a targeted behavior being repeated.

remedial action A correction or fix applied to restore a situation or equipment to an acceptable state or capability or to mitigate symptoms or effects of a problem. These could include steps addressing a deficient condition temporarily, until permanent corrective actions can be implemented. Additional corrective actions could be required to prevent recurrence.

repeat occurrences (1) Two or more independent conditions which are the result of the same basic cause(s). (2) An incident that includes failure modes, causes, or consequences that are similar to a previous incident. A repeat incident is one that reasonably could have been prevented by the corrective action(s) taken in response to a previous incident.

reportability Regulatory requirement to communicate certain occurrences or conditions to outside federal or state agencies.

result The outcomes of the enterprise in terms of production, incidents, personnel safety, performance indicators, and configuration.

rigor Completeness and correctness in a behavior or process; cautiously accurate and meticulous, exhibiting strict precision during the execution of an action.

risk-important step Actions in written instructions that are performed by plant personnel to provide reasonable assurance of plant safety. Actions may be made up of one or more tasks. The action exposes products, services, or assets to the potential for harm.

root cause (1) An underlying driver or reason explaining the existence in an organizational system of the triggering, aggravating, or exposure factors that resulted in a harmful business incident (and was not the effect of a more important underlying factor). *See also* underlying factor. (2) The basic reason(s) (i.e., hardware, process, or human performance), for a problem, which if corrected, will prevent recurrence of that problem.

root cause analysis A structured search for the underlying fixable reasons explaining the existence in an organizational system of the triggering, aggravating, or exposure factors that resulted in an adverse condition or critical incident so actions to preclude repetition can be initiated.

rule-based performance Behavior based on selection of a defined path forward derived from one's recognition of the situation. It follows an IF (symptom X), THEN (action Y) logic.

safety culture An organization's values and behaviors — modeled by its leaders and internalized by its members — that serve to make protection the overriding priority. *See also* culture, value.

safety significance Relative importance of a problem determined by considering actual and potential nuclear, radiological, and industrial impact on plant and personnel protection.

SCAQ Significant condition adverse to quality.

SCWE Safety conscious work environment.

self-assessment Formal or informal processes of identifying one's own opportunities for improvement by comparing present practices and results with desired goals, policies, expectations, and standards. *See also* benchmarking, performance monitoring.

shortcut An action, perceived as more efficient by an individual, that is intended to accomplish the intent of actions other than that directed by procedure, policy, expectation, or training. *See also* violation.

significance Conclusion regarding the implication of what an incident or situation could mean (or could have meant) to the future of the individuals, organizations, agencies, etc. that could be affected.

significance level Level assigned to a condition report providing an indication of the level of investigation needed to determine the cause(s) and corrective action.

significant condition adverse to quality (SCAQ) A situation or circumstance that, if uncorrected, considerably affects the safe, reliable, and economic production of electricity at a nuclear power station.

simultaneous, multiple tasks Performance of two or more activities, either mentally or physically, possibly resulting in divided attention, mental overload, or reduced vigilance on one or the other activities.

situation awareness The relationship between the operator's understanding of the plant's condition and its actual condition at any given time.

skill-based performance Behavior associated with highly practiced actions in a familiar situation executed from memory without significant conscious thought.

skill of the craft The knowledge, proficiency, and abilities possessed by individuals as a result of training or experience. Activities related to certain aspects of a task or job that an individual knows without needing written instructions.

slip A physical action different than intended. *See also* error, lapse, mistake.

standard Something considered by an authority or by industry best practice as a basis of comparison or judgment; an approved model of excellence; the behavior requirements of an expectation.

stress The body's mental and physical response to a perceived threat in the environment.

substitution test An assessment of a person's culpability relative to a performance problem to determine whether one or more motivated, comparably qualified and experienced individuals would take the same action under similar circumstances.

success Achievement of expected performance, behavior, and results in the areas of production and protection.

supervisor That member of first-line management who directs and monitors the performance of individual contributors (front-line workers) in the conduct of assigned work activities.

system An integrated collection of plant components and control elements that operate alone or with other plant systems to perform a function.

target A person, object, or animal upon which an unwanted energy flow may act to cause damage, injury, or death.

task A group of activities that have a common purpose, often occurring in close chronological proximity.

task analysis A method for describing what plant personnel must do to achieve the purposes or goal of their activities. The description can be in terms of cognitive activities, actions, and supporting equipment.

task demands Specific mental, physical, and team requirements that may either exceed the capabilities or challenge the limitations of human nature of the individual assigned to perform the job. *See also* error precursor.

task preview A review of procedures, other related work documents, and any job walkdowns that were performed to become familiar with the scope of the work, activity sequence, and critical steps/attributes. Provides a structured, risk-based review of the work activities from a human performance perspective.

taxonomy Systematic set of principles for the classification and arrangement of concepts.

threat An action or force from human error, equipment malfunctions, operational process malfunctions, facility malfunctions, or from natural disasters that could cause or trigger a hazardous energy release.

timeline Documented series of events from identification of problem through resolution and close-out.

triggering factor An action, situation, or circumstance that initiates, drives, or provokes an effect.

troubleshooting A systematic approach to data collection, failure analysis, and development and execution of a test/measurement plan to identify the cause(s) of equipment malfunctions in order to correct or repair a situation, component(s), or subcomponent(s) so the failure can be resolved and the component/system can be returned to operational status. Typically, troubleshooting will determine and correct the deficient situation but will not find the underlying factors or causes.

underlying factor A deep-seated reason for the existence in an organization of the triggering, aggravating, or exposure actions, conditions, or situations that provoked, released, influenced, or permitted an incident. *See also* root cause.

uneasiness An attitude of apprehension and wariness regarding the capacity to err when performing specific human actions on plant components.

value A central principle prized by an individual or the members of a group around which decisions are driven and actions occur. *See also* culture, safety culture.

verification The process by which the design is evaluated to determine whether it acceptably satisfies personnel task needs and design guidance.

violation A deliberate, intentional act to evade a known policy or procedure requirement and that deviates from sanctioned organizational practices. *See also* shortcut.

vision A picture of the key aspects of an organization's future that is both desirable and feasible — to be the kind of organization people would aspire to — that guides an employee's choices without explicit direction, but is vague enough to encourage initiative. *See also* mental model.

vulnerability Susceptibility to external conditions that either aggravate or exceed the limitations of human nature, enhancing the potential to err; also, the weakness, incapacity, or difficulty to avoid or resist error in the presence of error precursors. *See also* flawed defense.

wariness An attitude of apprehension and uneasiness regarding the capacity to err when performing specific human actions on plant components.

witness A person (observer or onlooker) who has information related either directly or indirectly to an incident or accident.

work environment General influences of the job site, organizational, and cultural conditions that affect individual behavior. These include distractions, awkward equipment layout, complex lockout/tagout (LOTO) procedures, at-risk norms and values, work group attitudes toward various hazards, work control processes, temperature, lighting, and noise.

work execution Those activities related to the preparation for work, the performance of work, and the feedback on work activities.

work practices Methods an individual uses to perform a task correctly, safely, and efficiently including equipment/material use, procedure use, and error detection and prevention. *See also* practices.

worker An individual who performs physical work on equipment, having direct contact (touching) with equipment, and is capable of altering its condition.

workload The physical and cognitive demands placed on job performers.

Index

Figures and tables are indicated by "f" and "t" following page numbers.

A

A-B-C model of behavior, 10–11, 10–11*f*, 11*t*

Abernathy, B., 10, 11, 176

Ability, lines of inquiry regarding, 69, 69*f*, 70*t*

ACA. *See* Apparent cause analysis

Accident, defined, 283. *See also* Incident

Accountability

    cause analysis of, 14–15, 14–15*f*

    in corrective action plans, 15, 227, 227–228*f*, 229

    decision tree, 70, 71*f*

    defined, 14, 283

    lines of inquiry regarding, 69, 70, 70–71*f*, 72–73*t*

    organizational. *See* Organizational accountability

    personal. *See* Personal accountability

    for safety, 161

Action plan. *See* Corrective action plan

Actions

    corrective. *See* Corrective action

    critical human action, 102–103

    defined, 107, 107*t*, 283

    immediate, 291

    initiating, 292

    interim, 292

    symbol for, 107, 107*t*, 109, 109*f*

    terminology guidelines, 210, 210*t*

Actions and factors charting, 106–110

    in contributing factor tests, 120

    of decision-making processes, 89

    defense analysis in, 107, 138, 139

    defined, 106, 283

    examples of, 110, 111*f*

    general guidelines for, 110

    methodology for, 108–110, 108–110*f*

    prerequisite for, 107

    problem statements in, 34, 34*f*, 108, 108*f*

    as report attachment, 258

    terms and symbols in, 107, 107–108*t*, 109, 109*f*

    as timeline, 87, 106, 106*f*, 108, 109*f*

    usefulness of, 87, 88, 106–107, 112

Activators, in A-B-C model of behavior, 10, 10–11*f*, 11, 11*t*

Active coaching, 229

Active error

    defined, 283

    lines of defense against, 151, 155

    worker reduction of, 156, 157, 157*f*, 159*t*

Active listening, 68

Administrative defenses/controls

    as contributing factors, 118

    defense-in-depth analysis of, 151

    defined, 283

    as external factor of behavior, 11, 12–13*f*

DO THE MATH

Combine more than 30 expert authors,
with 1,000 years of experience, and countless
problems solved for companies like yours…

Your definitive, current, comprehensive Business Continuity textbook and reference – based on international standards and grounded in best practices.

**Business Continuity Management:
Global Best Practices, 4th Edition**
by Andrew Hiles
©2014
494 pages + 200 pages of free downloads, illustrations, glossary, index, and instructional teaching materials.

ISBN 978-1-931332-35-4, paperback

ISBN 978-1-931332-76-7, eBook

ISBN 978-1-931332-83-5, ePub

**Root Cause Analysis Handbook
Third Edition**
by ABS Consulting
©2008
320 pages, plus accompanying downloads, glossary.

ISBN 978-1-931332-51-4, paperback

ISBN 978-1-931332-72-9. eBook

ISBN 978-1-931332-82-8, ePub

Complete all-in-one package for root cause analysis, including 600+ pages of book and downloads, color-coded, 17" x 22" Root Cause Map™, and licensed access to online resources.

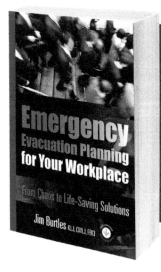

Be prepared! Follow this tested six-phase method to create a plan that you can activate at a moment's notice – to get everyone to safety from any workplace.

**Emergency Evacuation Planning
for Your Workplace**
by Jim Burtles
©2013
340 pages + 300 pages of free downloads, illustrations, glossary, index, and instructional teaching materials.

ISBN 978-1-931332-56-9, casebound

ISBN 978-1-931332-67-5, eBook

ISBN 978-1-931332-85-9, ePub

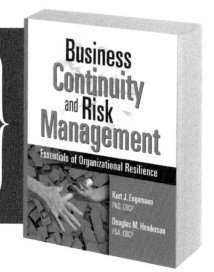
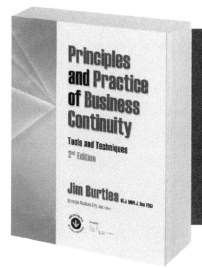

Credits

Kristen Noakes-Fry ABCI is Executive Editor at Rothstein Publishing. Previously, she was a Research Director, Information Security and Risk Group, for Gartner, Inc.; Associate Editor at Datapro (McGraw-Hill); and Associate Professor of English at Atlantic Cape College in New Jersey. She holds an M.A. from New York University and a B.A. from Russell Sage College.

Cover Design and Graphics:	Sheila Kwiatek, Flower Grafix
Typography, Layout and Graphics:	Jean King
Copy Editing:	Nancy M. Warner
eBook Design & Processing:	Donna Luther, Metadata Prime
Index:	Enid Zafran, Indexing Partners, LLC
Publishing and Marketing Intern	Sarah Patton

Title Font:	Haettenschweiler
Body Fonts:	Minion Pro and Myriad Pro

A Division of Rothstein Associates Inc.

Rothstein Publishing is your premier source of books and learning materials about Business Resilience including Crisis Management, Business Continuity, Disaster Recovery, Emergency Management, and Risk Management. Our industry-leading authors provide current, actionable knowledge, solutions, and tools you can put into practice immediately. Founded in 1984 by Philip Jan Rothstein FBCI, our company remains true to our commitment to prepare you and your organization to protect, preserve, and recover what is most important: your people, facilities, assets, and reputation. Rothstein Publishing is a division of Rothstein Associates Inc., an international management consultancy.

About the Author

Fred Forck, CPT, is a highly experienced incident investigator and self-assessment team leader who completed a 25-year career at the Callaway Nuclear Power Plant in Fulton, MO, in May 2007. He offers a rich array of root cause evaluation, quality assurance, quality improvement, facilitation, and teaching skills — including proven abilities to determine and correct the organizational weaknesses linking multiple adverse business incidents.

His background is impressive. Fred's first paying jobs as a young man were as a farm worker, janitor, and laborer. Fred began with dual undergraduate degrees — chemistry and secondary education — and he has put both into practice. For the first nine years of his career, Fred taught high school chemistry, physics, science, and math, while coaching varsity softball, junior high basketball, and Little League baseball. No stranger to hard work, when school was out, Fred found jobs as a bricklayer and bus driver. In the rest of his spare time, he served in Missouri National Guard military police units, advancing to detachment and company commander for four different units.

In 1982 Fred joined Quality Assurance (QA) at Callaway Nuclear Power Plant while the station was still under construction. As QA training supervisor, Fred developed the initial auditor and lead auditor training for the Callaway plant. He supervised the QA operations support group. As a certified lead auditor, Fred led inspections of vendors, chemistry, health physics, training, environmental monitoring, and corrective action. He also led the first self-assessment of industrial safety at the Callaway plant.

At Callaway and at Palo Verde Nuclear Generating Stations, Fred developed the root cause analysis (RCA) training programs and compiled root cause manuals for both stations (the latter for Palo Verde's regulatory recovery). At Callaway, Fred participated on over 90 root cause investigations generally as the lead investigator or the mentor. Besides participating in five common cause analyses, Fred developed and delivered the station's common cause analysis training. In 1999, Fred participated on a Nuclear Energy Institute (NEI) team that benchmarked best corrective action processes in the nuclear industry. Fred's final position at Callaway was root cause analysis coordinator. He has recent qualifications as a root cause analyst at Palo Verde, Ft. Calhoun, Tennessee Valley Authority (TVA), and Entergy nuclear stations. He was the lead RCA investigator for Fort

Calhoun station's Nuclear Regulatory Commission (NRC) 95002 inspection and qualified as a root cause subject matter expert at TVA's Browns Ferry nuclear plant to support the NRC's 95003 inspection. After Duke Energy completed its merger with Progress Energy in 2012, Fred consolidated the corrective action and cause analysis programs of both utilities into a single set of procedures. His most recent work has been with Entergy Nuclear as an investigator to support the Arkansas Nuclear One (ANO) 95003 regulatory recovery and the River Bend Nuclear Generating Station 95001 regulatory recovery.

Nuclear stations share information and people freely. Fred participated on corrective action audit and assessment teams at Davis-Besse, Indian Point, and Wolf Creek. While he served as Callaway's human performance supervisor, Fred helped facilitate a human performance gap analysis at Prairie Island. He was a member of the organizational effectiveness assessment team sponsored by the Institute of Nuclear Power Operations (INPO) at South Texas. He was on the industry team that developed and presented INPO training on performance indicators and latent organizational weaknesses.

Fred participated on INPO's first ever assessment of latent organizational weaknesses which was conducted at Grand Gulf Nuclear Station. His role was to complete the common cause analysis of the station's investigations. He supported other teams using common cause analysis to determine root causes of Diablo Canyon's and Point Beach's cross-cutting issues in human performance (HU). Fred has integrated HU fundamentals into Callaway's auditor and root cause training and into the corrective action program. He helped develop Callaway's first HU lesson plans. Later, he helped develop coaching training and taught portions of the supervisory skills training.

He has attended 16 national annual industry conferences of Human Performance, Root Cause, and Trending (HPRCT), and presented the following papers:

- *Human Behavior: Causes and Effects*
- *Before Dissecting an Event, Know the Anatomy of a Success*
- *Human Performance Problem Data Analysis*
- *Primer: Human Performance, Root Cause, and Trending*
- *Root Cause Analysis of an Adverse Trend of Recurring Problems*
- *Institutionalizing Behavior Changes as a Corrective Action*
- *Developing Performance Indicators to Measure Effectiveness of Corrective Actions*
- *Systematic Methods to Address Root and Contributing Causes*

Fred is a past secretary of the HPRCT. He was on the planning committees for the 1996, 1998, 1999, and 2008 HPRCT conferences and served as the chairperson of the 1999 conference. He was the conference lead for the Self-Assessment/Safety Culture track in 2007 and for the Root Cause track in 2008.

In 2007, Fred was designated as a Certified Performance Technologist (CPT) in accordance with the International Society of Performance Improvement (ISPI) standards. This certification is a reflection of Fred's work for over 35 years improving workplace performance by focusing on organizational assessment, incident investigation, continuous improvement, and safety culture.

Fred's hobbies include studying scriptures and researching the ancestors of his parents: the Forck and Wolters families on his father's side and the Taube and Schnieders families on his mother's side. He has completed a line-by-line study of every book of the New Testament except for Revelation. He loves languages and, in the distant past, has studied German, Latin, French, Spanish, and Italian. Most recently, he has become interested in Mandarin Chinese. But his most fun hobby now that his children are grown is reliving his childhood through the eyes of his four granddaughters and his brand-new grandson.

CPSIA information can be obtained
at www.ICGtesting.com
Printed in the USA
BVOW10s2016101216
470346BV00002B/2/P